HEYNE

CW01636416

DAVID GARRETT
WITH LEO G. LINDER

IF YOU ONLY KNEW

THE AUTOBIOGRAPHY

WILHELM HEYNE VERLAG
MÜNCHEN

If this publication contains any links to third-party websites, we assume no liability for their content, as we do not adopt them as our own, but merely refer to their status at the time of initial publication.

The publisher has made every effort to locate all holders of rights and to name and pay them as is customary for the publisher. If this has not been possible in every individual case due to the passage of time and a lack of availability of sources, we shall of course fulfil any justified claims.

David Garrett's memories served as the basis for the dialogue and events contained in this book. The conversations are reproduced mutatis mutandis. No claim is made as to the verbatim reproduction of actual dialogues that have taken place.

To protect individuals who are not public figures or family members, some names have been changed.

MIX
Papier aus verantwortungsvollen Quellen
FSC® C014496

Penguin Random House Verlagsgruppe FSC® N001967

1st edition 2022

part of Penguin Random House Verlagsgruppe GmbH,
Neumarkter Strasse 28, D-81673 Munich, Germany
Editor: Evelyn Boos-Körner
Advisor: André Selleneit, plan B – konzepte: Jörg Kollenbroich,
Weigold & Böhm International Artists & Tours GmbH: Tobias Weigold-Wimmer
English edition: booklab GmbH, Munich, Germany
Translator: Emily Plank
Editor: Diana Vowles
Typesetting: BUCHFLINK Rüdiger Wagner, Nördlingen, Germany
Cover design: Hauptmann & Kompanie Werbeagentur, Zurich, Switzerland
Cover photo: Christoph Köstlin
Picture editors: Sabine Kestler, Heike Jüptner
Printing and binding: GGP Media GmbH, Pößneck, Germany
Printed in Germany
ISBN: 978-3-453-21854-3

www.heyne.de

When can we speak of success?
When we succeed in making others happy.
With this in mind, I dedicate my book
to all young musicians.

As long as you love music
and keep up your curiosity,
you won't regret taking this path.

Content

Foreword

Before we get started, here's a brief introduction to my book.

Throughout my entire life, I've always steered clear of the beaten track. Of course, there have been times when it wasn't easy to forge an alternate path, but life is a journey of discovery, after all. It's true: I never seem to get tired of gaining new, surprising perspectives, and I always make sure that I pay close attention to the tiniest of details that ultimately make up the complete picture.

This is the attitude – one full of curiosity – that I have adopted when tackling any project in my life, be it in music or business. For me, a project always starts with an initial great idea, a sort of epiphany, and it was one of these that inspired the word 'phygital', which describes the concept of my book. It's basically a fusion of the physical and the digital, of the old and the new. I've always found it fascinating to combine them in new and exciting ways.

What it means in the case of this book is that all you need is a bit of curiosity, a smartphone for the QR codes, and you're ready to go. The many previously unreleased pictures, videos and sound recordings will give you additional insights into my life, beyond mere words. For the first time ever, I am unlocking my private archive of audio files and images that my parents and I have collected over the decades – so you'll be part of the journey as I recount my experiences, both the happy moments and the less enjoyable times. At the end of each chapter, you'll find a QR code that will take you to additional, previously unpublished photos and videos. If you don't have a smartphone handy, you'll also find the weblink to the additional material in the appendix.

As you will see, even in this project, there's no escaping a term I'm not at all fond of: 'crossover'. But this term has now also become a classic in its own right, so ...

I really hope you'll enjoy being part of my journey,

David

At the end of each chapter you'll find a QR code which holds as yet unpublished photos and videos. If you don't have a smartphone, you'll find a link for the additional material in the appendix.

I should have said 'no'

I should have said 'no' when Mascha ambushed me, asking me to go out with her that night. I knew, of course, that the long New York nights would end up even longer with her, and that wouldn't have bothered me except that I also knew I was expected at the Electric Lady Studio in Greenwich Village at 9 a.m. the next morning. The preparations for *Rock Symphonies* were complete. The following day, we wanted to start recording the pieces live; there would be a few corrections to be made, as usual, and it's even possible that some planned tracks would be discarded at the last minute and new ideas tried out. So there was a lot at stake; crossover productions keep things exciting right until the end, but that's exactly what I like about them, particularly as the crazy atmosphere at that studio always adds

Photo from the Rock Symphonies *album booklet, 2010*

a whole extra level of fun to the work. The ghost of Jimi Hendrix, who had brought the Electric Lady Studio into being, probably still lurks around the garishly painted rooms – who knows. In any case, things were finally going to be kicking off the next day at 9 a.m. I should have said 'no'. But I said 'yes'.

Of course, it turned out to be a very, very long night. Mascha loved to party, and once again there had been no stopping her – she was the embodiment of *joie de vivre*. I have to say I really loved that exuberance – in fact, it was one of the reasons why I found her so irresistible. We eventually fell asleep at 6 a.m., and, only two short hours later, at 8 a.m., I reached over to my phone, obviously still quite wasted, and called my producer. For the first time in my life, I had to cancel a studio session. What's more, that was the moment when I decided to break up with Mascha.

Was it her fault? It takes two to tango, I know. I was annoyed at myself more than I was at her, but I secretly would have loved, just this once, for Mascha to have reined in her unbridled zest for life – for her to have been the more sensible of the two of us, just this once. Except that wasn't Mascha. It was not in her nature to talk sense into me when there was partying to be done. I came to the realization that this relationship wasn't doing me any good. Things were heading in a direction I really didn't like. Of course, I still found her magnetic energy and lust for life hard to resist, and it was just too nice, just too easy to lose my head with her and end up making the wrong decisions. Yes, it had been an amazing night, but I had lost control. Now, my guilty conscience was almost killing me, and this conscience was right: the new album was the #1 priority. Music was more important. It was my life. When it comes to work, a lack of discipline is one of the deadly sins. I should have said 'no'.

Is that what you get for always being a wunderkind? No, I don't think you can put it like that. I must have been twenty-eight when I broke up with Mascha, and by then I had long started my second life – far away from Germany, in Manhattan, New York. In this new life, I could do and not do whatever I wanted. And I did just that, except that in the background there was still always that old friend that had dogged me since childhood, that voice I couldn't shake off: my guilty conscience. We don't particularly like each other, but we know each other very well. To this day, this conscience especially tends to rear its head in my dreams, and I'm once again that serious nine- or ten-year-old boy with his violin who was expected to achieve great things; who wanted the greatest violinists, the most famous conductors of the time, to recognize him as one of their peers; a boy who would therefore creep downstairs through the empty house at night, while everyone else was asleep, take out his violin and secretly keep practising, because, hours before, he had noticed the frown lines on his father's forehead – an indication that the day's goal obviously had not yet been achieved, and that perfection was still out of reach.

Settling for anything less than perfection was out of the question. It was the only acceptable goal. I had huge expectations to meet, and I certainly wanted to meet them. I just wanted to please everyone. But what happens when you can never ever please your parents or teachers? When, 24/7, 365 days of the year, you're required to perform well, to make progress, to be somewhat better than yesterday and definitely a lot better than the day before that – in other words, meet expectations that can never be met, because these expectations grow along with your abilities, and because the bar keeps being raised a few centimetres higher, with no end in sight? What happens when, despite all the progress you've made, you go to bed every night feeling that, once again, you are not enough? That's when the bad dreams come, and, with them, the fear of failure, of not passing the test, of being unprepared, and therefore disappointing everyone. Leaving Mascha was a panic reaction.

Was I still in love with her? Yes, absolutely. Did I want to continue the relationship with her? Absolutely not. What Mascha may not have known is that she had supremely powerful rivals. Prominent rivals, namely world-famous violinists and conductors, who would scrutinize me intently the first time they laid eyes on me as a young person with my violin. They all wanted to know: how serious is this lad about music? Is he aware of the scale of his task? Does he realize the amount of work and responsibility involved? Or does he come across as childishly flippant? If so, then he's out. He'll have no future, he won't make it, regardless of how talented he is.

Discipline and earnestness ... Some things never change. Even later in New York, I was no less strict with myself, no less focused on continuing to get better and better. This same discipline I had suffered from as a child was something I had also made a habit of in my second life. Never slacken the reins, otherwise it all goes awry, and a lack of discipline is punished with an extra shift – the fact that you overdid things last night is an excuse, but doesn't exonerate you, so get the violin out, make yourself an espresso and get going; it's time to spend the next three hours practising.

Looking back, I tell myself I would never have reached my current level of violin-playing without this pressure. Every other world-class performer will confirm that it is only the relentless pressure of expectation that leads to success. Today, I know that most things were right, even though there was also a lot wrong. But that's reason talking. My subconscious insists on a different, less comfortable version of the story. And that's why it's still not easy for me to open this door and step into the big, dark room where little David sits with his parents. He's four years old at the time, and near him, bathed in the golden light of the spotlight, there is a man dressed in black, holding a violin.

You can find videos and photos for this chapter here.

This impossible instrument

Do I really remember it? Or am I simply recalling the memories of others? I think I do remember ... Szeryng was going to perform in Aachen in 1985. Polish-born Henryk Szeryng, one of the greatest violinists of his time – and I would soon be able to see and hear this hugely acclaimed man in my hometown. Incredible! Being just four years old, of course I had no idea how lucky we were, but my father was adamant that we should go. So we bought our tickets, quite near the front, to be as close as possible to this Henryk Szeryng. But one thing first had to be clarified: should we take our youngest child with us? Will he be able to sit still for so long? Will he whine? My father made the executive decision: 'David is coming. He needs to listen to this.' Worst-case scenario, my mother would have to take me out of the auditorium.

With my father, on one of the first times I ever tried playing the violin

That night, I sat between my parents in the fourth row of the Eurogress concert hall, and, as Szeryng played, I started imitating the violinist I was watching up on stage – playing air violin, so to speak. I guess it must have looked pretty weird. Szeryng certainly noticed there was a child down there playing along, and, in the breaks between pieces, he would look at me and actually wait until I had calmed down again and was sitting still before nodding at the pianist and continuing to play.

After the concert, he came back on stage to play an encore. That's pretty standard. But what happened then, wasn't *at all.* As the applause died down, he stepped to the front of the stage, pointed his bow at me and said, 'When I was the same age as this little boy in the fourth row, I listened to Fritz Kreisler in concert.' Kreisler was a violinist from the 1920s and '30s, of the same calibre as Szeryng. 'Kreisler', he continued, 'saw me in the audience and dedicated his encore to me at the end, namely *Tempo di Minuetto*, which he had composed himself. And tonight' – he looked at me again – 'I am playing *Tempo di Minuetto* by Fritz Kreisler for you, young man.' This *Tempo di Minuetto* is a heartbreakingly romantic piece, a sweet little lullaby for a little prince, and he played it for me. Perhaps this moment was the initial spark. In any case, it wasn't long before my father pressed my first violin, a little child's violin, into my hands.

The violin is a curious instrument. Maybe this is something I should save for later, but then again I absolutely have to talk about it now, because – what would I be without my violin? I have asked myself this question again and again throughout my life, trying to imagine a life without a violin, and I haven't been able to, because I'm violin-obsessed. I just love violins; they have an irresistible allure for me, and not only because of the music – it's the violin itself that has me hooked, because I have experienced too much with it; the awful and the amazing. And anyone wanting to understand me needs to understand this instrument before embarking on my life journey with me. So for anyone who has never played a violin, I want to briefly explain what makes it different from other musical instruments.

If you want to make music, there are basically four different ways of creating sounds (leaving aside the human voice for the moment). You can press air through holes, in which case the sound is determined by keeping some holes shut and others open – that's how flutes, trumpets, clarinets and organs work. That's method #1. Or you can strike an object, whether with your fingers or with sticks or mallets – this is the case for pianos, drums, triangles and xylophones, and it's method #2. Then you can get strings to vibrate by plucking them, such as with guitars or harps. That's method #3.

Bowed instruments such as the violin and cello add a fourth option to this repertoire. It can be described as rubbing/friction, scraping or scratching, and doesn't really sound like a promising way of producing melodious sounds. As the word 'scratching' implies, this method can produce sounds, but very rarely are they nice ones, and so begins the torment of the young violin student.

There is probably no worse instrument for a beginner or, in fact, anyone living with or near them. Learning to play the violin requires nerves of steel from everyone involved. Even my father's nerves must have been shot after a while. And we haven't yet even spoken about the actual problem, namely intonation – that is, the process of actually finding the right note on your violin.

Let's compare it with the piano. Provided the instrument has been properly tuned, I only need to press down on a piano key to promptly get the note I want, pure and undistorted. Any small child can be taught to play a clean C-major chord on a piano within seconds. Achieving the same on a violin takes months. Why? Because a piano serves you every note on a silver platter;

you have a keyboard about two metres long, with keys on top that are so wide it's hard to miss them even during an *allegro furioso*. On a violin, however, the notes are not defined. You can't see them with the naked eye; you have to find them blindly. It's a case of millimetres, even micro-millimetres, often within milli-seconds! Instead of a two-metre-long keyboard, you have only a short fingerboard that packs in the entire range of notes over a few centimetres, meaning that the individual notes are all tightly crammed in next to each other. It is a mystery how, given these conditions, and often at lightning speed, anyone is ever able to hit a clear, sharp and clean-sounding note.

As if that weren't enough, when you have hit the note, you still haven't actually produced it. No sound comes out, because there is no friction. It is only once the bow is used that the violin comes to life, which brings you to your next problem, namely that of having to perform movements with your right hand that are completely different to what the left hand is doing. Your left hand is feeling its way along the strings more or less nimbly, while the right is performing upward and downward motions – at a completely different pace – with a bow. Well, now try coordinating these two movements! Not to mention the fact that, using this bow, you have to pinpoint the ideal spot between the bridge and fingerboard; in other words, that section of the string that gives you a smooth, round sound. You have to find this exact ideal point for every single note, and if you're looking for it in the same section of the upper string as it is on the lower string, you would be wrong – it's in a different place at the top.

To cap it all off – and this is where I will leave things for the moment – no physiotherapist would ever have invented such an instrument. Pianists have to be a bit careful of their backs, it's true, but a violinist needs to expect leg and back twinges after two hours, because they are forced to contort their bodies. After all, the violin needs to be held somehow, so you're standing there with your head turned to the left, the left shoulder slightly raised and the instrument clamped between your shoulder and chin. While the left hand offers a little support, it is also needed for acrobatic finger movements and therefore needs to be able to move freely, so holding the violin from this side is out of the question. What this means is that, on top of all the technical challenges associated with playing the violin, the body and violin also need to work together perfectly.

In short, it is a nearly impossible instrument. The degree of difficulty is brutal, and the prospect of becoming an elite violin player as likely as scaling Mount Everest alone without oxygen. So now comes the totally justified question: why would anyone encourage helpless little four- or five-year-olds to take on the struggles associated with this instrument?

The answer is: because experience has shown that, at later ages, the head and hands are no longer up to the task of handling the violin's tremendous demands. Someone who starts at age ten or twelve won't necessarily be a bad violinist, but they will never reach the summit of Mount Everest. Perfectly hitting a string with a finger of the left hand with millimetre precision is a fine-motor feat that can only be learned very young, and it's a similar story for developing a skilled 'ear'. Not even the best concert violinist in the world can hit every note exactly right one hundred per cent of the time. They will constantly have to make corrections within a fraction of a second, and these tiniest of corrections require an extremely precise ear trained all the way from childhood. So it's better to start when the brain is still able to absorb everything like a sponge, when every grip can still be imprinted into the subconscious. My father was right in this respect. No brilliant violinist, no world-famous pianist began playing their instrument as late as the age of eight or nine, and my father was probably envisioning an international career for me very early on.

For the time being, however, little David is standing in the living room of his parents' house in Aachen, grating away on his Suzuki fibreboard violin, making noises that, even to him, sound horrendous. For now, he has to learn to live with something that is torture for his ears. Thank God I can't remember my earliest beginner days. I can imagine the strain it puts on the nerves of everyone involved when I hear young people who are just starting out. It's so much more enjoyable when someone is learning to play the piano! The violin's fun factor is more or less zero; for months, sometimes even years, you produce nothing but rubbish, and yet you still have to persuade yourself to keep going – every single day. Where, from what corner of the universe, does a child find his or her motivation in such circumstances?

You can find videos and photos for this chapter here.

A childhood with violins

It's significant that even my earliest memories involve a violin. I cannot recall ever not having one in my hands. It's as if music is what brought me into the world, as if it was the Big Bang that created me as a thinking being.

But I'm not the only one standing here in the living room with a violin, doing my best to convert my father's instructions into sounds. Standing alongside me is my older brother, Alexander. I am five and he is seven, naturally a more advanced violin player than me. Still, I am probably the happier of the two of us. Most definitely, in fact. When my brother was given his first violin as a gift a year earlier, I was envious because he had this great new toy – I wanted a violin like that too! Now I finally had one and could emulate my sibling and role model. All my dreams had

At age five

come true, because there is a huge difference between whether 'you should' – as with Alexander – or 'you can' – as it was with me. He had to learn to play the violin, whereas I wanted to. Obviously I didn't have any idea what was in store for me, but I was certainly motivated.

So the two of us are now standing in the living room with our miniature violins, listening to our father teaching us by means of the Suzuki group-teaching method, which was the rage at the time. And for the next fourteen years, effectively every day in the Bongartz household will revolve around violin-playing.

My father, Georg Bongartz, is a qualified lawyer but a violin auctioneer by trade, and thus a violin expert. My mother is American-born Dove Garrett, a prima ballerina, who is responsible for organizing this not uncomplicated household. For the time being, my name is David Christian Bongartz. My sister Elena will become a new addition to our family many years later. Apart from violins in particular, my father's passion is music, especially classical music. He also has practical experience of it, having played in the German Air Force's entertainment orchestra and occasionally been a drummer at military funerals. Ideally, he would have become a violinist – that was his dream, but a career as a soloist was just a little out of his reach, and instead he turned his hand to trading in stringed instruments. Alexander and I were not his first violin students either; he had taught other children before us, so we could actually learn a lot from him.

And we did – but at what cost! Let's put it this way: as a child, you're on your parents' leash, but some leashes are long and some are very, very short. My father discovered that both his sons were remarkably talented violinists – me maybe a little more than my older brother. So what do you do with that? What measures do you take once you've realized fate has placed two golden eggs in your nest? It's not an enviable situation, because you're suddenly responsible for ensuring that birds of paradise, not quails, hatch out of those golden eggs. So are you going to just stand by and watch these talents go to waste? Or are you going to leave no stone unturned in your quest to secure this treasure?

My father decided to leave no stone unturned. Circumstances played into his hands, because he worked from home. He was basically always around and had a lot of free time. He gave us lessons, assessed our progress, provided criticism and didn't let up, always expecting more, even better performances, even greater progress. He became less of a father and more of a teacher by the day – a teacher who demanded discipline, hours and hours of regular practising, and tangible success. If we fell short of his expectations, the atmosphere at home turned sour. Everything was done according to his wishes, and he had very specific ideas – this is the fingering, this is the bow stroke, this is how you have to play it, and this is how it has to sound. The pressure never let up, and a year after I started, Alexander gave up.

Because he was bad at it? Definitely not. He was unhappy, absolutely miserable. He had completely lost interest; I would often hear him crying while practising. He was also barely able to cope with playing in front of people, at our house concerts, when other parents were also watching; he was plagued by stomach-aches beforehand and his face would be white as a sheet when he stepped up to perform. He eventually mustered up the courage to tell my father, 'I do want to play an instrument, just not the violin any more. I'd prefer the piano.' The piano was not my father's greatest passion, but Alexander got his wish and had his freedom back.

This could also have been my time to jump ship – but why did I stick to the violin? Because I was more stubborn than him, or had a thicker skin? Or did I have strong desire to please? That's probably more like it. I wanted approval from my father and my audience, and I definitely didn't want to fall short of their expectations. My need for harmony made me tolerate any ordeal. This need was both a blessing and a curse; above all, however, it would be one of the reasons I didn't fall to pieces over the coming years.

Because many do fall to pieces. Achieving a great career isn't just about talent alone; your personality, your motivation and your resilience are just as important. What you experience as a promising musician in your early years contradicts any notions you may have of a carefree childhood. You're basically a pro at a very young age, and are treated as such: as someone who does work that must meet the highest of standards. My brother was smart enough to pull the plug in time; my need for harmony was what saved me. But many others fall to pieces.

From then on, my father concentrated on me. He would be my main teacher until I was seventeen, and, over the coming years, violin-playing would develop into a twenty-four-hour job for me, meaning, of course, that father and son were working together 24/7. Plenty of time to squabble, because family life and work were now inseparable. Time and again I found myself sitting in my room at night thinking, 'I don't want to do this anymore, I can't do it anymore – ditch the violin, screw music ...' Except that was impossible, because my family's happiness, the atmosphere at home and, of course, my own wellbeing, my own peace of mind, all depended on how well I played the violin. If I practised diligently, if I achieved my targets, it was a harmonious day; but if I slackened off, there was tension, my father would get annoyed and twitchy, and everyone suffered. So not only was I responsible for my progress on the violin, it was also down to me to create a pleasant atmosphere in my family home.

That put a strain on me. On days when no one at home was in a good mood and I myself was thoroughly miserable, sleep would be out of the question until I had made my peace with the violin.

Then I would say to myself 'it can't be that hard, you'll manage it' – and, while everyone else was asleep, I would creep out of my room and down the stairs, take out my violin, not even turning a light on, and keep practising in the dark. I had to play in order to sort out my emotions. For me, at least, the day that was now almost done would have a harmonious end.

So me being a fast learner and making amazing progress was also due to the fact that, unless I was surrounded by harmony, I would keep working. I worked until everyone else was happy again. But this time left its mark on me, because, as a child, you want to be protected by your family, you want to feel safe and loved and cared for. But if this experience becomes overshadowed by being constantly under strain, relentlessly exposed to pressure and tension, and incessantly forced to perform exceptionally, that's when pain sets in. That's when your self-esteem suffers. That's when the sword of Damocles of inadequacy and failure constantly hangs over you. Even though everything ended up right, there was a lot that was wrong then.

You can find videos and photos for this chapter here.

Exceptional circumstances

Did I suffer? Yes, of course I did. But did my father make me a slave to the violin? No, absolutely not. It's not as if I was being condemned to child labour in a coal mine – I was making classical music, the most magnificent music on earth. This music is grand and overwhelming, but equally difficult and intangible, a glimmer of joy in the distance if you settle for mediocrity, but an explosion of blissful emotions within yourself if you work towards perfection.

No, it wasn't out of fear of my father that I demanded the most of myself. Naturally, no child likes uncomfortable silences at the dinner table, and they feel even more awkward when they are the reason for this silence. But my tenacity back then was driven by my love of music. Even as a child, I just knew that music was

There's nothing better than a relaxed day in the snow (with my brother Alexander)

the one great purpose and meaning of life. So no matter how dejected, how desperate or exhausted I was, music always took me in its arms, consoled me and made everything right again.

And every time, I knew I would be able to achieve what I expected of myself. I knew what was possible on the violin. Even as a child, I listened to any classical music recordings I could get my hands on. Browsing through Media Markt and coming out with five new CDs by great violinists would never fail to make my soul leap with joy. I devoured music the way other parents' early-maturing children perhaps devoured works by their favourite writers. I wasn't a bookworm; I was a record- and CD-worm. At home, I listened to these records over and over again and got goose bumps – I can't begin to describe what those hours of pure joy did to me.

And that's why my allies weren't literary figures, nor heroes from novels or movies. My allies were the great composers of history – Brahms, Tchaikovsky, Rachmaninoff, Beethoven, and of course Bach. But, and this is the crucial bit, they spoke to me through great interpreters, through people like Heifetz, Oistrach, Menuhin, Zukerman, Perlman and of course Szeryng and Kreisler. These incredible, phenomenal violinists – they were my ultimate heroes and idols. It was them I listened to, sitting by our stereo in Aachen; it was them I one day wanted to emulate, delighting my audience with my playing just like they were currently doing to me. In short, I wanted to become a magician. An enchanter.

Apart from that, there were more banal reasons for me to keep enduring this life of mine. One of them is that what you experience at home as a child seems normal to you. Even if you were to grow up in a cellar and never come out, you wouldn't question your circumstances because you simply wouldn't know any different. So for me, my life was normal, and, in fairness, I have to say it could have been a lot worse.

There were times I nearly forgot about the violin, such as when I would go on bike rides in the area surrounding Aachen with my father, or when I would play badminton in our garden with my brother. As a child, I was a ball of energy, and if I wasn't holding a violin, I had to get outside, away from it all. I romped around the garden like a tornado and was as adventurous as anything. My brother was the quiet, more level-headed one; I was extroverted and full of *joie de vivre* – at least until it was time to head back inside and practise again.

Then there was school. And even my schooldays seemed semi-normal to me, despite my circumstances being constantly exceptional.

My mother managed to obtain official permission that allowed me to attend Elementary School only four days a week. Thursday at noon would be the end of my week – but of course I didn't have free time after that. The extended weekend was spent having lessons with whoever my violin teacher was at the time, and many of them lived hundreds of miles away. Later in middle school and high school my mother obtained official permission for me to be privately tutored until final exams which enabled me to receive my high school diploma. That was a relatively laid-back affair: sometimes it would be five hours a day, sometimes only three, and occasionally none at all, because, for example, I would have to make a quick trip to Miami to see a famous violinist. And by quick I mean ten days.

Was I a lucky chap? I don't really know; my education was quite patchy for a long time, but the fact is that the violin was much more important than school. Most parents will check that their children have done their homework, but not in the Bongartz household – if I had practised well, no one gave a damn about homework.

As you can imagine, that casual attitude to my education frequently left me feeling embarrassed. I would often quickly scribble something in my notebook just before class – rarely the smartest thing to do – and my primary-school teacher would occasionally take pleasure in loudly sharing my notes with the rest of the class – or even writing my muddled sentences, complete with spelling mistakes and incorrect grammar, word for word on the big blackboard. Fortunately, that only happened once, but I felt thoroughly ashamed often enough. And while I barely scraped my way through school, my brother was a brilliant, straight-A student, which didn't exactly help matters.

Coupled with this was the fact that my classmates obviously found it difficult to make friends with me, and the feeling was mutual. My repertoire of conversation had nothing in common with that of other children my age. Honestly, I couldn't talk about the things my peers were talking about, and was the only one to be substituted in just a minute and a half before the siren when playing football in the schoolyard during lunch breaks. It wasn't because of my lack of sporting ability; it was just that no one wanted to have 'that violinist' around. That weirdo who knew nothing of real life, who ran around in his brother's hand-me-down pullovers and corduroy trousers, and, to cap it off, was exempt from any physical-education classes for fear of injuring his precious fingers.

In fact, I never worried about my fingers. My father did, though – that's why I wasn't allowed to play games that entailed throwing a ball. Even school excursions and youth hostels were things I only heard about through my brother. Every time my class went on a trip, I had to miss out. Skiing holidays were strictly forbidden, because at least one participant would always come back with their arm in a cast. But I still got involved in little fights because I would cop a lot of banter for my violin, and also I would defend the innocent, primarily girls, who were nudged and teased and had their hair pulled. Bullying was against my morals, and as I was very tall even at a young age, I pushed back. I certainly made a point of ensuring justice in the schoolyard, regardless of my fingers. As an outsider, you have to make a valuable contribution to society somehow, after all.

In other words, elementary school and playing the violin is a tricky combination. And if, on top of all that, you don't leave the coolest of impressions, if even your appearance and the way you express yourself are completely out of place in a primary school, then 'outsider' is a term that barely comes close to describing your role in Aachen school life. If someone had to draw the word 'uncool', they might as well have just put a photo of David Christian Bongartz there. But, honestly, even then, my involuntary special status didn't really bother me. After all, I had my own circle of oddballs, namely violin students my age whom I met at my teachers' houses.

You can find videos and photos for this chapter here.

Bring on Tchaikovsky

It wasn't long before my father felt he needed support, and he began looking around for a good violin teacher. Later on, I was to have the most amazing violinist, a living legend, as a teacher, but even for a *wunderkind*, learning to play an instrument is a step-by-step process, and my list of tutors starts with Coosje Wijzenbeek. She was Dutch, and her name was pronounced in such a way that, even for child, it ran easily off the tongue: 'Koshe Weizenbek'. Known for successfully teaching small children, Coosje Wijzenbeek in Hilversum would be my teacher for now, from the age of four to six.

What I remember most are the car rides to Hilversum at the weekend. My brother was initially there too, so the backrest at the back of the car was removed to allow space for us to

With my teacher Zakhar Bron

sleep – my father found this preferable to us fighting in the rear seat, which would have been the alternative way of whiling away the travelling time. With Coosje, I worked on the basics: practising scales, playing easy studies and performing mini student concerts. But, even back then, the pieces could not have been that simple, because at the age of five, I had already come first in the *Jugend musiziert* [Youth makes music – a competition for children and adolescents on a regional, federal and national level in Germany] music competition with Beethoven's *Romance in F Major*. So my rendition of this romance, a not entirely unchallenging piece, must have sounded at least half-tolerable.

It's possible that, even with Coosje, my father made the point that his son didn't like spending all his time on studies and finger exercises, but also enjoyed playing serious compositions. After all, his great idols – Menuhin, Oistrach and Heifetz, all of whom were also child prodigies – started performing great works at just six or seven years of age. A ten-year-old Menuhin was on stage playing Beethoven's violin concerto, while at the age of eight Heifetz performed Tchaikovsky's violin concerto with an orchestra – in other words, a high bar had been set for me.

I also remember meeting Janine Jansen, who would later similarly go on to have a great career, at Coosje's. But the rest of my memories of this time are hazy, because I didn't spend long taking lessons in Hilversum. After a year and a half, my father decided I had outgrown my first teacher, and set about finding a new one.

It is worth pointing out here that my father always sat in on every lesson with Coosje and indeed with all the other childhood teachers yet to come. He would initially note everything down on the spot, but later switched to recording every lesson with a small video camera, so he could go through and analyse it meticulously at home. So my father was effectively continuing his own learning with my teachers, himself playing the student, albeit also acting as a supplementary teacher during the week, thereby exercising complete control over me and my musical development. There was no downtime for me, particularly as he also had to drive me to and from lessons – yet another opportunity for him to once again go through everything point by point.

From then on, I would go twice a week to Saschko Gawriloff, without my brother, who was now totally finished with the violin. Gawriloff taught at Cologne's College of Music, was himself an acclaimed violinist, concert master and soloist, and was thus the perfect choice to expand my musical repertoire. What I, as a seven-year-old, particularly liked about Gawriloff was that this likeable, warm-hearted and highly skilled man opened his doors to a little boy like me. I even felt comparatively comfortable in his home. I would arrive in the early afternoon, we would spend an hour working together, he would get me to stop for an afternoon nap, and then we would continue.

I had of course long moved on from my Suzuki child's violin. During those early years, children grow out of their violins as fast as they do their clothes. I started with a 1/16-size violin, which wasn't much bigger than an adult hand. By the time I was with Coosje, I had already moved on to a 1/8, a Hornsteiner, a very fine instrument indeed. My violin during the Gawriloff days was a Jombar, produced by a French violin-maker in the late 19th century, varnished in a glorious red.

Not only did my teachers want me to succeed, they expected me to succeed, and these successes had to be tangible and demonstrable. Gawriloff, for example, primarily honed my mastery of the instrument, my intonation, my vibrato, how I held my bow. That's what the études he had me practise were for – violin compositions comprising a terrifying array of difficult and fiddly exercises for both hands. Playing études is simply fine-motor tuning; boring repetition to get the fingers and brain into shape. While Gawriloff made me do this cheerless task, he did know that practising also needed to be fun, which is why he never forgot to give me something enjoyable: a little piece by Handel, an early sonata by Mozart, a Dvořák sonatina. Getting the hardest stuff over with first, then having fun and playing something beautiful is the ideal balance. That's what any good teacher should do, and the friendly Gawriloff was a very good teacher – just like all the other teachers I've had in my life. Some were strict, but no one ever shouted or was short-tempered. I felt totally comfortable with all of them, and enjoyed working with every single one.

However, I did make their lives pretty easy, because I'm a teacher's pet. I would never wait to give them a chance to criticize; I would cut them off, saying 'I know what you're thinking', and then play the same passage again, but better. Heaven forbid any teacher should think I hadn't noticed the weak areas ... The truth is, I craved encouragement and recognition. I couldn't expect praise for a grade-three school essay filled with spelling mistakes and scribbled down barely half an hour before, but, when it came to playing the violin, I was good, I sought enthusiasm and was happy to help draw it out a bit.

Okay, now that I've made that admission, it's time to move on to my third teacher. By the age of eight, I had reached a good technical level, and my father had heard about a Russian music teacher from Novosibirsk who had come to Germany. His name was Zakhar Bron, he had a reputation of being an excellent teacher and, in the little world of ambitious parents, the news of his arrival spread like wildfire.

How can you tell if a teacher is excellent? From their amazing students. Bron hadn't come from Siberia on his own – he had brought brilliant students such as Vadim Repin, Maxim Vengerov, Natalia Prishipenko and two or three others, all aged between ten and fourteen. Only Bron himself knows how he managed to get visas for all of them from the Soviet authorities, but they were now all in the West, where everybody was raving about the man who had students the likes of whom had never been seen before.

The news of Zakhar Bron's spectacular talent academy had piqued my father's interest, and he decided that this Bron would replace Gawriloff as my teacher. He managed to get me to play for Bron, and at the age of eight I joined his group of students in Lübeck. This marked the start of a hugely exciting, eventful time, packed full of proper, great music. My father and I would start heading to Lübeck on Thursday evenings, him at the wheel and me putting one classical music CD after another into the CD player – I would take a stack so large it would have lasted a trip to Portugal and back. We would ride a wave of the most wonderful music, played by the greatest artists in the world, to Lübeck every two weeks.

Our repertoire contained not only violin concertos, but also operas, chamber music, piano concertos and all manner of symphonies – though sometimes, after barely five minutes, we would both agree that this or that piece was not worth listening to and didn't appeal to us at all. It was on those highways that I experienced the most enjoyable times with my father – the music united us, made us like-minded, made us father and son.

It was just as nice, if totally different, to make this trip with my mother. If my father could not be available, she would get behind the wheel and the two of us, or three of us if Alexander came along – and later there would even be four of us, because my sister Elena was born in the meantime – would head to Lübeck. We rented an apartment, cooked dinner at night, and thus briefly created a homely atmosphere, an unusually relaxed family life, in the faraway city of Lübeck. I would spend three days working with Bron, and progressed faster than I ever had before.

Just as my father had thought, Bron's mission was to get his students playing the great works by the great composers as early as possible, and, that same year, he said to me, 'Let's try the second and third movement of Tchaikovsky's violin concerto.' We avoided the first movement of that concerto for the time being; it was super-complex, and was long considered unplayable in the 19th century. But Bron was confident I could handle the second and third, because he knew about my finger skills.

He would constantly feed me pieces that allowed me to shine technically – compositions such as the '*perpetuum mobiles*', short but breathtakingly fast pieces in which the violin is not still for the entire three minutes, racing to a furious end in semiquavers and demisemiquavers. Anyone who was able to manage that would not have any problem, at least at a technical level, with the last movement of Tchaikovsky's concerto. And I managed them – first the *Perpetuum Mobile* by Czech composer Nováček, and soon after the *Moto Perpetuo* by Paganini, both extreme examples of virtuoso violin music.

So, bring on Tchaikovsky's concerto! And, after I had mastered movements two and three, Bron even allowed me to tackle the lofty peak that was the first movement. Astonishingly, I scaled it relatively quickly, and, at the age of ten, I was able to play that virtuoso first movement without any major difficulties.

I wasn't doing too badly at all, and Bron took me through a load of repertoires. But, for him, there was a limit. He kept me away from Brahms and Beethoven, probably not wanting to demand those of me at my age. My father may have had a different view. I suspect he found Bron too hesitant– after all, weren't Heifetz and Menuhin already playing Brahms and Beethoven at that age? It's possible my father even tried to get Bron to move at a faster pace. But Bron stuck to his conservative approach and, looking back, I think he was right. You have to grow musically in order to be able to play great music; you have to mature and understand the music. While I had acquired a high degree of musical instinct by now, I still had very little musical understanding.

And speaking of Menuhin ... Did his teachers really advise him to play Beethoven's concerto at the age of ten? Menuhin himself wrote in his memoirs that he was the one who really wanted to play the concerto. But is that the whole truth? I can imagine it was more his parents pushing him, with Menuhin then selling their wish to his teachers as his own. In any case, something about Menuhin's version of events didn't sit right with me. Who, at that age, is able to comprehend the plethora of ideas and experiences that Beethoven transformed into music in that piece?

However, while Bron steered clear of Brahms and Beethoven, he otherwise ensured an active musical life. This included his student concerts, in which his Russian pupils Maxim Vengerov and Vadim Repin were the headline acts. Concerts need to gradually reach their climax, which is why the pair would be the last on stage. But I was also put on towards the end, which I took as recognition of my skills. Then there was my first public performance in the greatest possible concert format – as a soloist with an orchestra!

At the age of nine, I performed Mozart's *Violin Concerto No. 1 in B flat major* to an audience at Bad Kissingen's Kurhaus. Bron and I had rehearsed this concerto intensively, and the applause at the end was overwhelming; plus, the write-ups afterwards were also full of praise. After my performance, I collected my first fee of 500 marks. In my childish naiveté, I thought this money would go straight into my savings account. But no, my father pocketed it instead. Today, I understand why he did that. As he had invested huge sums in my training over the years, a little repayment from me was not inappropriate. And yet ...

You can find videos and photos for this chapter here.

Very proud of my first concert poster for my debut in Hamburg

David Bongartz becomes David Garrett

If it seems like everything went very quickly, indeed it did. My life had become something of a race against time – but this, too, is normal in the strange world of child prodigies. You're probably wondering at what age my great idols, the child prodigies of the past, played this or that challenging piece. Eight? Nine? And how did I compare?

The competition was indeed fierce. My fellow students under Bron were not only hugely talented, but also extraordinarily ambitious and willing to put in every effort required, so it goes without saying that everyone pushed themselves to their limits when practising. And that's why, after starting with Bron, it all came thick and fast, especially in the beginning – but, since then, I have constantly asked myself what I would be without my violin.

I used to be scared of getting carried away. In my sort of life, so much falls by the wayside, so much has to be neglected! There was no Mascha in sight until I reached the age of 16. I didn't even have normal contact with peers or classmates, let alone boring any girl to death with my musical vocabulary. So I long braved the high seas alone with my violin. The current had swept me far out, and I got a sense that the way back was longer than the way to the next coast beyond the horizon. This was also coupled with the fear that I couldn't actually make it there, and would somehow simply sink and drown in the middle of this ocean.

Returning to square one, taking a new direction and focusing on other things was out of the question. As it was, my general knowledge was so pitiful, I would probably never have caught up on everything I had missed. Playing the violin was really the only thing I could reliably master; so, I told myself, keep rowing towards the horizon with your violin, stick to it, don't let up even for a minute.

And I did stick to it. New, unimaginable opportunities started opening up for me when I got a professional manager at the age of ten.

How did this happen? Yes, I knew my mother had received a letter from Berlin, perhaps even a telephone call. Either way, she went there and came back with a contract from the Hans Adler concert management agency, which I presumably signed as a purely token move. I still didn't quite grasp what I was getting into – but agency boss Witiko Adler wasn't just anyone. His agency's clients included the Berlin Philharmonic Orchestra, Anne-Sophie Mutter and even Yehudi Menuhin! So this step taken by my parents was nothing less than my ticket to the big wide world of classical music. But my contract didn't refer to me David Christian Bongartz – the name shown on the contract was David Garrett.

What was that all about?

There were several reasons for my new name. First, having an 'artist name' is nothing unusual in the music world. Secondly, my father was probably worried that the name Bongartz was too difficult for foreigners to pronounce. And thirdly, he may have felt uncomfortable with the idea of me performing under the family name. He would have thought: I, Mr Bongartz senior, have a reputation in the music business as a violin dealer, and I don't want people to think young David only made it because he had an advantage in his choice of instrument. So no one was to get even an inkling of it; there would be no quiet whisperings of 'no wonder; of course he would get the best violins, while other kids have to try to keep up with the Bongartz boy on second-rate fiddles.' For this reason, and also with a view to my international career, my father kindly had enough foresight at the time to think that the surname of my American mother would be more suitable. So, in the music world, I was David Garrett.

Unfortunately, this did not go down well among my classmates at primary school. Aha, they now said, it's not enough for him to just look weird, talk weirdly and play a weird instrument; now he has also needed to adopt an artist name ... That was the last straw for them, and my fate at school was sealed. I, on the other hand, couldn't have cared less. Garrett? Didn't bother me. The name was just suddenly there, similarly to when, overnight, someone starts wearing glasses. Word of the new name of course got around in my hometown when the name Garrett appeared on a church concert programme instead of Bongartz, but it's not like it made my life more difficult.

Back to my agency.

Witiko Adler had fantastic connections in the music world, and in the years that followed he ensured I was constantly given the opportunity to play in front of famous conductors or star violinists. He organized my first encounters with the world-renowned conductors Zubin Mehta, Kurt Masur, Lorin Maazel, Giuseppe Sinopoli, Seiji Ozawa and Claudio Abbado, as well as with virtuoso violinist Itzhak Perlman, who would later become my teacher in New York. The mind-blowing thing was that all these famous personalities were willing to listen to an eleven- or twelve-year-old! I would have expected them to say, 'Tell him to call me again in five years.' But no. If they had half an hour spare between orchestra rehearsals, they would ask me to come in and allow me to play a couple of pieces. Not all meetings resulted in a collaboration, but Witiko Adler had at least made them possible and opened countless doors.

Circumstances were also favourable because that decade saw the re-emergence of child prodigies. In the 1990s, there were several young violinists who were marketed that way, such as Sarah Chang and Hilary Hahn, both of whom would go on to have international careers. This was not a new phenomenon. Mozart, Paganini and Liszt had sparked a similar sensation among event organizers and audiences in their day; even in the early 20th century, Europe experienced a golden age of great virtuosos. Towards the end of that same century, the 'wunderkind' legend was once again enchanting record companies and conductors alike, which benefited me. But the 'wunderkind' or 'child prodigy' label has always bothered me.

I became acquainted with it at an early age – and it's true I had good intuition and was a fast learner. But I found the terms 'wunderkind' or 'child prodigy' almost insulting, because they ignored my hard work and took away from my performance; as if I was just born with it, as if my skills just fell into my lap! This was absolute nonsense, and, ultimately, a betrayal of audiences, because what goes on behind the scenes, what goes on at home, has nothing to do with prodigal wonders. Instead, it's all about sweat and tears, to be honest. It was no different for Mozart or Paganini, to name just the two most famous child prodigies of all time.

Because even a surprising talent is only seed capital. You need someone to discover you, you need someone to encourage you, but it's you who has to scale the mountain, and it doesn't matter if you want to keep climbing or not; you have no choice – you have to keep climbing every day in order to be that much closer to the summit every night.

And on top of all that, every wunderkind is a product. Anyone sitting in the audience thinking they're lucky enough to be watching a natural wonder on stage is being deceived by the music business. Sure, there is a little person up on stage doing something special, and I can now totally understand the fascination. But I will never forget what happens behind the scenes, what is carefully hidden from public view: both the self-torture and the efforts invested by others in your career.

But anyway, 'wunderkind' David Garrett was in the best hands with Witiko Adler. Right at the start of our collaboration, he arranged for me to play for Gerd Albrecht, chief conductor of the Hamburg Philharmonic Orchestra. I was, of course, determined to impress Albrecht, and prepared *Zigeunerweisen (Gypsy Airs)*, a rather lively, virtuoso, catchy piece by Spanish violin virtuoso and composer Pablo de Sarasate – perfect for impressing a chief conductor, and equally perfect for delighting an audience and prompting standing ovations. Albrecht was indeed impressed enough with my playing to hire me to perform *Zigeunerweisen* at Hamburg's Laeiszhalle in a concert that would kick-start my stage career.

The Laeiszhalle ... When it comes to concert halls from around the year 1900, you can never be disappointed, because they all have the same ceremonial character of a grandeur-loving, décor-obsessed era. While I would later perform in even more magnificent halls, the Laeiszhalle was certainly an imposing concert building, with its epic stage, mighty organ and Great Hall seating more than 2,000. Performing to a huge audience here with the Hamburg Philharmonic requires a ten-year-old to have a certain, well, let's say, uninhibitedness. And I did. I had an inherent sort of childish self-command. That would change a few years later, but, that night, the only thing bothering me was what I was wearing.

To better understand this, I need to talk about Yehudi Menuhin. Until the age of 13, Menuhin performed in shorts as a way of emphasizing his youth and milking the 'wunderkind' mystique for as long as possible. As he started to reach puberty, his parents even shaved his legs, because bare, hairless legs made him look younger. My father was a huge fan of Menuhin. There was even a photo of him, aged around thirteen, with his violin and shorts, hanging in our living room. So guess what I wore on stage – that's right: black shorts, Menuhin-style.

There is a video recording of that concert, which my mother secretly made. Her mission that night was to smuggle a little video camera into the hall in her bag. The bag had been prepared as if for a spy operation; my mother had used nail clippers to cut a hole in the front, then all she needed was to stick the lens through and turn on the camera. The result is unfortunately so blurry it makes you dizzy to watch it, but otherwise the evening went down nicely. My performance actually caused a sensation. Imagine: a ten-year-old playing with the Hamburg Philharmonic in the Laeiszhalle, against the backdrop of the awe-inspiring great organ.

There were standing ovations, the applause erupting straight after the final note of the third movement was played. But what I most clearly remember is that it initially took me ages to tune my violin on stage. The audience was starting to get restless. No connoisseur of classical music would expect Sarasate's *Zigeuner-weisen* to feature on a ten-year-old's repertoire; it requires a high level of virtuosity. And, after two minutes of fiddling around with my G string, amused whispers started rippling around the audience – if this kid can't even get his violin tuned, we're really in for something. Things could get really hilarious ... but they were wrong, falling into a relaxed silence as soon as I had got through the first difficult section at the start of the piece.

This success brought me many more concert invitations. From then on, the spirit of Menuhin constantly surrounded me and my father, and I had no issue moving on to a Beethoven concerto as my next challenge. That meant saying goodbye to Bron, and, for the fourth time, my father set about looking for a new teacher – one without any reservations, who would allow me to try my hand at the works of an absolute great such as Beethoven.

But one final word on Zakhar Bron. Some people might imagine a Russian violin teacher to be a merciless disciplinarian. Bron was anything but. I remember him as a good-natured Russian teddy bear. Of course he was demanding, sometimes even strict, but in me he had found a highly motivated, easy student. After my concert in Hamburg, he even went as far as making the flattering comment that I 'was no less talented than ... ' I won't mention any names here. But, suffice to say, it was a huge accolade for me.

You can find videos and photos for this chapter here.

Ida Haendel

Speaking of Menuhin's concert shorts – until the age of 15, I had little say in what I wore on stage, which meant that I didn't always like my outfit. Thinking of Mr Koslowski, our tailor, makes me slightly uncomfortable. The Bongartz family home was of course filled with pictures of 19th-century violinists, of Paganini, Sarasate and many others, and it was now Mr Koslowski's task to make suits for me inspired by those role models. He definitely put a lot of love into it, but the choice of colours was sometimes questionable, such as when the new suit would turn out to be canary yellow or fir-tree green. No disrespect to Sir Elton John, but you're really up against it when a photo of you ends up doing the rounds at your school – not to mention the fact that you want to feel comfortable in your outfit on stage.

With Ida Haendel in Miami

As it is, it requires a lot of effort for a pubescent twelve-year-old to take to the stage of a magnificent concert hall; and if they also have to do this in a suit made from snow-white moiré silk, the effort needs to be Herculean indeed. I would have preferred a black suit, and got my way on one single occasion at the very start of my career with the rather odd request to perform in tails.

My request wasn't easy to fulfill, because no shops had tails in my size in stock. Twelve-year-olds didn't generally ask for them, but it was a special occasion, namely my first performance playing Tchaikovsky's *Violin Concerto in D Major* in Hilversum, including a radio orchestra and television broadcast. And that's how the tailor Mr Koslowski entered our lives. To a certain extent, I had been asking for trouble by wanting to wear tails, but, when I watch the live TV recording today, I have no regrets: there's something touching about a twelve-year-old in tails, and, even if I do say so myself, they really suited me.

Anyway, these are just sideline observations. To discuss the main event, I'm going to jump into our red VW Kombi with its CD player. It even had an extendable outdoor shower.

This vehicle is zooming its way through the landscape of southern England, with the entire Bongartz/Garrett family on board. Our destination is Dartington in Devon, not far from Exeter, which would prove to be an ancient village with houses built of grey stone. So what happened?

A violin-dealer friend of my father had given him a recording of the famous Polish violin virtuoso Ida Haendel. He was so impressed by her performance with the Israel Philharmonic Orchestra that, to use his own term, he had been 'agape'. He contacted her management and eventually spoke to Haendel herself on the phone. She was 67, a long career already behind her, and was quick to point out to him that she was not a teacher. 'But', she added, 'if your David wants to play something for me, he is welcome to do so. I'm going to be giving a masterclass in Dartington, England, soon.' So we were in, and I was just as excited about meeting a world-class violinist as my father was.

Later, Ida would often recount the story of our first meeting as an unforgettably strange occasion. My version goes like this. There were a good dozen young violin students sitting in a room in Dartington with their parents, along with the Bongartz/Garrett family. Each of the students had prepared a piece, and Ida went to them one by one, asking 'What would you like to play?' The response would be something like *Spring Sonata* by Beethoven, or Johann Sebastian Bach's first *Partita*. And while the student played, Ida would listen silently. It was eventually my turn, and Ida of course asked, 'What would you like to play?'

Now, I'm known for being an ambitious lad, so I answered with, 'What would you like to hear?' I was, of course, perfectly prepared and dumped a whole pile of sheet music on the piano: six violin concertos, five sonatas, a few Bach solos and Paganini *Caprices*. Ida thought I was an arrogant little nobody who was just bluffing, but just asked me to play the first movement of Tchaikovsky's violin concerto. This movement is a huge challenge for violinists of any age, and there would have been quite a few people in the room thinking, 'If he can pull this off ...'

Ida let me play the entire movement through to the final note – a clear sign that she saw me more as a colleague than a student. I had won the doubters over, and Ida intimated that she would make an exception for me – that I didn't need a teacher, but, in future, would still need someone to encourage and challenge me, a role she was happy to fill. And so it happened that the admirable Ida Haendel would be part of my life for the next four years. I would be her only permanent student, and would remain so until her death in 2020. She refused to take any payment; my father would repeatedly offer her money, but she would never accept it.

Ida and I would meet all over the place – sometimes in London, where she would spend a lot of time, or in Germany, if she was performing there, or in Miami, where she actually lived. Her approach was different to Zakhar Bron's; she didn't say, 'You have to wait before playing Beethoven.' No, she herself was already playing Beethoven at the age of eleven. In her view, maturity had nothing to do with age, and in my case, she explained that my soul was actually much older than my age suggested. But her generation didn't have the same teaching-oriented mindset we tend to see today.

She had an uncommonly friendly manner. It was something I noticed that very first day in Dartington, when she commented forgivingly on the young students' playing, saying 'I would do it differently – I would do it like this', before picking up her violin and playing the same piece in such a way that nothing further needed to be said. She treated me as an equal. 'You're not a wunderkind', she would say, 'you're a musician.' After I played something for her, she would often comment kindly, 'Very nice, but I have a few more ideas ...' And if a piece wasn't yet quite right technically or musically, you didn't even have to go and see her. I once made the bold move to see her in Miami, even though my version of Wieniawski's *Violin Concerto No. 1* was still a bit wobbly. 'Let's take my dog out for a while,' she said to me. 'That will be enough for today.' She then picked up her tiny fluffball of a pet dog called Decca (inspired by her record company), and never said another word about my debacle for the rest of the walk.

She was a wonderful woman; fluent in eight languages, she had travelled the world, played with the great conductors, and was the perfect person to be working with if I was now to be tackling the likes of the Beethoven and Brahms violin concertos and, later, Beethoven's sonatas – everything that represented the absolute zenith, not necessarily of virtuosity, but of musicality. But she would limit herself to showing me phrasing (means of expression) I would never have thought of, or explaining the way each passage breathed, how to fundamentally approach an interpretation.

At a technical level, I was on my own from now on, and had to teach myself the most difficult passages. Every concerto requires its own playing technique, and an experienced teacher could show me how to make the tricky sections easier. But my parting from Bron also marked the start of the days that saw two autodidacts in Aachen – my father and me – trying to solve the technical problems of virtuoso pieces without any instruction. You can imagine the friction that our lack of experience caused. Looking back, it's a mystery how autodidact #1 still managed, with the help of autodidact #2, to develop that immense repertoire independently.

Time to bring the curtains down for a moment and take a breather. After all, my life story has another leading actor who wasn't in as much of a rush as I was, and that's my instrument, the violin. Good violins have their own story too, and they're no less exciting than my own, which is why I want to push open the door to the past a little wider and creep a few floors lower. This journey into the past starts with my passion for collecting. You see, between practising and performing, I do actually have time for a hobby, and when I finally put my violin down, I focus on – violins.

Yes, I'm serious. What else would you expect from someone who has grown up with tons and tons of violins of all kinds? Who was born into the world of violins? Every year, my father would run two violin auctions; twice a year, up to 400 stringed instruments would arrive at our house, and, throughout my youth, there would be violins, violas and cellos in their cases stacked up in the cellar and all around our home, including in the bathroom. I felt like a kid growing up in a sweet shop, and would run around the house flipping open the violin cases, picking up the odd instrument and examining the finest ones more closely. My father was, of course, enough of an expert to show me the unique features of each violin. One look and he could tell which workshop it had come from: this one is a Vuillaume, this one is a Pressenda, this one is a Santo Serafin, a Klotz, and an Amati. I got infected with a rare disease: a violin obsession.

From the age of six onwards, I devoured every book relating to violins or violin virtuosos. I trawled through old catalogues from violin auctions at Sotheby's or Christie's from the 1960s and 1970s and memorized the contours of every single instrument; the F holes, the wood grain, the varnish and the way the scroll at the top of the neck was carved. I even collected and catalogued them by violin-maker. This meant that, much to my father's chagrin, I would cut the pictures out of the catalogues, place them in plastic wrap and sort them into the relevant folder, like a botanist cataloguing his dried plants. Each famous violin-maker had his own folder; there was one each for Amati, Pressenda, Guadagnini, Stradivari, Vuillaume and Bergonzi, but my favourite folder, my greatest treasure, was for violins made by Cremonese violin-maker Guarneri del Gesù, whom I admired the most.

Later on, my father took me to see the most famous violin dealers – Étienne Vatelot in Paris and Charles Beare and Peter Biddulph in London. 'Have a look at this violin,' they would say, and, even then, at the age of ten, I was able to classify every instrument. You see, for me, violins have a face. Sometimes the face is ravishingly beautiful, sometimes less attractive, but still always unique and full of character. And just as you rarely forget a person's face, so I rarely forget that of a violin. Charles Beare, the greatest violin expert of our time, even told me I had the best eye for violins he had ever seen, and advised me (as he continues to do to this day) to give up violin-playing and come and work with him, as it would also be much more lucrative.

When I started earning money, my passion for violins took another turn; I wasn't comfortable with the idea of having large sums of money sitting around in a bank account, which is why I have been investing in violins ever since. They don't necessarily have to be Stradivariuses; there are hundreds of great violin-makers from Italy, France and even Germany, so the last twelve years have seen me build up a pretty nice collection I am extremely proud of. I occasionally allow myself to make purchases on sentimental grounds. A few years ago, for example, I bought a wonderful Pressenda, partly because, back in Hilversum, a twelve-year-old me wearing tails performed Tchaikovsky's violin concerto on another Pressenda.

In other words, I have probably spent just as much time in my life examining violins, admiring violins and identifying violins as I have practising and playing. That's why I'm pretty relaxed about my future; even if I were to break my arms and legs, a single phone call would be enough to secure myself a permanent job as a violin dealer.

While my travels today often take me to London, New York and Amsterdam, my first journeys took me to the best violin dealers in the cities, to the Tarisio auction house, to Tim Ingles, Charles Beare and Andreas Post. I didn't want to buy anything; I didn't even want to play anything. I just looked around at what violins these dealers had on offer. I was like a car enthusiast in a car museum; just the sight of them all gave me the greatest pleasure.

To this day, I continue to maintain the collections and catalogues of violin images I started in my early Aachen days, albeit now on a computer. I'm currently in the process of digitizing all the instruments crafted by my favourite violin-maker, Guarneri del Gesù, in their order of creation. He must have made about 200 violins in his day, and of course not all of them still exist, but that doesn't bother me – I just add an annotation such as 'missing since 1920', and make do with an old black-and-white photo as the picture. The main thing, even in this pursuit, is to try to get as close to perfection as possible.

You can find videos and photos for this chapter here.

Luigi Tarisio and the Messiah Stradivarius

At the age of ten, I could finally move on from children's violins. I started playing an adult violin for the first time – a replica of the legendary Messiah Stradivarius, crafted by famous French violin-maker Jean-Baptiste Vuillaume around 1870. And I was completely captivated. I was over the moon. The initiated will understand why; for everyone else, I'll explain it by telling the relevant story. In fact, I would have told it anyway, even if I had never been obsessed with a copy of the Messiah Stradivarius, because this incident provides a look behind the scenes of a business that follows its own, not always clean, rules: violin-dealing. So here's the story of Luigi Tarisio and the Messiah Stradivarius.

In the early 19th century, there lived in Italy a fly-by-night violin dealer. Perhaps this is being harsh on him, but that is how

With my replica of Vuillaume's Messiah Stradivarius

he is described in history books. He was actually not a violin expert at all, having only trained as a carpenter, but, one day, he decided to specialize in procuring rare, valuable violins.

The man's name was Luigi Tarisio, and he actually did have a good eye for violins. He had the gift of being able to distinguish a high-quality Cremonese violin from a mediocre instrument at first glance. He began travelling all over Italy, the land of great violins – because, back then, the best violins were not being sent in huge quantities to America or China; they were staying in Europe, and were still abundant in their homeland, sometimes found in churches, sometimes in monasteries, sometimes in manor houses, and often just placed anywhere, in a store room or ramshackle cupboard, possibly gathering dust, rotting away and basically forgotten about.

But Luigi Tarisio had an eye for premium violins, regardless of the condition they were in. He would travel around, browsing churches, monasteries and villas, always dressed in nondescript, almost tattered casual clothes so that no one would think he was a businessman. And wherever he went, he would seek people out, insistently asking them for old violins and often getting them to show the instruments to him. If a scratched Stradivarius or dusty Landolfi happened to catch his sharp eye, he would take out one of the five or six polished, nicely crafted but completely worthless run-of-the-mill violins that he carried with him in his bag and offer this brand-new, shiny violin in exchange for the musty old one. 'That one has really had its day. It's totally scratched ... But have a look at this beautiful instrument! Can you just imagine, Signore (or Reverend or Padre), the joy this violin will bring to your house (or community or convent)? No, no, don't say anything. I don't want any money. Just let me have the old thing – perhaps it can be restored, after all – and take this gem of an instrument in return. It's yours.'

And the trick worked. Many people were taken in by this barter, with Tarisio constantly wangling the valuable violins out of them, and so it was that, over the decades, he came to possess a number of the finest violins. In the mid-19th century, Paris was the capital of the European music scene, and nearly all of Europe's prominent violin dealers were based there. So Tarisio took his treasure trove of half a dozen Guadagnini and Montagnana violins and made his first trip to the French capital, where he visited the shop of renowned violin dealers François Gand and Gustave Bernardel. He took out his violins and was met with disappointment: the dealers offered him a price well below market value. He had expected a lot more; what had gone wrong?

'It's my impoverished appearance!' he told himself – no doubt a grave error when dealing with the French, who place so much emphasis on sophisticated looks. When he arrived in Paris with his second haul, wearing professional attire, he decided against going to Gand & Bernardel, instead heading to their largest competitor, Jean-Baptiste Vuillaume. And, guess what! He received his asking price, and it was a considerable sum indeed.

So began a friendly business relationship between the most famous violin-maker and dealer of 19th-century France and our little crook Tarisio. Vuillaume would fawn all over him, probably because he was having sleepless nights worrying that Tarisio could start doing business with Gand & Bernardel. Then, one day, Tarisio mentioned an utterly wondrous violin, a Stradivarius, so incredibly beautiful and well preserved, it was as if it had only just left the master's workshop. Vuillaume pricked up his ears. 'Bring it along then,' he said, and, the next time Tarisio visited, he asked, 'Have you got it with you?' But no, he hadn't. Tarisio kept fobbing Vuillaume off, and so it went on for years, until, one day, the dealer flew off the handle. 'Your violin is like the Messiah! It's always "He's coming! He's coming!" But he never comes!'

And in fact Tarisio died before Vuillaume got to see the violin. No sooner had Vuillaume received the news of Tarisio's death than he made his way to Milan, Tarisio's hometown, found Tarisio's family, negotiated the estate with them and discovered a vast number of top-class instruments in Tarisio's home – but the mysterious Stradivarius was not among them. Vuillaume was ready to give up hope when he stumbled upon a double violin case under Tarisio's bed and opened it.

Now, Vuillaume had seen a lot of violins. He was an expert, and had even seen some very unusual ones. But what he saw here took his breath away: one of the two violins was the Alard Guarneri del Gesù from 1742, today on display in the Musée de la Musique in Paris, the best-preserved Guarneri known to man. But the other was the very Stradivarius Tarisio had been talking about the whole time, and, as it turned out, Tarisio hadn't been exaggerating. This 'Messiah Stradivarius' was indeed different to all the other Stradivariuses around – because of its immaculate, orange-red varnish. Any other Stradivarius shows the normal traces of violin wear and tear, but this one looked brand new, as if no one had ever played on it; as if it had barely been touched in a century.

Of course, Vuillaume bought up the whole estate. He paid a laughable amount for it and must have done good business out of it, but there was one violin he kept for himself: the Messiah Stradivarius. He kept it in his shop to preserve it for posterity in the condition in which he had found it, but did allow copies of it to be made – and one of these amazingly beautiful copies ultimately ended up in my hands, courtesy of my father.

It's a marvellous object. It is not the original, of course, and if anyone claims there's no difference anyway, that all the fuss about Guarneri and Stradivarius is based on pure fantasy, then I fiercely disagree. It would mean all of us who work with such violins are wrong, that the likes of Isaac Stern, Yehudi Menuhin, Henryk Szeryng, David Oistrach and Arthur Grumiaux are wrong. No, the fact that great violinists prefer to play on such instruments has very little to do with prestigious names.

While much less valuable violins have nice tones, only an original Cremonese violin can create the tonal nuances a top violinist needs. You must, of course, also be able to play such an instrument. Anyone used to driving a Fiat 500 won't be able to step straight into a Formula 1 car with success. Behind the wheel of such a racing vehicle, they'll do a lap of Silverstone slower than they would in their little city-centre car, and in the same way a Stradivarius needs immense skill to be mastered, challenged and played. But when that happens, that's when it produces all the tones of the universe – or of your imagination.

You can find videos and photos for this chapter here.

Mind over matter

You can't get me off the topic of violins any time soon. Here, briefly, are my memories of what was my favourite time of year as a child: my father's violin auction and the weeks leading up to it.

For weeks ahead, I would get more and more excited as the violins started to pile up in the Bongartz household. Where do you put 400, sometimes even 450, instruments and their bows? When there was no space anywhere and even the cellar was full, then in the bedroom? Eventually, every room would be packed full, completely barricaded, with violin cases, cello cases and viola cases, to the point that we had to carefully weave our way around them. Everything was different to usual. Our home was like that of a compulsive hoarder, and us kids had a bit of downtime, because my father was totally caught up in his business activities, photographing every instrument and poring over the catalogue text. Beyond him, we could see our mother sitting on the ground preparing the catalogue layout with scissors and glue. Eventually, however, everything would be ready. That's when the truck would stop outside our house, and be lined with Styrofoam and loaded with stringed instruments. For us, that meant it was time to head to Cologne to prepare the auction rooms.

So we would put up tables, push them together, put cloths over them and set up the opened violin cases. Alexander would pitch in, as would I, albeit, much to my brother's annoyance, only half-heartedly, because – look at all these violins! All these bows! And right in the thick of it all was my father, running back and forth, recounting things, explaining things ... these were exciting times. But the whole thing would reach its emotional climax when, two days before the actual auction, interested buyers from New York, Tokyo and all over the world, but primarily from Europe, would fill the showroom.

There would be a special smell as soon as you stepped in. Human sweat mixed with the paint and wood vapours – an intense mixture indeed. Dozens of people would come in, crowding between the rows of tables, moving from violin to violin, picking up an instrument, giving it a few strokes with the bow, putting it back down and picking up the next one. There were hundreds of violins on display, creating a veritable cacophony of background noise. The room would hum with sounds, much like before an orchestra rehearsal; everyone fiddling away on a different instrument, and each person playing a little differently, some better, some worse, a scale here, a snippet of Mozart there, topped with a few bars of Tchaikovsky – all a bit of a nightmare, because violin dealers don't necessarily have to be able to play the violin. I found it exciting, but my father found it painful to listen to.

Many years later, I would sometimes sit in on the auction, put in a bid and even buy a fine violin – after all, auction prices are generally cheaper than dealer prices. Incidentally, it's always amazing to see who exactly is collecting all these violins: architects, industrialists, bankers, people from the IT scene, and completely normal, lovable loonies. I often observed these people coming in, some of them raggedy, dishevelled types à la Tarisio, others dressed totally inconspicuously – a potpourri of characters that even a Balzac couldn't have brought together better. For some of them, you would think, 'Why didn't anyone stop that guy at the entrance?' But it was often precisely those types who were the experts. Curiously enough, my father's first-ever violins came from the collection of an Italian steelworker from Lüttich, who had had his foot amputated. He, too, would have fitted in perfectly here.

Ok, that's enough – time to raise the concert curtains again. Two years have since passed, and I'm now in the Vatican in Rome. There's a big religious event taking place, and a fourteen-year-old me is standing in front of a television camera in the Sistine Chapel, violin at the ready. Although I had so far managed to maintain my childish self-composure, I could feel my sweaty hands trembling slightly, and my breathing was also speeding up; but I would have had to be completely numb for my heart not to be racing in such circumstances: Michelangelo was looking down on me from high above, and down below, a camera was pointing at me – if there was one place on the planet where you didn't want to play a wrong note, it was probably here. 'When am I on?' 'Red light – you play. Okay?' I spent twenty long minutes staring at the camera before kicking off and playing Bach's *Andante*. And after four minutes, it was all over. I didn't even see the Holy Father. There probably was a ceremony outside in St Peter's Square, but I must say it was quite something nevertheless. An engagement like that was of course not highly paid. Even a Witiko Adler couldn't negotiate fees with the Vatican.

As you can see, my agency in Berlin didn't just sit around doing nothing. It arranged concert performances for me, and, most importantly, constantly gave me opportunities to demonstrate my talent to top conductors. Witiko Adler literally pitched me to every conductor who came to Berlin and performed with the Philharmonic. Some would listen to my music with a happy expression on their faces, others would occasionally look as though they had had to be coaxed into it, and there was even one who invited me in on the spot. That person was Zubin Mehta.

I experienced a lot with him over the following years. He took me with him to India, he gave me the chance to perform with the Munich Philharmonic, he hired me as a soloist for concerts with the Los Angeles Philharmonic, and even warmly recommended me to the organizer of the Ravinia Festival – the largest outdoor music festival in the USA. Zubin himself wasn't even going to be there; he did this sort of thing purely out of kindness. That's why I would like to say a few words about this special man, who would become my musical mentor.

Zubin Mehta has had an impressive career, with stints in Los Angeles, Israel, Munich and Florence, but he has never been one for flamboyant behaviour. He embodies a combination of sublime skill, humility and a love of music. Every sentence he utters conveys a sense of inner peace and level-headedness, as well as kindness and humour. And he loves company; after rehearsals, he would never lock himself away in his room, and would instead always leave his door open. In a word, Zubin doesn't just impart music; he also imparts life – true, great life, making him the ideal person to guide a young musician. I also learned something else – something very important – from him, namely a basic rule of the music business, which is: there's no getting sick; minor illnesses are not allowed.

It was 1997 and India was celebrating fifty years of independence. Zubin, idolized in his homeland, had been invited to perform two concerts with the Munich Philharmonic in Bombay and New Delhi to mark the occasion. And Zubin asked me to come along as a soloist – a massive honour for me.

We were put up in a grand hotel in Bombay – it could well have been a former maharaja's palace – and on the day of the first concert, we had lunch at the buffet. There would also have been an à la carte menu, but my father found this absolutely fabulous buffet too good to resist, so we tucked right in.

Now, in the tropics, there are bacteria and viruses that European stomachs are not familiar with, and all hell broke loose two hours later: I was throwing up, had a fever and the chills – classic food-poisoning. In short, I felt absolutely miserable, and it was 5 p.m. The concert was starting soon and my father was worried sick. He went to Zubin and told him, 'I don't know if David can perform tonight. He's running a 40-degree fever. What do we do?'

The concert should really have been cancelled, but Zubin is old school, and advised my father to give his son two aspirins. These days, fifty virologists would all start screaming, but these were different times, and anyway, the show must go on. The audience had paid, there was no refund, the boy could still stand up, so up on stage he must go.

And that's what I did – white as a sheet. The amazing thing is, when the excitement builds up and you need to start concentrating, you no longer feel your own body. All discomfort melts away into the background, and you forget you're sick – the rest is just a case of gritting your teeth and getting on with it. Anyone watching the video recording of this concert must have noticed I wasn't in the best shape, but I somehow managed to muddle my way through that night. I didn't throw up in front of everyone on stage, and was at least fortunate enough not to have to perform the following night.

Life just does throw a tough situation at you from time to time, and this is where my mother comes in. She was a dancer, after all, and was familiar with the problem from her experiences in ballet, where things are possibly even harder than in the music business. There's one phrase I would hear her say right from the time I was a child, and continue to hear today, and that is: 'mind over matter'. The mind does not let itself be dictated by anything, not even the body; regardless of the circumstances, it has the final word. Your will always prevails over anything you may be feeling. Now, one might dispute this fact at an older age, but, as a young person, it was absolutely something I lived by.

Today when I go on stage with a heavy cold, I use a little trick. After all, I don't want to be blowing my nose hard in front of 10,000 people, so I tell the lighting staff to turn off the lights briefly after every piece and leave the stage in darkness for ten seconds. And these ten seconds are enough for me to pull out a tissue, sniffle away into it and shove it back in my pants – then the lights are turned on and I'm back there smiling.

You can find videos and photos for this chapter here.

Isaac Stern

When I think back to the years between 1994 and 1996, I end up having doubts about some of the memories – what life was that in? My current one or another? Was it really me performing Brahms' double concerto at Dresden's Semperoper as a fifteen-year-old?

Yes, I'm sure. The Semperoper is a good example of the wonderful world I had suddenly found myself in. My performances with Claudio Abbado at Milan's Scala and London's St Martin-in-the-Fields almost feel surreal to me – and I cannot forget my performance in Paris, when President Chirac was sitting in the audience with his wife and came to see me backstage afterwards. When I think back now to that time, those places, the names of the conductors and orchestras, I'm

During a tour of Italy with Claudio Abbado

incredulous. I know I experienced it all, but I really have to dig those events out of my memory. I certainly enjoy admiring the findings I unearth, but I also know why I buried them.

The fact is, it all came way too quickly. My departure to New York a few years later was an escape from that dazzling world, riddled with relentless expectations. Coupled with it was, of course, the normal life of a student in Aachen, who, while being home-schooled, still had to do maths exercises. Plus there were the trips to my teachers and the recordings with Deutsche Grammophon (which I will talk about in the next chapter but one). I must have been craving peace. It is no coincidence that you hear of so many child prodigies who, after brilliant beginnings, end up having mental breakdowns and quitting. Stretching between the wunderkind and adult artist is a shaky suspension bridge that spans a vertiginous abyss, and, as a young person, you have to cross this scary bridge alone.

But anyway, we'll get to my New York life soon. Readers will probably have been wondering if I ever got to perform Beethoven's violin concerto. The answer is: yes, on German Unity Day in Frankfurt an der Oder at the age of thirteen. Did I pass the test?

Let's put it this way: my rendition was definitely not comparable with that of a well-versed violinist who brings life experience into the music. I also have to admit that Yehudi Menuhin had been faster and had done it at the age of just ten. But I was still proud. After all, that Beethoven concerto is a huge challenge, because it was originally written as a piano concerto. On a violin, you don't have the clear keyboard you get on a piano. When Beethoven later switched to the violin, he didn't factor in the particularities of that instrument, instead retaining all the aspects that cause great inconvenience to violinists as a result of the piece being intended first for the piano. It's still a great piece of music, though, and Beethoven may not have even written it for his time; perhaps he was thinking of a future in which violins would have developed further.

So anyway, that was achieved and done. At the time, there were also some great concert tours to Japan. Whether my father was unable to come because of work or because his fear of flying overcame him I do not know, but it was my mother who accompanied me to the Far East on a recital tour (piano plus violin) of four or five cities with Israeli pianist Itamar Golan. I had two really uplifting experiences during that time in Japan. The first surprise awaited me when I left the stage after a concert and entered my green room – myriad large bouquets of all kinds of flowers, and baskets of fruit, too. What an overwhelming and touching expression of joy!

The second surprise was my audience. In Europe, I was used to seeing older, rather wealthy people; I was usually thirty years younger than the youngest attendee. I noticed it, and found it odd, but knew no different until I came to Japan. There, I saw so many young people sitting in the audience! Yes, there were lots of women, but also quite a few young men. And then came my first encounter with the onslaught of fan appreciation ...

After the concert, we left the building through a back exit, where a car was waiting for us. I got into the back seat with my violin, my mother next to me, and we took off. Not long afterwards, the driver pointed out three cars that were obviously tailing us. Even then, there would often be fans wanting to know the name of the hotel I was staying at, but I couldn't understand why – only years later was I able to work it out – and when the driver asked whether he should shake off the pursuers, I said yes, acting purely on a James-Bond-esque whim. It was a cinch. Full throttle through traffic lights that had just changed to red, and we were free of our pursuers, who had most likely been female. That would have been something.

While I remember those concerts fondly, what I'm about to recount continues to make me cringe to this day (and probably has the same effect on others too).

Back in 1994, Zubin Mehta had contracted me for three performances with the Munich Philharmonic at Munich's Gasteig. I was to play Mozart's *Violin Concerto in G Major*, and during the rehearsals, Zubin kept asking me to play Mozart's music 'like champagne'. It may not have been age-appropriate (after all, I didn't have the foggiest idea about champagne), but it was funny – unlike what I had the cheek to do on stage.

You see, before one of these concerts, someone had unfortunately let me know that world-famous conductor Daniel Barenboim would be sitting in the audience.

Once the concert ended, there was applause, and I got the crazy idea into my head that, as Barenboim was sitting somewhere down there, I would impress him and play Bach's *Chaconne* as an encore! A solo violin piece that, in my version, lasted nearly twenty minutes and, for a variety of reasons, was entirely inappropriate as an encore at that time – firstly, because the orchestra wanted to have a break; secondly, because the conductor wanted to start the second half quite soon; and thirdly, because the audience had already been listening to music for the past fifty minutes and wanted to drink their champagne or go to the toilet.

Now, everyone knows an encore lasts only about three minutes, but this one did not. Eventually, I noticed a sense of restlessness in the room. Eventually, it struck me that the orchestra musicians were sitting on their chairs with frozen facial expressions, as if they were paralysed. And eventually, I realized Barenboim had probably snuck out, thinking 'I'm not putting up with this!' Today, I can only imagine how much I must have made poor Daniel Barenboim and the whole Gasteig suffer. I had definitely way overstepped the mark, and my only consolation is to assume that never before in the history of music had a fourteen-year-old dared to send his audience into a state of shock by playing a twenty-minute encore.

So much for the concerts.

In the meantime, I kept having the occasional session with Ida Haendel, who had helped me prepare the Beethoven concerto. No matter how well prepared you are, as a violinist, or as any kind of artist, you are never totally ready, and certainly not at the age I was then. Anyone wanting to be measured against the greats needs to learn from the greats, and Ida was definitely one of them. But during those years, other true legends also came on board, and the first one I want to talk about is Isaac Stern.

My personal encounter with him has a back story. Stern was to give a recital in Oxford, my father went with me and, that night, I witnessed one of the most defining concerts of my entire life. I sat there and had goose bumps from the very first note to the last. Stern had captivated me so much that I was quivering with emotion. It was the same for my father; he would later admit that Stern's *Sonata* by César Franck had completely 'blown him away'. How do I explain this effect?

What I particularly liked was that Stern spoke with his violin. Not literally, but the pair of them, him and his violin, seemed to be in a deep, uninterrupted conversation with each other. He also had an incredible instinct for the dramatic dimension of his musical expression. For the rest, he was like any other outstanding violinist in that he had his own unique sound, his own personal tonal nuances. Every great violinist has a musical identity, perhaps a unique vibrato, their own amount of pressure applied to the bow, and their own way of playing glissandi. All this made him as distinctive as the brushstrokes and colours made a Van Gogh, a Rembrandt or a Monet unique in art. I would definitely be able to pick out Isaac Stern even if a thousand violinists were playing.

My father contacted him after this prelude, and, weeks later, we were on our way to see him in Switzerland. What do you play for someone like Isaac Stern? I felt Édouard Lalo's *Symphonie Espagnole* was fittingly difficult, so, at around 11 a.m., and well prepared as ever, I joined my father in Stern's room in a grand, old-world Swiss hotel dating back to the turn of the 20th century.

And Isaac Stern was sitting there in a regal armchair, behind a little desk, dark glasses on and a fat cigar between his lips – sitting there as the godfather incarnate, exactly the way Marlon Brando had played him in the film. No one would have been surprised if, at that moment, he had opened his mouth and said, 'David, I'll make you an offer you can't refuse.'

Obviously, he didn't, but he sure knew how to cultivate a look and create an aura of aloofness. He also had an unusual way of speaking, sometimes downright aristocratic, other times indeed quite vulgar. I was impressed. Never before had a teacher greeted me with sunglasses and a cigar, seated in what seemed a throne rather than a chair. He indicated for me to take out my violin, and I played the first movement of *Symphonie Espagnole*. The entire movement, mind you! It is not uncommon for an aspiring violinist to start playing, only to be told within ten seconds, 'Thank you, you are very talented, but unfortunately I have to go and rehearse now' – translation: we will never see each other again in this life. Stern didn't say much at the time, but the fact that he had let me play the entire movement was to be taken as a huge compliment. He probably arranged a time with my father afterwards and that was it.

It was, of course, impossible to work continuously with Isaac Stern, but that wasn't our intention for our collaboration anyway. We would just meet for a few days occasionally, always outside Germany, because Stern refused to set foot on German soil. We even travelled to New York for him, and I remember German Consul General Erhard Holtermann kindly allowing us to use the guest room in his stunning, spacious home. This house right near Central Park must have impressed me just as much as the man himself, who, it turned out, was a lover of classical music and owned a fine Jean-Baptiste Vuillaume violin.

During the day, as soon as Isaac had time, we would go over to see him, and I would play him a piece from my repertoire. I would then have to brace myself for a different manner to anything I had experienced with my previous teachers. Partly, of course, because I was awestruck by him, but also because the personal, friendly tone my other teachers had used was just not Isaac's style, nor was any notion of paying compliments. If he needed to make mention of something, he could be harsh, even patronizing; but he would always get straight to the point – no diplomatic beating around the bush, no friendly remarks, just plain language; Isaac never left you in the dark about his displeasure.

But he was usually inscrutable. You could never tell for sure if he liked something or not. As a student, you would think, 'I've given it my all this time, this time I was absolutely brilliant', but the master's face would not show any sense of enthusiasm. Indeed, it would show nothing at all. Is this the way he himself had been taught? Had he made a point of not paying compliments? In any case, when he was not pleased, he was good at expressing his dissatisfaction in clear, unequivocal words.

He was a fascinating character, and I put him on a pedestal. Being in the presence of this aloof man made me realize just how long and arduous the road to the top was, and how distant the ultimate goal still remained. But I also got a sense of what it had taken Isaac to achieve this degree of mastery. Every note he played was hard-earned. He certainly was not one of those violinists who exude ease and effortlessness, from whom the music seems to flow out of the violin of its own accord; with him, you always knew that every note was extremely hard work. This perception of violin-playing somehow fitted the imposing vibe he gave off as a person. He was proud of his life achievements and cultivated his look accordingly.

And when it came to him as a teacher ... if there's one great lesson that great musicians can give you, it's the habit of using your own brain. An average teacher will tell you, 'Come, use this fingering, put your bow like this, be more passionate here', but that's not what it's about. As I said, every outstanding violinist has their own unique sound identity, and good teachers will always ask questions to make their students aware of their own sound: 'Why did you play this section that way?' They force them to look inside themselves until they find their own musical language. And this was true of Isaac, whose criticism, incidentally, would be limited to just a few comments or simply hammering my forehead with his index finger like a woodpecker, uttering only one word: 'Think!' and then again, 'Think! Think!'

But he also got me to bear in mind the spirit of the age, as well as the composer's personality, in my interpretations. That meant playing Tchaikovsky passionately, Beethoven with a mix of energy and restraint, and Mozart with a precise sense of ease. It was also important to make a distinction as to when to bring your own personality into the performance and when to take a step back out of respect to the composer – with Beethoven, for instance, Stern warned me against trying to distinguish myself as a violinist, because the greater the music, the more humility it requires from the performer.

In short, there was once again a lot for me to learn here. Stern was a completely different character to Ida Haendel, and it was for precisely this reason that he was all the more important for me and my development. In the end, it was actually he who gave me the crucial nudge I needed to finally leave Germany and move to New York.

You can find videos and photos for this chapter here.

Yehudi Menuhin

All of my lessons were conducted in English, though surprisingly most of the great violinists I met could also speak German. Polish-born Ida Haendel was fluent in eight languages, and even Isaac Stern would switch to German if I hadn't understood his English during the lesson – just like Yehudi Menuhin, whom I remember particularly fondly.

Along with Jascha Heifetz, Yehudi Menuhin was the 20th-century violin wunderkind *par excellence*. I knew his autobiography by heart right from the age of nine, and I mainly used my DJ duties during the hours-long car trips with my father to put Menuhin CDs on. I particularly found the combination of Furtwängler and Menuhin second to none, and, to this day, I can still hear the sound of his violin in Brahms' *Violin Concerto*

My first meeting with the wonderful Yehudi Menuhin at age ten

in D Major conducted by Wilhelm Furtwängler. Don't ask me why, but Menuhin made the violin sound otherworldly. When he played, it ceased to be a violin; it was an instrument from a different, much more beautiful world, and it was not until his last concert as a soloist in the early 1990's that this sound left our planet forever.

In 1992, Menuhin gave a guest performance as a conductor in Aachen, and however my father had managed to swing it, I soon found myself in Menuhin's room at the *Quellenhof* hotel. 'What do you want to play?' – the usual question, but not a usual situation, because it was just before his concert, and he would soon have to be getting changed and preparing himself... No matter, Menuhin was cool as a cucumber and let me play.

I must have left a good impression, because, over the next six weeks, we met more regularly. First off, though, I want to mention an amusing detail; the only thing Menuhin had on the table in his room at the *Quellenhof* hotel, which consequently caught the eye straight away, was a cut pineapple. As I've mentioned, Menuhin was one of my father's huge idols, and my father was a health-conscious person who always tried to keep me from the dangers of the big wide world. When he saw the pineapple, he probably came to the conviction that, if this great man eats pineapples, then this fruit will also be beneficial to the development of my son David. From then on, there were definitely more pineapples around for me in the Bongartz household. It didn't do any harm.

But that's just an incidental anecdote. What really caused a stir was when, in 1996, Menuhin contacted my agency in Berlin to ask if I would play Elgar's *Violin Concerto in B Minor*, conducted by him, at the Wiener Musikverein concert hall in Vienna.

Now, it is important to know here that Menuhin had a special relationship with this violin concerto. On the very first recording of this concerto, created in 1932, you can hear Menuhin himself playing as a teenager, a sixteen-year-old soloist, while Sir Edward Elgar himself is conducting his own work. So, sixty-five years later, I was, in a way, following in Menuhin's footsteps, but with Menuhin himself filling Elgar's role as a nearly eighty-year-old conducting the concerto – a huge honour for me!

But I hadn't yet mastered this concerto. Even Menuhin wasn't sure I would be able to manage it; after all, it was an epic, fifty-minute piece riddled with pitfalls. So Menuhin's reservations were only too justified, which is why, soon after, we went to Switzerland, where Menuhin had lived for a long time, for the audition. What can I say? Menuhin tapped his foot along to my playing and absolutely loved it. He promptly sent my manager, Witiko Adler, a fax saying he wasn't worried in the slightest, because I was 'phenomenal' and would play Elgar's concerto 'superbly'.

I went to Vienna and I now need to say a few words about Vienna's Musikverein concert hall. Opened in 1870, this classical temple of music is one of the most magnificent performance venues in the world. Its showpiece, the Golden Hall, with its ceiling paintings and ornamental sculptures, all actually gold-plated, is a particular feast for the eyes. So the setting for this concert couldn't have been more stately; except, all of a sudden, on the day of the concert, there was a problem: Menuhin had arranged an orchestral rehearsal with me for the afternoon, but, before that, he had to rehearse a symphony for the first part of the programme, and that had run over time. It never seemed to end. The time of the performance was approaching, and Menuhin was still rehearsing – we now only had fifty minutes, then only forty, and, once the stage was finally free for me, there were only twenty-five minutes to go. How long did we end up rehearsing? Ten minutes! Only the most difficult sections. Yet

I was about to make my debut here ... That night, I went up on stage in the world-famous Golden Hall of Vienna's Musikverein concert hall without having played this piece through a single time with the orchestra! But I had thought to myself beforehand: if Menuhin isn't worried, you don't need to worry either.

Well, our timing was not always perfect, but the reviews the next day were positive ... and here's a little story that may explain Menuhin's composure that night. Back in 1932, before that first-ever recording of the concerto, when he came to London to play for Elgar, he went to Elgar's estate. They briefly greeted each other, Menuhin took out his violin, and, no sooner had he played a few notes than Elgar waved him on: 'Fantastic; see you at the studio for the recording; I'm off to a horse race.' So Elgar also appears to have been one of those more relaxed contemporaries; in any case, Menuhin himself had similarly performed without rehearsing with the orchestra beforehand, and, in Vienna, he may well have thought, 'I managed it without rehearsing, so why would David mess up?

Never before nor since have I experienced anything like the night of that Elgar concerto in Vienna. Nor would it likely have happened with any other conductor in the world. But, for Menuhin, music was a break from life, and who agonizes over trifles like a missed orchestra rehearsal when they're on holiday? In his dealings with me, in any case, he was always cheerily self-confident. I do know, however, that he would occasionally be overcome by sadness – which is probably nothing unusual for a larger-than-life character like him, who devoured life's moments, and whose vitality and zest for action were boundless. But Menuhin was also very health-conscious; he was not a fan of alcohol, nicotine nor meat, and was always mindful of his body, which had managed to cope with the incredible stresses and strains that came with his on-the-go lifestyle. Not only did he give hundreds of concerts every year, but, during World War II, for example, he also performed with the forces and at military hospitals, and, after the war, played for concentration-camp survivors.

He eventually lost control of his right bow arm and was no longer able to play at his usual level of perfection, switching to conducting in the early 1990s out of necessity. Until the end of his life, he must have sought ways of getting the mind and body back into that balance he had maintained in his early years. He was never able to, but it might be that without his physical affliction, Menuhin may not have reached that marvellous human maturity I witnessed in him.

He was essentially a happy soul. Anyone who reads his autobiography will get a sense of this merriness, and it is also amusingly demonstrated by the story I mentioned earlier, with him performing as a shaven-legged 13-year-old in shorts, lest anyone think the wunderkind Yehudi had outgrown his childhood. As an adult, you could be forgiven for regarding this warily – who knows what other unsavoury tricks his parents came up with? – but Menuhin would talk about it frankly and with genuine humour.

It should be clear by now that you could hardly get a pair of more polar opposites than Isaac Stern and Yehudi Menuhin. If I had to compare them, I would say that Menuhin was a humanist, a philanthropist and a lover of life. He was the only Jewish violinist, who, after the war, accepted Wilhelm Furtwängler's invitation to perform concerts in Germany, whereas Isaac Stern refused to set foot in Germany right until the last. I believe both attitudes deserve respect. For Menuhin, reconciliation went above all else, while Stern had the most justifiable reasons in the world for his lack of forgiveness. Despite this dichotomy, however, both took German David Garrett under their wing. They were also polar opposites at a musical level. Menuhin was pure emotion, embodying something divine for me, whereas Stern represented all that was profoundly human. It is impossible to imagine more contrasting violinists, but, in their own way, both were great.

You can find videos and photos for this chapter here.

The piano is too loud!

For one last time, I'm going to return to the twelve-year-old me. Back then, at the start of my wunderkind phase, Witiko Adler called me to say that Deutsche Grammophon, a prestigious record label in the classical music industry, wanted to contract me. This they did, resulting in me symbolically (as usual) signing an agreement for five CDs just under a year later. In turn, this sparked an influx of concert requests, culminating in recordings for Deutsche Grammophon, with Claudio Abbado and the Chamber Orchestra of Europe, and with Mikhail Pletnev and the Russian National Orchestra in the Tchaikovsky Hall at the Moscow Conservatory. It's a miracle I didn't get swept away by all the excitement and nerves at the time.

But first things first. CD #1 was a recording of Beethoven's *Spring Sonata*, Mozart's *Adagio* and Bach's second *Partita*, with

With German president Richard von Weizsäcker during my concert at Villa Hammerschmidt in Bonn

violin and piano only rather than an orchestra. I was thirteen. On CD #2, I played a purely Mozart repertoire alongside the English Chamber Orchestra led by Claudio Abbado. I was fourteen. That same year, I recorded virtuoso romantic pieces, including *Polonaise* and *Faust Fantasy* by Henryk Wieniawski, L*a Campanella* by Niccolò Paganini and *La Capricieuse* by Edward Elgar. I was accompanied here by the amazing Russian pianist Alexander Markovich, who was only a few years older than me, and this CD was to be released as the third album. But it wasn't.

What happened? Shortly before our CD went into production, my father was sent the digital audiotape of the recording. He listened to it and said, 'The piano is too loud!' He felt the mix wasn't right, that his son didn't have enough of a presence, that he was drowned out by the piano. In other words, my father was very displeased, and, at my next meeting with the Deutsche Grammophon representatives, I was under express orders to stop the whole venture. Just imagine it: the photoshoot in Paris is done, everything is all in place and ready to go, the recording is to be released soon, Deutsche Grammophon has already spent a lot of money on travel, hotels, food, photographers, studios and so on, and a fourteen-year-old is now telling them the recording is unusable and the whole venture is a failure ...

This was extremely ill-received by the people at Deutsche Grammophon. It was not difficult to tell what they were thinking from their expressions – something along the lines of 'This lad is clearly off his head. What kind of a diva have we been nurturing here?', no doubt. And I understood their struggle to contain their annoyance, because I liked the recording, and cancelling the whole thing did not sit well with me at all. I actually had to muster up all my courage even to go to the meeting, but what was I supposed to do? I was my father's mouthpiece, and it was better for there to be anger at the record company than at home.

In short, the recording was banished to the archives, and the relationship between Deutsche Grammophon and me was clearly damaged. But a contract is a contract, and we met up again soon after to discuss the musical repertoire for CD #4. I was sitting at the table during this meeting, so I heard it when my father suddenly said, 'What about Paganini's *Caprices*? My son plays them beautifully ...'

This made me wince, because so far I had played only seven of the twenty-four *Caprices*. So I had never touched seventeen of the twenty-four, and, collectively, these twenty-four made up the most technically difficult piece ever written for violin. As if that were not enough, no one had ever recorded the *Caprices* at my age; it had been hailed an amazing achievement when Japanese violinist Midori recorded all the *Caprices* before her eighteenth birthday, five years earlier. In other words, the suggestion my father was making was rather foolhardy and probably intended as a way of making amends for the little affair with the shafted CD #3.

And Deutsche Grammophon agreed. They jumped at the chance. 'When do we start recording?' 'In four months. In summer.' Yes, everything had to move quickly now. Deutsche Grammophon was on a tight time frame, it was in a hurry, particularly as David Garrett seemed to be perfectly primed for the *Caprices* ...

Actually, David Garrett was not primed, but he was now practising like crazy. Every spare minute I had, I would grab my violin and tinker away at the passages that demanded the most ludicrous fingering. No teacher was advising me on the fingering; I was improvising. I didn't even have time to consider fingering that would make the most complicated sections at least a little less scary, so inexperience meant I made the whole thing even more difficult. But, this time, my sweat and tears were rewarded, and you'll have to forgive my lack of understatement here when I say that, by teaching myself seventeen Paganini *Caprices* in the shortest of time frames, and recording them in the studio as a fifteen-year-old to a level that pleased everyone involved, I earned my place as a titan among autodidacts! That was more than twenty-five years ago now, and I still consider those twenty-four Paganini *Caprices* as a truly glorious chapter in my previous life as a wunderkind.

There are two reasons in particular that keep these two weird albums – both the hapless third and the successful fourth – in my mind.

The first reason is a pleasant, albeit curious, one: many years later, having long moved into crossover, I received a call from Deutsche Grammophon: 'Mr Garrett, we've still got an unreleased recording of yours. Do you have anything against us releasing it now?' I advised my father, we listened to the tape again, and he promptly said, 'The recording is great! I have no idea what came over me back then ... I must have been dim.' Today, he readily admits he made a mistake. And so it was that, in 2013, CD #3 finally made its way into the world as album #14.

The second reason is an unpleasant one that really, really got to me – to the point that the entire wunderkind house of cards started to wobble and ultimately collapsed.

You couldn't really tell at the time, because wouldn't all the effort eventually pay off? I was giving concerts, had teachers like Ida Haendel and Isaac Stern, was contracted by the most reputable record company, and was now even playing on a Stradivarius. Yes, I almost forgot to mention that, but it's only a quick story ... Germany's president at the time, Richard von Weizsäcker, who was a classical music enthusiast, had invited me to perform at his office at Villa Hammerschmidt in Bonn. After the concert, he was in a caring mood, and came over to me and said, 'Listen,

I could help you get a nice violin.' And indeed he managed to convince the Talbot family in Aachen to give me their Stradivarius. It was very generous of them, even though I would have held out for another few years without one – and it wasn't as if I immediately started playing better on the Stradivarius anyway.

So you would think all my dreams had come true. But something wasn't right. It all started soon after the Paganini recording. I suddenly noticed pain in my left hand and left forearm. I couldn't move my fingers properly anymore. The little finger was the worst, but it wasn't just that one – the whole hand was no longer behaving like it usually did; it felt like some sort of fatigue that ran up the arm to my elbow, and this pain, this weakness, wouldn't go away. Was it because of the Paganini CD that I had worn myself out over? Who knows. I had never experienced anything like this before. What I had experienced, however, and had been suffering from for a long time, were the most severe migraine attacks the night before a concert.

These were equally a mystery, as I would usually go into concerts totally relaxed, full of naïve self-confidence, unperturbed by the spotlights and audience. Beneath the conscious perception threshold, however, I must have sensed the responsibility I had, the lofty expectations I had to fulfil. Then I would wake up in the middle of the night with a pain that felt like someone was driving a butcher's knife into my head, a pain so horrendous I wanted to dig my nails into the wall. Getting back to sleep was out of the question. Sometimes my mother, other times my father, would sit by my bed, racking their brains as to how to help me. Put a cold cloth on my forehead? Give me a cup of chamomile tea? No, nothing helped, except throwing up. Once I had done this, the migraine would let up soon after, as if I had released all the stress in my body, as if this was my body's treacherous way of ridding itself of its high tension. Despite the relief, I would often be so exhausted the next morning that my body couldn't even muster up the energy to feel nervous.

So I had experience with all that, but now there was suddenly this problem with my left hand. It was exasperating, because the concert performances continued on their merry way, but I was no longer the same. I suddenly became nervous before the performance, and even while playing. My sense of ease had gone. I no longer felt confident, because my fine motor skills were suffering, and this meant I gradually lost my passion for playing. Oh, I kept playing, and even did pretty well over the following years, but something alarming was happening: previously, when I had worked with world-famous conductors and played with orchestral musicians, their eyes would light up, as if they were about to experience something great, or at least out of the ordinary. Over time, however, this light in their eyes grew dimmer and dimmer, like a shooting star burning up. As if the wave was breaking.

And now? Violin-playing was my whole purpose – aside from the fact that I was a little cog in the machine that was the music business, which was running at full speed. And the only people I had around me were those who believed in me! There was no one I could confide in, no one who would perhaps have given me the obvious advice to just take a break for a year. On the other hand, that wouldn't have been an option, because tours were planned eighteen months in advance.

In any case, my father didn't think too much about the issue for the first two years. And my mother? 'Mind over matter.' So I rehearsed Camille Saint-Saëns' *Violin Concerto No. 3* with great discomfort and pain, went on stage and jittered my way through the concert. At the age of sixteen, I also recorded CD #5 with Mikhail Pletnev and the Russian National Orchestra in Moscow. You can't hear my distress in the recording, and both

Tchaikovsky's *Violin Concerto in D Major* and Julius Conus' *Violin Concerto in E Minor* sound marvellous and full of ease, but I know how I struggled through that recording, how difficult it was for me to put on a brave face.

Eventually, all I could think of was: why are you suddenly finding the easy stuff hard? Why does your confidence drop before a performance? Playing the violin has never been an effort for you! What will happen to you? A rude awakening, perhaps?

You can find videos and photos for this chapter here.

Of love and heartache

Fortunately, it wasn't all bad at that time. I became acquainted with love, for example. But it wasn't in Japan, nor was it in Aachen – it was in Israel.

As you know, we had a habit of seeking out prominent people in the world of music – my father would make the contact, and I would play for them. And this was once again the case, straight after I had finished doing the Paganini recording for Deutsche Grammophon. Shlomo Mintz was chief conductor of the Maastricht Symphony Orchestra at the time, and Maastricht is just a stone's throw from Aachen, so paying a courtesy call to Mintz was an obvious decision. And what did he ask me to play when we sat down with him? The Paganini *Caprices*! 'I know them all,' I blurted; I wasn't one for false

At the Keshet Eilon Festival with Ivry Gitlis, Shlomo Mintz and Cihat Aşkın

modesty back then, and my left arm hadn't yet started to cause problems.

'Very good,' was his short-and-sweet verdict once I had played the twelfth *Caprice*. There was a slight Isaac Stern vibe in the room, because Shlomo similarly did not beat around the bush. And he then made me a proposal: 'Come to Israel. I'll be there for three weeks in the summer; it will do you good and we can work together.' What was he talking about? A music festival specially for violinists, which had been held at the Keshet Eilon kibbutz on the Lebanese border since 1990. Shlomo Mintz was the patron of this festival.

So, would I go to Israel? Shlomo, a student of Isaac Stern, was one of my idols, and Israel would of course mean I would be away from my parents, away from my father. So off to Israel I would go! But not totally alone. My brother Alexander, who was not at all keen, was forced to be my babysitter at the kibbutz; being the very amiable person that he is, he swallowed the pill and came with me. However, it was the first time in my life I was largely unsupervised, and I discovered that, apart from playing the violin, I had absolutely no idea about the world. Thank God the kibbutz was such that you couldn't get completely lost – if the complex had been larger, I would probably still be roaming the border area between Israel and Lebanon looking for my kibbutz. In short, these three weeks were my first foray into freedom, and this unfamiliar new situation felt good.

We did of course work during this time too. Shlomo taught me techniques I had never seen before – and this is hugely important if you want to do justice to the different personalities of different composers. But we also bonded with our teacher at a more personal level during those few weeks, because, in the evening, we would all sit around the campfire, tell stories and entertain each other with jokes that sometimes were actually rather dirty. Shlomo was a leader in this field – he would tell the sauciest of jokes with such a straight face that it would take a while for you to laugh. Plus, of course, our respect for this man was too great for us to burst out in guffaws.

We even danced on Saturday nights. There was a larger space that had been converted into a disco, and Shlomo liked stopping by there too. At forty, he was still a young man who enjoyed life away from music and was the picture of fulfilled contentment when, at special moments, he would sit with cigar in hand, as was his habit. Telling a joke during a lesson would have broken all the rules, but, after work, he was up for having fun with the young people by the campfire and sometimes even popping into the disco. Music wasn't everything in life for him, but as soon as someone started making music, everything else faded away, and music did become everything.

Upon my return to Aachen, as it was apparent that the Kibbutz sojourn hadn't caused me any harm and my fingering wasn't rusty, it was logical that I started to consider going back. So I returned to Israel the following year, without my brother, and, this time, exactly what you might expect would happen in such circumstances did happen: a young Israeli girl came into my life. Her name was Sara Zuckerbaum.

And Sara was lovely. What am I saying: she was phenomenal! Around the same age as me, she was a brilliant violinist. That was a good enough reason for me to find her captivating, but she also had the face of an angel and an amazing temperament. Her attitude to violin-playing alone was completely different. No one forced her; Sara played purely out of a love of playing, a love of music, and her violin normally lay on her bed – she only practised when she felt like it. And yet she was good! She was pretty baffling, that girl. She actually had a life, and a zest for life, outside of music! In other words, she embodied everything that I didn't; she was easy-going and relaxed, witty and cheery, and I fell head over heels in love with her. She was just wonderful. She was the love of my life. I was seventeen, and we grew closer.

Or, more specifically: I spent perfect, blissful days and nights with Sara Zuckerbaum, and we kept in contact even after I left Israel. I was convinced nothing could shatter that love, that it would last a lifetime, and I would happily chat away with her on the telephone, much to my parents' chagrin, because calls at that time cost (if I'm not mistaken) 2.20 marks per minute. Eleven months later, we were in each other's arms once more, smooching away, ending up in her bed. The next morning, she uttered the fatal words 'we need to talk' to me.

I am now familiar with this phrase. At the time, however, I thought nothing of it, and encouraged her: 'Sure, fire away. What can I do for you?' To which she responded, 'I've met someone.' Cool, still no reason to panic. 'Yes, but it's more than a friendship. Tim and I are together, and he's coming tomorrow to stay for the rest of the festival.' Aha. Oh God. The next three weeks were going to be interesting. The love of your life enjoying herself with Tim while you watch on ...

Fortunately, Harry Karr, a British violinist, gave me a shoulder to cry on. And Harry, a man with experience, advised me, 'make friends with Tim'. This would ultimately be my undoing, because my efforts to be friends with Tim resulted in me having a front-row seat to watch the couple kiss and cuddle from morning to night. In the end, I sat in my darkened kibbutz room, feeling nothing but doom and gloom, listening to Bryan Adams' sad ballads on my headphones, eyes filled with tears. It's no surprise that the word 'love' brought me no great sense of euphoria those next few months.

But hey, there was at least one glimmer of light during those three grim weeks; I had brought my Stradivarius with me to Israel, and there was to be a concert at the weekend. People from the surrounding area had been invited, including the patrons who had made the summer camp possible, and the programme included Beethoven's *Violin Concerto in D Major*. We had spent days practising, and Shlomo, who was to be the conductor, now had to decide who would play the first movement, who would play the second, and who would play the third. So three violin soloists were needed, and he assigned me the first movement, which, being eighteen minutes long, was the showpiece of this concerto. 'But,' he said, 'I don't want you having an advantage over the others because of your Stradivarius. So Amnon will give you one of his violins.'

Amnon Weinstein was the violin-maker who had been running a violin workshop over the last few days, and he had a few cheap French violins with him, good student violins worth between 5,000 and 15,000 euros – so not a patch on the Stradivarius, which was worth millions. I protested feebly, but Shlomo was adamant. 'I want you to be the one who generates the sound, not your instrument. And one more thing: don't tell anyone. This stays between you and me.'

I didn't like Shlomo's idea at all, yet I have Amnon's violin to thank for giving me one of the best moments of my life. For, after the concert, many people came up to me, beaming and congratulating me on my magnificent instrument – 'I wish I had a Stradivarius too! What a wonderful sound!' Boy, did that make me happy! Shlomo refrained from making any comment, but I could tell from his face that he was just as pleased with himself as he was with me – it was precisely the outcome he had been aiming for. After all, there was no better way of demonstrating that the violinist is the one generating the sound, and that the Stradivarius is effectively a luxury item; it makes life easier, but it is not crucial.

The rest of the time, however, was more or less spent hungover. I definitely couldn't envisage a fourth stint in Keshet Eilon, but I had liked life at that traditional kibbutz, with its farming, its canteen open to everyone, and its simple two-bedded rooms in the kibbutz school. Until the second day of my third stay, I had found Israel beautiful all round, but the unfaithful Sara could never diminish my love for Israel, partly because I owe Israel an incredible amount. For example, it was Israeli orchestras who, after my time at the Juilliard School, when no one else wanted to know me, invited me to give concerts in their country. So I cannot thank them enough; they did a lot for my career.

But I also have to credit Sara with something I haven't yet mentioned: she sowed a life-saving seed in my brain by informing me in the first place about the Juilliard School, the college for musicians, actors and dancers in New York, which became a great hope for me, because Sara had told me about it. Strangely enough, she herself had felt so uncomfortable there that she had quit after just one semester and returned to Tel Aviv. I, on the other hand, had been dreaming of studying there ever since, and the longer the pain in my left arm continued, the more intensely I yearned to move to New York.

Which brings us back to the issue that preoccupied me more than anything else during those years. Curiously, Israel played a part here, indeed it actually played the most absurd part of all in that drama.

In my desperation, I had contacted Israeli doctors during that third stay in Eilon. They had advised me to undergo magnet therapy, and had recommended a tube into which I was to stick my injured left arm for one hour every day. I bought the thing – it wasn't exactly cheap – did what I was told, spent weeks, months, ultimately an entire year, putting my arm in it, and it did nothing. I might as well have stuck my arm into a toilet roll. Yes, there was a power socket and a plug, but that magnetic tube didn't get hot or cold, it didn't vibrate, I didn't feel any pinpricks on the skin – perhaps the machine was still being evaluated, but whatever the case was, it was a flop.

You can find videos and photos for this chapter here.

The secret tape

Who do you turn to when you have a concern that is gradually turning into a torture for you, but everyone else thinks it's trivial and not worth talking about? When everyone around you says it will pass? As ridiculous as the matter seems in hindsight, my Israeli magnetic tube was a way of trying to address the problem physically, and was, for a long time, my only hope. The people closest to me expected me to function properly. They knew nothing else. They still saw me as the golden wunderkind who had never disappointed them. Someone like that certainly belongs on the top step of the podium – but then they naturally also have to deliver the victory.

My father had initially downplayed my condition as a phase of puberty, as the temporary dark mood of an adolescent, perhaps

With the unique Isaac Stern at the Verbier Festival, 1995

as a phase of self-discovery. He eventually realized I was no longer the cheerful boy I once was, that it was eating away at me, that I really was suffering. He contacted Dr Müller-Wohlfahrt, who worked with elite athletes at his Munich practice, and had an excellent reputation. But even he couldn't deliver satisfactory results. It wasn't tendonitis, it wasn't anything specific at all; so that ruled out the Paganini *Caprices* as being the cause. Besides, my father was convinced that I was a perfect, outstandingly trained, acclaimed soloist at the highest level – there was nothing more anyone could achieve in that field.

But there was one person who clearly knew more about me than the others; someone astute enough to recognize what was wrong with me. And this person was, of all people, the unapproachable Isaac Stern. There are usually several factors at play when a messed-up story eventually has a happy ending, but, in my case, it probably really was just Isaac Stern who decided it.

Let's go back two years. I was fifteen. International stars of classical music had all come together for seventeen days at the Verbier Festival in Switzerland. Isaac Stern was giving a masterclass, and I was one of his students. At one point, he said to me, with my father standing alongside him, 'David, I want to speak to you privately.' Aha. He wanted to take me aside – why not, it could be interesting. But my father announced, 'You'll take a tape-recorder with you to record the conversation. I want to know what he has to say to you.'

I wasn't comfortable with this, but, at a technical level, it was more than feasible. I would simply have a tape recorder in a little bag, attach a tiny microphone inconspicuously to my clothes, and away I would go, like something out of a spy movie.

Isaac was naturally oblivious to this undercover operation. He spent two whole hours talking to me, on tape, his every word being captured for posterity. How did I feel about it? Uncomfortable, but I wasn't very confident or assertive at that age. And Isaac was strict with me. While his choice of words was not abusive, he wasn't easy on me either. I was already familiar with this special treatment from his masterclasses, where he would often be more restrained in his criticism of others, yet would regularly go hard at me – 'Why do you do it like that? Can you give me one good reason why you play this section like that?'

Our entire conversation boiled down to the question of what had to happen in my life in order for me to safely navigate the swing bridge spanning the abyss between wunderkind and adult artist. 'You need to be yourself,' he said. 'You need to become a self-styled musician. How often I have seen highly gifted children simply disappear into the ether. I don't want the same thing to happen to you. You need a proper education ... Come, conduct in common time!' I couldn't. 'See? The time to learn this and much more is now.' His tone here was serious, almost cutting.

I eventually plucked up my courage and interrupted him, 'Isaac, am I really that much worse than the others?' To which he responded, 'I'm not interested in the others. I'm strict with you so you don't fall into the trap of thinking the hardest bits are behind you. No, they're still yet to come. I want to give you something to help take you further. Why? I'll tell you. Because you're one of the most talented violinists I have ever heard, and you're only fourteen.'

One of the most talented? That was music to my ears. And it's perhaps what made me deaf to Isaac's lectures. Yes, my father listened to the tape afterwards. He may have also realized that Isaac had hit the odd nerve. But, barely a month later, it was once again all just about practising – business as usual. Should

I have insisted on taking Isaac's admonitions seriously? Well, I didn't.

And I later discovered I could no longer answer my own questions. Purely practising was no longer helping me advance musically. I started doubting my instinct; I lost confidence. Then nerves, even helplessness, crept in on stage, to the point where I suddenly wondered, 'What's the conductor actually doing?' At twelve, you play uninhibitedly. You stand on stage and think, 'My dad taught me this like so, plus I have great teachers – so, let's go!' But when the rational mind starts kicking in as you look at the score, and you realize the notes in front of you don't necessarily have anything to do with what you're doing at that moment, that's when self-doubt starts to creep in.

But you've got a new contract with a record company, and a load of people shoving the reviews in your face after a concert! And it begins to dawn on you that people want to celebrate you as an artist at all costs, that you have tremendous responsibility, that people expect veritable wonders from you, while you're still just emerging from wunderkind land. And one day ...

I must have had a very bad day. Maybe a concert write-up had been tepid, maybe a conductor had cancelled on me, which would previously have been unthinkable – in any case, I was moping around the house looking for something and mindlessly reached into the archive cupboard containing the rehearsal and concert recordings. What should fall into my hands but the tape of my conversation with Isaac Stern. I was seventeen at the time, and could only vaguely recall our conversation, so I thought to myself, 'Let's give this a listen.' I waited until everyone had gone to sleep, then played the conversation quietly, and, once Isaac had uttered his final sentence, I knew what I had to do. 'You need to watch that you're the one steering your ship into port', were his words, 'because, at the moment, you're heading for a dead end.'

My father probably didn't even notice this dead end. There was too much love in it for him. His belief in me was too strong; the positive responses to my playing also seemed to validate his view, while criticism was cast aside – 'they have no idea; they don't understand anything about music'. But I knew the critics were right. And, secretly, without my father knowing, I applied to the Juilliard School in New York.

You can find videos and photos for this chapter here.

Digging deep

As quickly as things seemed to be moving along in the last chapter, this didn't continue to happen. There was still an intermezzo in London. But before I get to that, before taking the leap from Aachen to New York via London, I want to draw a line under those first seventeen years from today's perspective.

It was certainly a very unusual childhood and adolescence; my behaviour was often baffling, and some may be thinking, 'How did he put up with it all?' I get it. But, although I don't like the term 'wunderkind' or 'child prodigy', if you are one, you can expect a life so far from normality that you have no benchmark. You live this life alone, for yourself, your only reference points being role models who come from the same peculiar world – those child prodigies of the past who made it to the summit of Mount Everest.

As a baby with my grandmother and parents

Honestly, I could spend hours, days, poking around my past, critically going over everything that happened – this was useful, this was complete nonsense – and will share a few thoughts on this in a moment. But first I want to make it clear that I have experienced some of the most amazing things, but I have also had bad experiences, and both of these come out in every note I play. There are some things that I could have done without, but am I still happy, in hindsight, to have also felt sadness, anger, frustration? Yes, because that is also a win. The more emotion you have experienced, processed or even not processed, the more you can channel into your playing. You can dig deep, even if it's just for a single note in the third movement of a César Franck sonata. You can't measure this win, nor can you produce this very personal sound by applying a superior playing technique; it comes from life, from the heart, from the soul, and that's why I lament little and regret nothing.

Did I feel like some kind of 'chosen one', superior to my peers? No. I simply lived a different life in a different world, sheltered and wrapped in cotton wool – I didn't even have to help out at home. Different rules applied to me around the clock. And in that world, I didn't have the slightest reason to be arrogant, because the people of my world were the luminaries of classical music to whom my father and I would pay courtesy calls, for whom I would play, with whom I worked. Right from the start, I saw the greats of my field as colleagues; it was just that they were infinitely more advanced, head and shoulders above me. I, on the other hand, was tiny, which is why I would spend day and night trying to reduce this gap, whatever the cost.

I knew, after all, who would be waiting for me behind the door whenever we went to visit one of these towering figures. I would be familiar with their records, I would know their story and life achievements. And when I entered the room, I would be filled with emotion and awe. In those moments, I was no longer myself; I would transform into the person I wanted to be someday in the distant future. So I knew all about humility. And I particularly knew the feeling of inferiority; I was used to thinking of myself as being imperfect and in need of improvement. Anyone who steps out of this world and into the everyday lives of their peers doesn't have much to talk about, and I would then become taciturn and introverted, almost shy, and definitely not arrogant.

There were essentially two David Garretts existing at that time. There was the wunderkind who wanted to be taken seriously by the greats of his craft, and who, when it came to violins, whether on stage or off stage, therefore did everything with deep sincerity and earnestness. And there was the kid who, the rest of the time, was, and needed to be, just a kid. There was a huge discrepancy between the two, and it wasn't easy to handle, particularly as I had virtually no social contact with any peers.

Conversations, exchanges of ideas, communication – most of this all happened with people much older than me, in a serious, responsibility-filled environment. Everyone around me was four or five times my age, and therefore discussed topics that were just as irrelevant to me as the stuff my classmates chatted about. I nearly died of boredom at one post-concert dinner, surrounded by arts directors and agents. Nothing they talked about meant anything to me; they might as well have been speaking in Latin. But there's nothing you can do. There's no way around it, because it's part of your training. So you live in two worlds: the adult world you've fallen into through a weird twist of fate, where you try your best to keep up, to not embarrass yourself, your teachers or your parents, even though it's a world that's utterly foreign to you. And the child's world, where you can joke around all you like, but knowing full well that, once you got on stage, all the childish stuff suddenly had to stop. Without my brother Alexander, I would often have felt lonely.

This extraordinary life was as normal for me as the pressure I was constantly under. There were rational reasons for this pressure, put on me by my father. First, behind every highly gifted child aspiring to have a successful career is an extremely ambitious parent. This is usually not talked about, because many people like the idea of child prodigies who personified perfection from the moment they were born. For my part, I have to admit, twenty-three years later, that my father went all out for me. He took the time to work with me every day, when he may sometimes have preferred to be doing something more enjoyable. He was the most important person in my life; I wasn't convinced by all his methods, and my sense of free will was really put to the test, but I was the epicentre of our family. You could even say I had power. But I never made the most of this power, never exercised it; on the contrary, I loathed it.

Wolfgang Amadeus Mozart, who had a similar experience with his father Leopold, would mostly counter doggedness with humour. Without wanting to compare myself to Mozart, I like this pragmatic attitude. I wasn't able to adopt it to the same extent. While there was never any major falling-out, I did often argue with my father. There was no distinction between his role as a loving father and that of a strict teacher. And when you hit puberty and get everything dictated to you, down to the tiniest of details, then you very quickly start to feel the frustration and anger build up – not to mention the fact that your self-esteem suffers when you've got the cold wind of criticism blowing in your face every day.

One thing I absolutely did not like was that my father not only recorded many lessons with his video camera, but also tape-recorded or filmed nearly all of my concerts from earliest childhood.

Many concert halls had a strict no-recording policy at the time. These days, you can't stop it, and when I go on stage I'm staring into 2,000 mobile phones in front of 2,000 faces. Back then, however, it was made clear at the entrance that concert recordings were not permitted. But a DAT recorder is super-easy to smuggle in on your belt under your jacket, the little microphone on your lapel can barely be seen, and no one ever noticed that my father used this method to tape-record virtually every concert.

That's why Aachen today has an amazing archive of concert recordings, all unpublished, of course – and I'm happy about it. At the time, however, I was mad at my father, because I knew that, apart from his pride, there was another reason for his pirating: picking up errors. So I would be sitting in the passenger seat next to him on the way home and, instead of enjoying the moment, instead of the two of us celebrating my great performance, he would replay the concert on the car stereo and give me a debrief. Perhaps someone more intense would have appreciated it, but I figured that, if everyone was satisfied, why would you want to go through it all again and pick out tiny imperfections – especially straight after the concert, on the way home? No, those moments definitely do not rank among my favourite memories.

And now to the question of my other family members – my mother and brother. Were they at least on my side? Did they protect me?

Let's start with my mother. She has a wonderful nature, she's an optimist. She always tries to make the best of everything. So, cut the self-pity! Don't let things get you down! As such, no one encouraged me more than her, and she used this same combination of perseverance and empowerment to ensure order in a household that was permanently in a state of exceptional circumstances. Imagine: all the business activities, plus the private lives of a five-person family, plus my school lessons, plus my violin lessons – which could drag on well into the evening, that alone making normal family life impossible – under one roof.

My mother did her best to co-ordinate everything and particularly to make my life easier by making arrangements with the school and teachers or giving me occasional freedom. But her influence ended at the closed sliding door, behind which I would practise with my father, behind which there was no such thing as Saturday or Sunday, and which no one would have dared open from the outside. She was outside, I was inside – that was the situation, which is why a lot of what she did for me and for our family peace was lost on me at the time.

Alexander, my brother, has always been my best friend. He knew I had a difficult life. He suffered from the strain and tension just as much as I did. When my father was particularly strict with me, he sometimes didn't know what else to do but retreat to his room and put on his headphones. But he stuck up for me whenever he could. Alexander was always fair, thoroughly decent and reliable, a gentleman; he acted as the substitute for all the friends and playmates I never had. And there was someone else, too: my paternal grandmother.

She was awesome. In the 1940s, she had fled Stalin's secret police in Ukraine, settled in Aachen and made an admirable life for herself. A clever and educated woman, she had a room full of books in her little flat, which, fortunately for me, was only a fifteen-minute bike ride away. If I had had a falling-out with my father, I would often hole up at her place until the storm had passed. With her, I could have some peace, she would cook for me and serve up the world's best borscht – in other words, my grandmother was my comforter, my safe haven, my little slice of paradise, and for once I didn't have to talk about music – although, as a little geek, I did sometimes take my violin with me to her place.

Without her, I wouldn't have known where to turn in those early years when things got uneasy at home and I felt like I was walking on eggshells. I loved her dearly, and, to this day, I still remember her telephone number and will never forget it – 6331.

Those three people – my mother, my brother and my grandmother – created something of a family atmosphere, but they were powerless to prevent serious trouble. My sister Elena, eight years younger than me, was too little to figure in this situation. But there was a fourth person here, someone who wasn't a relative, but who slipped into the role of father for me on at least one occasion. I'm talking about Isaac Stern, and a particular conversation we had.

It wasn't until later, when listening to a recording of it at night, that I understand what he meant. It wasn't about comforting or encouraging me; it was about my future as an independent artist. Not unlike my father, he believed in taking life seriously, but he spoke as someone looking down on my life from far above, and his core message was:

First, compliments spoil one's character. If you are very good at something from a very young age, you hear a lot of positive things said about you. But at that early age, you don't yet understand that success primarily means work, and that nothing will ever change that. In other words, success can make you lazy; flattery can stop you from developing further. Of course it is tiring to see every day as a new incentive, but, as an artist, you need that mentality, that will, every night when you go to bed, to be better than what you were when you woke up – that's the only way you'll be able to maintain your level. Being a comet is not particularly difficult. Being a star takes time and effort.

And secondly, there comes a point when instinct will no longer suffice. Until then, I had relied solely on my gut feeling when playing the violin. In future, however, I would need another reason to keep believing in myself. This other reason is musical knowledge, well-founded musical training that allows you to control your instinct and make any necessary corrections. Otherwise, you'll eventually find yourself facing a load of questions and realize that you can't answer any of them because you don't even understand why you're doing a particular thing.

So what did that mean now? Simply continuing down the same path was out of the question; after all, having to keep putting on a happy face when you feel like crying because the thing you've spent your whole life preparing for, the thing that should now be bearing the finest of fruit, is drifting further and further away, is unbearable.

It's a grim, lonely situation that floods your brain with self-doubt; coupled with a father who continues to lead your lessons and oversee your practice schedule ... No, I was absolutely done with all that. So I would either give up or find a way out of this labyrinth.

You can find videos and photos for this chapter here.

Intermezzo in London

The Royal College of Music in London is a huge brick building designed in historic style with turrets and Victorian scroll-work. It was erected directly opposite the no less imposing Royal Albert Hall in 1894. I had been working within these walls with my teachers for some time, and I have to say, the lessons could have been rather more exciting. In any case, fascination is something quite different, but perhaps that also had something to do with me: I often didn't even listen.

I just wasn't into London; the two-class society alone made me uncomfortable. In London, it was a case of 'What do your parents do?' and your answer would determine how you were treated. For me, what counted was: 'What have you achieved?' Not 'Where do you come from?' I'm not a fan of elites, society

Christmas in Aachen during my London days

parties or snobbery – plus, the weather is abominable. There's no denying the city has a lot to offer, but it definitely has one major fault: it's not New York.

London was instead the typical compromise. I had long made up my mind about the Juilliard School, but my parents didn't want to hear of New York; my initially feeble, later more forceful, attempts to bring up the Juilliard School in conversation at home failed miserably. 'You're an established artist, you can't go off radar for four years, no one will take you seriously any more' – end of discussion. So the Royal College of Music was the woman my parents found for me, not the girl I loved; my relationship with her was consequently quite a frigid one, and came to an end after nine months. To give you an idea:

The rehearsal rooms there had paper-thin walls. As you're unpacking your violin, you're hearing oboes on your left, pianos on your right and a string quartet opposite you. I don't want to sound like a snob, but I could not concentrate amidst that cacophony. Fortunately, there were also empty and therefore wonderfully quiet rooms, but they were locked. And then the hapless Harry Karr came back on the scene – the one who had given me the idiotic advice in Israel to befriend Sara Zuckerbaum's lover. He was a fellow student at the college, and, when I think back now to how we got into one of the locked rooms unnoticed …

As I said, it was an old building, with old doors and old locks. I remember how Harry and I went over to the quiet corner room I had scouted out, him taking a credit card, passing it through the gap between the lock and the door and, voilà – the door burst open. You could learn something from him after all. In future, I would go in whenever I wanted using my Student Travelcard.

Unfortunately, word started to get around. Someone didn't approve of my method and ratted on me. But I had to practise, and it was impossible to do so in my London basement flat because the neighbours didn't like it. The upshot was that I got two warnings from the principal, and, after the third one, I received a blue letter that said something like, 'Dear Mr Garrett, take a break for six weeks. You will not be permitted at the college during that time ... ' In other words, I had been barred from the Royal College for six weeks. My parents got the letter and were very upset, but I was free.

What else is there to report from my time in London? At the most, a love story. This time, her name was Tessie Yamada, and she was another great love. A pianist who was also studying at the Royal College of Music, she moved in with me, so we ended up sharing that basement flat where all you could see of people through the window was their shoes. One night, several months later, we were due to go to a party but there was no sign of Tessie. I waited an hour, I waited another hour, the clock struck midnight, the clock struck one, and finally someone told me Tessie had headed off ages ago with some guy. I spent the next seven days trying to contact her – to no avail. On the eighth day, I happened to bump into her at the college entrance where, for the second time in my life, I heard the words, 'I need to talk to you.' But this time I knew what was coming.

As I said, Tessie had been living with me. Her little suitcase stood in my dark basement flat. That sounded like a relationship to me. But now it turned out she had met someone (please, no) and was now with them (for God's sake), plus: 'Is it okay if I leave my stuff at your place for another few weeks? You're rarely at home, after all.' 'Yes, of course that's okay.' (I love harmony above all else ...)

But Tessie made no effort to move out over those next few weeks. On the contrary, I would come home to find more and more of her things lying around, and then suddenly her boyfriend's things too. But to cap it all, one night there was a framed photo of him beaming at me on my bedside table, and Tessie's sexy underwear was strewn all over my duvet. Now, it takes a lot to set me off, it really does, but enough was enough. Unfortunately I didn't have the guts to ask her straight out if she had lost all her marbles. Instead, I called my mother, who said, 'Get some cardboard boxes, pack her stuff into them, go to her student residence, hand everything in to the concierge and catch a train back to Aachen.'

Tessie had an ego the size of California. She certainly had a more dangerous streak than me, so direct confrontation was a no-no. I ended up doing as my mother had said and neatly packed all her things into boxes. I had to smile at the fact that all traces of her fitted easily into a London black cab. As I didn't want to go back to the music college either, I took the Eurostar to Aachen and that was it. The moral of the story? While my time in London wasn't exactly a success, it did teach me a valuable life lesson – it made me more aware of non-music-related problems.

Unfortunately, the London debacle did no favours in terms of my parents' attitude towards my New York plans – why would my New York adventure be any different to how things went down in London? My father's doubts weren't unwarranted and, at the time, there was nothing I could do to dispel them.

In any case, I still had my high school diploma to sit, and, considering how little time I ended up dedicating to my education, my results weren't too bad. So I could now finally have a crack at the New York plan.

I had requested the application forms for the Juilliard School, which turned out to be a sizeable stack of papers. My father was completely oblivious. My mother was in on the secret, but I didn't want to bother her with all the practical arrangements for my move to New York, so instead I called on my English teacher, Mrs Marquardt, to help me compose answers to the questions on the application form. There were three sections I was able to understand even without Mrs Marquardt's assistance: *first choice teacher, second choice teacher, third choice teacher.* I cheekily wrote the same name three times: Itzhak Perlman, because it had to be him. I had met him years prior in Berlin, and had even played for him. He was awesome; I worshipped him. Perlman had been teaching violin at the Juilliard School for a year, and, given a considerable problem had cropped up, I even called him from Aachen, at half-past two in the morning, to be on the safe side.

You see, the entrance examination – the audition – meant I had to make a brief trip to New York beforehand. 'Mr Perlman,' I said, 'could we not make an exception in my case? Would you perhaps accept me without an audition? If I fly to New York, my dad will find out ...' But no, not a chance. 'Sorry. You have to come; I can't change the rules,' was his response. In other words, I wasn't going to be getting any red-carpet treatment there just because I had recorded five albums with Deutsche Grammophon.

So what now? My departure to the US definitely wasn't going to be a source of euphoria at home, that was for sure ...

But considering these last few months had been my first real exposure to the harsh realities of life, I came up with an amazing idea: Alexander had gone to Boston a year before to study at Harvard – his straight-A school results meant they accepted him immediately. I shared my thoughts with him and, together, we came up with the following plan: I would fly to America because I was missing him and wanted to check how he was doing. I would of course arrange my stay so that I could quickly also dash over to New York to do the audition at the Juilliard School without the authorities in Aachen knowing. Boston wasn't more than five hours from New York, so I would be able to take the first step towards my new life without rocking the boat.

Good, sorted. At that time, people still went to a travel agency to book a journey, so my mother and I did just that. We were happy to sit around and wait for the travel agent to check her computer and perform all the mysterious operations. Forty-five minutes later, we stepped back out with a plane ticket to Boston in my hand. I would spend ten days there – I wanted to have some time with my brother, after all – so, one morning in February 2001, I found myself at Brussels airport boarding the plane to Boston.

You can find videos and photos for this chapter here.

New York in the snow

Snow flurries in Manhattan

What exactly was I hoping to get out of Perlman and the Juilliard School? The answer is to move forwards, because two things had become clear to me over the last year. First, I wasn't going to give up. I had no other interests I could indulge in when I put my violin away. I played because I couldn't imagine any other life, and because my violin and I had been inseparable since my childhood. And secondly, I wanted a theoretical foundation. I needed to broaden my horizons and think about subjects such as conducting, composition, harmonics, counterpoint and ear training. I also needed to be able to play chamber music and work as an orchestral musician. In other words, I wanted to take a proper, structured course, which was just the thing for a 20-year-old, except that this was at one of the most prestigious music schools in the world. I wanted to acquire that knowledge, those experiences there, to regain my confidence, because there's no room for doubts when you're up on stage.

So that was my focus, my plan for the future, when I arrived in Boston. I spent three days with my brother first. I hadn't given any thought to how I would get from Boston to New York – by train? Bus? Plane? My brother reckoned the cheapest and easiest way would be to take the bus, which would cost only 16 dollars. The cheapest option suited me just right, so we arranged that I would take the bus that ran daily from South Station near Harvard to Chinatown, Manhattan.

As I was still a bit unworldly, my brother took me there and ushered me to the right bus (I'd had bad experiences in the past when my train hadn't gone where I wanted to go, which can happen when you're caught up in your thoughts with your headphones on). My brother also drummed it into me that I had to get off at the last station, though in reality there were no stops before Chinatown, so getting off at the terminus was something I figured I could do.

So I headed off south-westwards, New York-bound. It had been a cold, clear winter's day, but the skies outside my bus window soon clouded over and snow began to fall. The snowflakes were the size of a silver dollar, and I had my first encounter with the dreaded East Coast winter. But American bus drivers didn't slow down in that kind of weather, and we sped through the snow flurries so incredibly quickly that we arrived in Chinatown on time.

Manhattan was all in white. Normally New York was teeming with yellow taxis; in those days, you didn't even need to look at them – just lift your arm and three yellow cabs would pull up two seconds later. But every New Yorker knows that when it starts to snow, it can really come down, and the piles of snow disrupt the traffic before long. This was one of those days when virtually everything was at a standstill, and there I was in Chinatown, shivering, a lonely figure with a violin case, the snow doing what it always does in New York – swirling and fluttering incessantly, blanketing everything. So I trudged off northward, up Bowery and along 4th Avenue, through the snow, through the cold. Get there an hour before the audition, warm up, tune my violin and start playing – that's how I had imagined this day would play out, but it was only after a seemingly endless half-hour of walking that I managed to hail a taxi, by which point I had nearly made it to Union Square anyway.

I collapsed onto the back seat, happy to be in a warm taxi. I was thoroughly frozen, so I turned up the rear heating even more. Off to the Lincoln Center we went. I got out at the Juilliard School, which was located in an elongated, late-1960s building that tapered like a ship's bow – sleek, minimalist architecture.

And then? Once I had found the entrance, there were people who could help me out. 'The audition? Straight ahead, then ask whoever you see there.' I asked my way through to the Green Room, where everyone was waiting for their turn to perform, where fifteen violinists were all warming up, resulting in a cacophony of sounds spanning the full classical music spectrum from Bach to Sibelius. There was no time to lose. I unpacked my violin and was just about to start tuning it when I heard my name called out over the loudspeaker. After a hasty tune-up, I headed down the corridor to the concert hall with my violin, stepping into the blinding white spotlight of the stage. My fingers weren't yet at operating temperature, but they were able to move.

Now I could do the audition process blindfolded, but back then, the conductors were patient; this time was different. Waiting for me upstairs was a pianist I had never seen before, and I had barely placed my music on the piano when a commanding voice came booming out of the impenetrable darkness of the hall:

'We'd like to hear some of Bartók's second violin concerto.' The pianist played the first few bars, then it was my turn to come in. I got going and, just before the end of the first page ... 'Stop please! Thank you very much. We'd like to hear a bit from Beethoven's violin concerto.' Same thing again, after half a page ... 'Thank you very much. You prepared some Paganini, which caprice do you want to play?c I played a bit of Paganini, and then ... 'Thank you very much. That'll be enough. We'll get back to you.'

I left the stage feeling so lost, baffled and empty. Was that how they did it with everyone? Was that normal? No comments, no praise, no criticism, nothing to indicate what the judges thought – just a bland, business-like 'Thank you very much?' You played into blackness; there was no one in the auditorium apart from six or seven shadowy judges in the background, basically in the last row, and they would ultimately be the ones to decide your fate. It made me feel uneasy.

So then it was just a question of waiting. I decided to spend the next ninety minutes on a couch behind the main entrance to distract myself with scenes from American daily life. As in every large building in New York, there was a security door system with a turnstile, security checks and security staff. It was calming to watch them do their monotonous work.

I went back at 6 p.m. 'How's it going?' 'It'll be a little bit longer.' But then a woman appeared and affixed a list of names to the blackboard in the lobby. 'I have the recall sheet!' Everyone raced in, including me. There were eight names on it, and mine was one of them, but what did 'recall' mean? I didn't know. My English was only average at the time – I had occasionally spoken English with my mother, but my vocabulary was still pretty limited. My first thought was that 'recall' meant a second go. That the list contained the names of people who hadn't totally impressed and had to perform a second time. Crap ... There was a young woman standing next to me. I pointed at my name and gave her a questioning look. 'Hey,' she said, 'good news!' 'What do you mean "good news"?' 'You're nearly there. Anyone not on the list is out. But you're on the shortlist.'

So I wasn't entirely wrong. At any rate, I was one of the eight lucky ones who had to take to the stage again that same night to determine the best of the best. So once again a bit of Tchaikovsky, once again a 'Thank you very much', and, at the end of the day, we were told, 'you'll get a letter'. 'And where will this letter be sent?' 'Well, to your house, to your home address.' Aha. Where did I live? Aachen. Who lived there? My parents. And who checked the mail at our house? My father. Things were about to blow up, and all I could do was watch it all unfold as coolly and calmly as I could.

You can find videos and photos for this chapter here.

David Garrett becomes Christian Bongartz

And things turned out exactly as I had feared. Annoyed by the name of the sender on the envelope, my father opened the letter, scanned it over and, let's just say he was not amused 'Congratulations,' the letter read, 'you have been accepted, and Itzhak Perlman will be your teacher ...'

As for me, I had mixed feelings – of course I was over the moon, but my enraged father now had to be calmed down, at least enough for him to agree to the venture I had orchestrated behind his back with a certain amount of cunning and the support of secret helpers. But I would have had to come clean to him sooner or later anyway. The matter was eventually sorted and my father found a compromise he could reconcile with in his mind: 'You can do it. I don't share your opinion, but

After a performance with the Juilliard Symphony Orchestra

if that's what you've decided, then go – but you need to pay for it yourself. We won't put anything towards it.' Now I was upset. Hadn't he paid for my brother's Harvard studies? Yes, but, he added, how much money have I already put into your training? Today I admit he was right. Back then, however, I resented him quite a lot for it, and our relationship soured.

So my father certainly didn't approve of my plan. I vividly remember him saying things like, 'Who knows if you'll even make it. I can see you regretting your decision.' But comments like these were actually extremely valuable, because nothing motivates a son more than the desire to prove a sceptical parent wrong. When I boarded the plane on 10 September 2001, I was sure that, this time, I wouldn't be back on my parents' doorstep in Aachen after nine months. I would make it through the whole four years, and even scrape together the money for the astronomical course fees.

I had even got myself a new name for the Juilliard School, which I would be using from day one. From then on, teachers and students would only know me as Christian Bongartz. Now, this name wasn't actually new – Christian is my middle name and Bongartz, of course, is my family name – but the advantage of having this different identity was that, in the small world of classical music, I could be virtually unknown. Many people would have already heard about David Garrett, and I didn't want my artist name to give me any privileges, nor did I want anyone to think I had been given a free pass by the Juilliard's directors because of my prior successes. In short, I was determined to do it the hard way.

So there was no David Garrett in New York. Christian Bongartz was the name on my door in my residence, on my ID card, in my documents, and even my teacher Itzhak Perlman, who I had called at the start of the year still as David Garrett, thought he was simply teaching a nobody called Christian Bongartz. As it so happened, one morning, after three months and many lessons spent working together, I arrived at my lesson to find him with an odd smile on his face.

'Listen,' he said after greeting me, 'I've been wondering for months ... I haven't liked to ask, but I can't get the thought out of my head: are you perhaps,' – long pause – 'David Garrett?' I looked at him, nodded and nearly exploded with joy; I now had proof that Perlman hadn't accepted me just because I was David Garrett – he had accepted me because this total stranger Christian Bongartz played the violin so damn well that he wanted to have him in his class! He must have had this awkward question going round and round in the back of his mind the whole time while giving this 'Christian Bongartz' his lessons ...

This story gives me great pleasure to this day. By the way, it also came out in that conversation that he actually remembered our very first meeting. It had been twelve years prior, but he still knew which piece I had played for him that day backstage at the Berlin Philharmonie: *La Capricieuse* by Elgar. I was absolutely blown away and delighted to have made an impression on him. When it came to Perlman, my game of hide-and-seek was of course entirely over, but most of the others would remain in the dark about Christian Bongartz's true identity right through my studies.

Incidentally, I had previously revealed myself on one other occasion to prove my trust in my best friend, Dort Bigg. We were browsing albums at Tower Records, rummaging around in the pop section before moving to the classical music shelves, and there they were – David Garrett CDs in a specially designated David Garrett section! Curious to hear Dort's opinion, I pressed my Paganini *Caprices* into his hand. 'Yes, I know this one,' he said, glancing briefly at the cover. 'It's a good record.' The photo on the cover showed me as a fourteen-year-old, but he didn't notice any similarity, so I helped him join the dots: 'The guy on the front, that's me.' As I said, the world of classical music is small, and Deutsche Grammophon was not just some backyard label, so he knew my name, and was familiar with this recording, which made him all the more stunned. But as I definitely did not want my secret getting out, I asked him not to blow my cover – 'Please stick with Christian Bongartz. It's important for me; being here is a fresh start for me.'

And speaking of starts. It had almost – through no fault of my own – gone wrong. You see, I had been in New York thirteen hours, the day had flicked over to 11 September 2001, when ...

But first things first. On that first morning after arriving in New York, I was sitting, brow furrowed, in the Financial Aid office, which was something like a support service for students. I had to somehow cough up course fees of 37,000 dollars per semester, otherwise I would likely find myself on a plane back to Aachen.

But keeping afloat by giving concerts was not permitted. The Juilliard School had a strict policy that, during the semester, no one was allowed to give performances outside the school, and it was a policy they kept an extremely close eye on – first, because we were supposed to be concentrating on our studies, and secondly to prevent a two-class society situation where there were musicians with stage experience and normal students, that is, artists who hadn't really appeared much in public. So I had spent days, no, weeks breaking my head over how I would round up the money.

Now some of you might say that a Christian Bongartz, alias David Garrett, surely couldn't have any money worries!

It's not like he played all those past concerts for free! Correct, he didn't, and money did indeed come flooding in. But my lifestyle at the time involved huge outgoings – there were private tutors to pay for, violin teachers, travel expenses, plane tickets and accommodation, often for me and my parents, and sometimes even for my siblings, plus the insurance for my violin ... in short, there wasn't a lot left over, and by the time the London episode had happened, the money had all dried up.

But try telling a student-support service in the US that your parents aren't paying for your studies and your own income is nil! No one will believe you. Here in the US, parents always pay – if nothing else, out of pride to have a child attending the Juilliard School – and it's not like my father didn't earn well! So, I now also felt like a scholarship fraud, and that's not something the Americans take well – but, at that moment, the door flung open and someone burst in with the news that a plane had flown into the World Trade Center.

What did I think this meant at the time? That a light aeroplane had hit and shattered one of the World Trade Center's windows – typical America, things are always blown out of proportion. Heck no. All hell broke loose. Everyone who was in the building at the time was led into the concert hall and not let out until the evening – who knew what else was going to be flying around. Today when I think of September 11, there are two sensations I feel instantly. First, it had been a glorious late summer's day with clear blue skies; the whole city had been the picture of peace. In disaster movies, there is usually an atmosphere of impending doom, with squalls, fierce storm clouds, lashing rain and dramatic music, but there was none of that on this bright morning when – and this is my second memory – there was suddenly a smell of burning metal pervading the air. Never before or since have I smelt that odour, but I knew what it was. Something very sinister must have gone down in the city.

What a situation! As someone who had had a very sheltered life up to that point, I suddenly found myself in a room full of loud people, all sitting around baffled, nervous, and imagining the most nightmarish of scenarios. And among all this chaos, I had only one thought: how do I find the money to pay those course fees? If it weren't so tragic, you could simply shake your head at my misjudgement of the situation. But put yourself in my shoes: I had barely set foot on American soil to spend the next four years there, and didn't have the slightest clue of what was going on outside (this was still the pre-smartphone world) – naturally my main concern was how I was going to finance my studies. So there I was, hunkered down in a windowless room full of distraught people, breaking my head over utterly trivial things. I was probably the only person in the whole of New York who had other worries that day.

The situation that greeted us as we went back to the residence that night was no less surreal. Dead silence on the streets, interrupted only by the sirens of the New York fire brigade and police. You couldn't see a thing; 66th Street, where the Juilliard School was located, was three or four miles from the financial district where the World Trade Center had stood. You couldn't even make a phone call because the network was overloaded, so I couldn't phone home to say something horrific had happened here. Most shops stayed closed the whole of the following week. And lessons were out of the question too – everywhere was still on red alert. We students were required to temporarily stay within the school precinct, so we would spend the evenings sitting around in our residence's common rooms, watching the news aghast.

Once the dust had settled over the collapsed Twin Towers, my scholarship application was processed, and I ended up having to pay 25,000 of the 37,000 dollars per semester, which was still quite a lot. It was 5,000 dollars more a month in addition to my living expenses. Where was I going to get that money from?

You can find videos and photos for this chapter here.

Dinner with Itzhak Perlman

My answer to that last question would, after many twists and turns, eventually lead me into the craziness that is New York's nightlife, but I'll get to that story later. For the moment, I'd rather focus on my circumstances at the time – things like where I lived, how I ate, the people I mixed with in my new life. And: what I actually did at the Juilliard School.

First, a few general facts: the Juilliard School was founded in Manhattan in 1905 as a means of creating an American training centre that enabled musicians to keep up with the famous conservatories of Europe. After World War II, it also opened its doors to actors and dancers, and, in 1969, moved from Claremont Avenue in Harlem to a modern building at the Lincoln Center on 66th Street, where it remains to this day.

New York, Upper West Side, where Itzhak Perlman lived

At the time I was there, there were around 100 professors and some 600 students.

If you look at the list of its alumni today, you'll see a host of famous names, of which I'll mention just seven here: dancer Pina Bausch, jazz greats Miles Davis and Thelonious Monk, violinist Nigel Kennedy, singer Nina Simone, actor Robin Williams and, last but not least, my teacher, violinist Itzhak Perlman. You could certainly say it was a privilege to be able to study here.

How can I describe the set-up? Let's start with the school. The main building encompassed the classrooms, the concert hall, the musicians' rehearsal rooms, the ballet rooms, the actors' area and several theatres, and it was here that the most hopeful of artistic talents on the planet would converge every day during the week. But this elongated six-storey complex was just the work area – we lived in a high-rise building barely 50 metres away on the same campus.

At the entrance to this building, there was the usual security door system that turned away anyone without an ID card. Guests were required to leave the building by 11 p.m., though there were ways and means of getting around this rule, and it didn't take long to hear about them. Once you'd got past security, you'd be at the lifts, and pressing the button for the 36th floor would take you right to the top, which, even by New York standards, was pretty high above Manhattan – and, fortunately for us, our living quarters were in the top half, so from the 18th to the 36th floor. This meant that, as a Juilliard student, you had fantastic views over the city from every room, which, to a certain extent, made up for the cramped, stinky student digs, where the bedrooms were the size of a prison cell and, for security reasons, only had a tilt window.

In other words, I would have to spend the next few years sharing 10 square metres of space with a bunk bed, a table, a small cupboard and a roommate. My roommate at the time was an acting student named Phil. When we could no longer stand the musty smell and pokiness of our room, we could head to the common room, because all the bedrooms on each floor would run off a central common room where things were a little more pleasant. It was a decent place to hang out. So that was the residence; now for the food side of things.

For lunch we would go to the canteen on the ground floor of the residence – a large, nice, if spartan room. We didn't necessarily go there for its culinary delights, because the choice here was usually pizza or salad. Pizza on the left, salad on the right. The ballet dancers would generally make a beeline for the salad bar, though if one did go astray and end up at the pizza counter, she would use ten napkins to soak up all the oil as she made her way to her table (whether or not it worked, I still have no idea). The musicians preferred pizza; their mindset was a bit different. Our motto was: just make sure you're full, because who knows when the next meal will come.

The school didn't profess to offer luxurious rooms or Michelin-star cuisine. Anyone enrolling here just wanted to learn as much as possible. The Classical Music department encompassed all orchestral instruments plus singing; Dance included classical and jazz ballet, and the third department was Drama. This was the best part about the canteen, because it was where all three departments would come together. At the Juilliard School, it wasn't just about focusing single-mindedly on your own art; musicians could also mingle with dancers and actors. So the canteen really came into its own when you saw it as a place of broadening your horizons rather than just a dining area.

And, twice a month, we Perlman students experienced a little slice of heaven on earth, because, every two weeks, Perlman would invite us to a meal at his house.

You can't imagine how happy these invitations made us. This violinist was utterly adored, effectively worshipped by his small circle of students, which consisted of Ilya Gringolts, Arnaud Sussman, Giora Schmidt and Christian Bongartz (me). We were all only about twenty years old, we all felt that we were on the verge of a breakthrough, we all hoped that the doors to a bright future would soon be opening for us, and now our teacher Itzhak Perlman was already giving us a preview into the private realm of a world-famous violin virtuoso – it was flattering, exhilarating and uplifting for us.

So, every two weeks, at around 7 p.m., we would make our way from the residence to a large brick building – one of those traditional New York townhouses – on the Upper West Side, just next to Central Park. Perlman's home, where he lived with his wife, extended over all five floors, but we of course never ventured further into his private quarters on the upper floors. He would greet us in the entry hall, and we would follow him up the stairs to a cosy dining room, where we would all sit at a large table. We would also be joined by the 'pre-college kids' – music students who were under 17. Meanwhile, Perlman's wife Toby and a helper would be busy cooking away in the kitchen. We would then become acquainted with our teacher's second great passion; apart from music, he absolutely loved anything to do with cooking and eating.

Now dining pleasure isn't just about the quality of the dishes, but equally also about the time you take and the company gathered at the table. Perlman knew this, of course, and encouraged us to talk. For the first time ever, I had a teacher I wasn't just meticulously studying sheets of music with, but who instead appreciated me as Christian Bongartz the person. Perlman would talk about life, he was interested in his students' childhoods and youth; he wanted to know about our previous experiences, the things we were particularly fond of. No teacher had ever asked me such questions, and it did me good. When you were around Itzhak Perlman, you felt as if you were breathing in the fresh, rarefied air inhabited by the great minds.

By now, the dishes would be ready and set up in the kitchen. We would each take what we wanted and then Perlman would get to the main point, namely the world of pleasures beyond music. His connoisseur's knowledge extended to composing and preparing a dish, to recipes and ingredients and tricks that make the high art of cooking easier, and it was clear to see that he was just as at home among pots and pans, or at the grill, as he was on stage. He didn't have a particular style or cuisine; for him, it was all about quality and ensuring everything was in abundance, lest the feasting and indulgence have to end prematurely. When it came to wine, however, he was more restrained. Anyone who was older than twenty-one was allowed to have some, but, as an American, encouraging people to drink alcohol was quite a foreign concept to him. None of us younger ones would ever risk touching a wine bottle in his presence, if nothing else just out of respect and awe.

Talking about food was something that had never occurred to me; I would not have dared to talk to my teacher about personal things! Just being at this table was a dream, particularly as we would also touch on other topics, from sport to movies, theatre and literature, before getting to the best bit: once our bellies had been nicely sated – a feeling they were not altogether used to – we would play music, and this was when we would see our host transform back from gourmet to musician.

My father was of the opinion that you shouldn't eat before playing because it affects concentration. Perlman thought differently. For him, it was more important to satisfy physical needs before reaching for the violin. So it was not until after the meal that we would all head to the music room upstairs. Rohan de Silva, his pianist, would sit at the Steinway, and, for the rest of the evening, each of us would be given the opportunity to play something. Music was of course also part of the good life in this household, and since everyone had their violin with them, they would each get a chance to play – if they wanted to. Perlman would refrain from making any comment afterwards, instead asking us all, 'What did you like? What did you not like so much?' His students would then have to help the performer along a bit, either with well-considered praise or cautious criticism. Perlman would then make his own comments on these assessments, because they possibly revealed more about the speaker than the performer. And here, he wouldn't stint on recognition or criticism.

Each of these social music nights would have a theme. It would be chosen spontaneously, and if it happened to be 'virtuosity', then everyone would play something virtuoso. This would be followed by comments along the lines of: there's precision lacking here, you need more expression here, you should use different fingering there, maybe use less bow here. After which Perlman might actually admit that he himself had initially had similar difficulties with that particular piece – and knowing that was also helpful.

In other words, those two-weekly events at the Perlman household were an incredible, gratefully accepted luxury, especially as student life at the Juilliard School was otherwise pretty basic. Another positive effect of this was that we developed a great sense of community. We all trusted our teacher, so we didn't rip each other to pieces – because, during those nights in Perlman's music room, we were stripped bare, and an artist will only ever go that far if they know for sure there's no risk of losing face. In actual fact, none of us had to fear any slander or backbiting; in our group we were of the conviction that the world of classical music had enough space for all of us.

Itzhak Perlman has of course always been an amazing teacher. Above all, however, he is a wonderful person, a man filled with a zest for life. When he told jokes, he would have us rolling around laughing, and he enjoyed being a raconteur, telling not just jokes, but also anecdotes from his life, which to us all sounded like the stuff of legends. He'd played concerts with Isaac Stern, he knew Yehudi Menuhin, he had met Jascha Heifetz, he had played with all the world's top orchestras and worked with all the great conductors, plus he had won a Grammy for his interpretation of the theme music in Spielberg's film *Schindler's List*. In short, he has always embodied everything that we saw as being larger than life in music. To us, this man's greatness had no limits.

You can find videos and photos for this chapter here.

Rebel Rockers

The Juilliard experience

The evenings with Perlman are some of my most favourite memories. But, even then, we still had to prove ourselves. It's not as if there was no competition between us students; even in Perlman's music room, everyone wanted to be the best, which is why we all prepared as thoroughly as we could behind the scenes, regardless of how spontaneous the performance ended up looking. In any case, I actually sought this competition, because it's important to measure yourself against others. I ultimately learned just as much from my classmates during this time as I did from my teacher, partly also due to the fact that we generally didn't practise behind closed doors, so anyone could approach someone else at any time if they had a problem, safe in the knowledge they would be supported. It was all about give and take.

After a concert at the Beacon Theatre, New York, with Itzhak Perlman

But one unexpected benefit for me was also the evenings spent at the residence, or occasionally also out at a bar, because that's when we really could have a proper chat. I wasn't at all used to hanging out in such a large group of peers, and now, for the first time in my life, I was able to put my experiences into words and compare life stories with others – how had they grown up? How had they discovered music? We would sit together until well into the night, and I was fascinated at all the different paths that had led to the Juilliard School; every life story was a movie in itself!

This is where my roommate Phil comes in. We didn't have a lot in common, but we couldn't avoid each other either, which brings me back to the living conditions: Fourth-year students were lucky enough to get a room to themselves, and everyone of course wanted to eventually be part of this elite group – what a relief to finally have some privacy! For us first-year students, meanwhile, not only did we have to deal with the aforementioned cramped space, but it also reeked to high heavens because we couldn't properly open the window. The only thing that made the situation more bearable was when the window was tilted open in the summer and the air-conditioning was on at the same time, whereas it was kept closed in winter, with the heating remaining on.

Phil the acting student was nice and sweet, but very extroverted. For example, right from the first semester, he would often have ladies over. In these instances, he would throw my blanket and pillow at me before I had even stepped through the door – his way of telling me I would be spending the night on the couch in the common room. In other words, I was being evicted, which was actually okay with me if it meant avoiding quarrels at such an early stage.

In the fourth week of the first semester, however, I came back from a lesson and was hit by the worst stench I had experienced to date. Phil was sitting on the floor, surrounded by six buckets of wall paint, and was painting the first wall yellow, red and blue. I was shocked. 'Phil, what are you doing?' To which he replied, 'Don't tell anyone but I'm doing up our place in Seventies style.' Yeah, he had a thing for the 1970s, sported an afro and listened incessantly to Janis Joplin and Jimi Hendrix. That was all cool, but, firstly, the wall paint stank like a beast, and secondly, Phil was spending so long on his renovation project I could see we probably weren't going to be getting any fresh air in there for weeks.

The vapours coming off his buckets and hanging in the room's air were enough to make you feel ill. And he couldn't even leave the door open, because then everyone would find out he was doing something that was strictly not permitted. The vapours couldn't escape through the gap in the window either, so I spent the next two nights back on my couch in the common room.

By the morning of the third day, Phil had finished only a quarter of the job. And he didn't seem to be in any rush either, so I grabbed the brush myself and said, 'Phil, you won't get anywhere like this. I'll help you and we'll have the room done by twelve.' And it was. Our room now looked like the Electric Lady Studio with its garish colours, but that didn't last long. There was a room inspection a week later – I had no idea there was such a thing – and our room was reported to the principal (Phil of course hadn't been able to keep his mouth shut. He had even showed his work to some of the interested ladies). I was lucky to get away with just a warning for being complicit, but the room naturally couldn't stay the way it was, and I hardly have to explain how long you have to paint to turn bright red or dark blue walls white again ... Anyway, a life lesson: don't go painting strangers' walls without asking; it causes problems. But as time went on, our relationship deteriorated. I asked to move rooms in the second semester, and, from the third semester, I started sharing a new but same-sized room with Cody the ballet dancer – a much more preferable solution despite his habit of rubbing intensely odorous coconut oil over himself every day.

To say my life had changed completely since swapping Aachen for New York would be an understatement. Nothing was like before. My left hand was behaving again. Was it because I was breathing in the fresh air of freedom in New York? Was it because I had finally entered reality? In any case, I had never met anyone like Phil, nor had I ever seen anything like the dancers in the canteen. And I had never had a teacher like Itzhak Perlman. While we did work here – and we worked a lot – it wasn't like the work I used to do.

I'll briefly describe what my lessons entailed. Perlman was my violin teacher for the entire four years, but he wasn't the only one; I had others for ear training and piano-playing, there were conductor courses and chamber-music courses, we learned how to write music on the computer, and we also had composition lessons. I particularly looked forward to the lessons with my composition teacher, Eric Ewazen. He was convinced I had a talent in this area, he encouraged me in every respect, and our relationship soon became so good that we would also meet up in private to talk about things like harmonics, melody and twelve-tone music. I just loved composing, and, over time, this part of my training would become just as important to me as the actual violin-playing.

In a word, my experience at this school was four great years of non-stop inspiration. But Itzhak Perlman was the crowning glory for me. To understand his greatness, his importance to me, you need to know what a violinist considers as being the absolute zenith in terms of perfecting their skills. I've already said a bit about this, but I want to go into it in more detail again here.

You see, your hands are not the critical thing. The critical thing is what plays in your head, like a sonic vision, the idea of what your playing should sound like. So you spend a lifetime searching for the tone, the sound, you hear in your head. After all, there are infinite tonal nuances – some are lighter, some are darker, some are more metallic, others are warmer – but every violinist has their own personal ideal sound that they want to nail as closely as possible. You try to create this sound with your hands, and this entails making the tiniest of variations when playing. For example, where you place the bow – closer to the bridge or closer to the fingerboard – or how much pressure you apply with the bow. The range of expression options on a violin is endless, and you might spend your whole life focusing on your own unique sound, but some people find it right from an early age, and Itzhak Perlman is one of those exceptional violinists.

I only need to hear two notes, and I know it has to be Perlman. He is brilliant, technically perfect, and has a distinct sense of musicality. But on top of all that, there's something else that's special; a melodiousness, a charm, a silkiness that makes every note he plays a declaration of love to the violin – and to music in general. No other violinist comes close to achieving such a relationship.

Plus, he was a real teacher. Ida Haendel and other great violinists had influenced and inspired me on my occasional meetings with them, and I had assumed I would also be seeing Perlman in person only once a month, tops. But I was well and truly proven wrong: this man, despite his wealth of successes, put on no airs and graces, and met me for lessons once a week, sometimes even twice a week – not to mention the fact that he also acquainted us with the finer, and indeed the funny sides of life. No wonder his class was the crème de la crème of highly gifted teenagers and already established young stars, which for me in turn meant I definitely couldn't be overconfident.

During our partnership, Perlman primarily focused on the technique of my right bowing arm. Isaac Stern and Shlomo Mintz had criticized my bowing motion in the past, but it had been a long time since I had been under constant observation, to the point that I had lapsed back into old mistakes. Those days were now over. Perlman monitored my progress, placing utmost emphasis on fine-tuning my bowing pressure to allow me to produce that round, warm sound he was so fond of. He called this sound 'lilt'. When the notes dripped from the violin like delicious honey, that's what he meant by lilt, most likely preferring to its zest, its creaminess – pretty logical for someone who loved thinking about food.

He was incidentally extremely generous when it came to the way we played. He gave us total freedom and let anything go, as long as we could provide good reasons for it. He dreaded the thought of someone sounding great but not reflecting this in their playing style. He lamented the fact that the personality of sound had been neglected over the last thirty years, and feared that all good violinists might eventually sound the same.

In a word, Perlman imparted to us a love of music and a love of the instrument – the love that had kind of gone AWOL on me in the past. And my initial low spirits weren't lost on him. 'You come with lots of baggage,' he had said to me after Christian Bongartz had revealed himself to be David Garrett. And he was right, of course; but, after six months at the Juilliard School, I had nearly forgotten about it all. And yet it was here in New York, of all places, that I experienced one of the saddest moments of my wunderkind existence.

I had paid my last visit to Isaac Stern in that city four years earlier. 'Come over,' he had said. There had been no mention of violins, but of course I usually took my violin with me. Not this time. This time, I didn't dare; I already had pain in my left arm, and Isaac would have immediately noticed from my playing that something wasn't right.

'Where's your violin?' was the first thing he said to me after I stepped into his house. And I played dumb: 'I didn't know if ...' Of course I knew; it went without saying. Anyway, instead of playing, we chatted, talking for about an hour, before he thrust his own violin at me to set things right. It was naturally a super unique violin – the Ysaye Guarneri del Gesù from 1740. What an honour! And what an awkward position he had put me in! I could deal with going on stage in pain, but embarrassing myself in front of Isaac?

I wriggled my way out of it by inventing some excuse. I wouldn't have been able to bear seeing the disappointment in his eyes. But today I regret not having shown the necessary courage; perhaps even humiliation would have been better than this inhibited, unresolved situation because after all I knew him. He would never have asked, 'What's up with you? Can I help you?' No, he would have looked at his watch and said something like, 'I've got other commitments now. Have fun in New York.' Unlike Ida Haendel, he didn't have a dog but he would probably have invented one just to get rid of me.

You can find videos and photos for this chapter here.

Five ways of earning money in New York

For the first eighteen years of my life, I had worn clothes I hadn't bought and didn't necessarily like. So I didn't put up the slightest resistance to the suggestion of 'let's go shopping'. As a male, you may soon become your girlfriend's fashion project, and, in New York, I was often a fashion project – and gladly so.

So, those years saw me elevate myself not only musically, but also in terms of my outfits. I was only just starting to take an interest in what was stylish. When I first got to the school, of course I looked around to see what the others were wearing and what was cool. My fellow students came from various parts of the world, everyone was trying to find their identity in this crazy city, and I was no different. 'Let's go shopping' was a signal that new beginnings were afoot.

One of my first photo shoots in New York

Sure, there was the occasional bad buy. I was initially friends with a group of people who liked going to 1980s clubs, which meant black clothing. *The Matrix* was on at the movies, and I entered a Goth phase; I needed a black leather trench coat, I needed a tattoo, I needed a tongue piercing. In those first few days after the piercing, your tongue is so swollen you can only eat stuff that's been basically puréed, and I slurred my way through lessons with Perlman. He wasn't shocked, but he did look at me with a bit of bewilderment. But none of this was the result of a bad mental state; it was simply an adventure, a brief foray into this eccentric world. I went even further too, using eyeliner and dying my short hair black.

I remember flying home during the holiday break and having my parents pick me up at Brussels airport. The poor things! Their son, the wunderkind, approached them shrouded in darkness, black from head to toe – what a year in New York can do to a person! They may have been somewhat confused at that moment, but there were no lectures. I had expected a worse reaction.

My mother was different to my father; she had had an interesting life. I had been watching the ballerinas' work at the Juilliard School from the sidelines, and knew they were vivacious people. My mother was also a child of the late 1960s and early 1970s, which wasn't exactly a time of contemplation and introspection either. She was there in the crowd in Washington D.C. when Martin Luther King uttered the unforgettable words, 'I have a dream', and Jacqueline Kennedy had been a regular guest at her ballet classes. The winds of change that were starting to revitalize cultural life in the US were what blew her across the Atlantic as an eighteen-year-old to Germany, where everything was foreign to her, including the language – a shortcoming that her energy and zest for life made up for. Following commitments in Kiel, Lübeck and Frankfurt, she ultimately came to Aachen, where she gave up dancing after twelve years upon falling pregnant with her second son, David.

Whenever she told her stories, I could imagine her as an adventurous young woman zooming around in a convertible VW Beetle. But no one wants to hear the details of their mother's excursions to Paris and other pleasurable ventures. Let's just say she embraced life, and if I temporarily ran a bit wild in New York, I wasn't alone.

But now to more serious topics, for example my finances.

My first job paid seven dollars an hour. It was a dream job. New York was the epitome of freedom, and later, when I would often earn 1,000 dollars in a night, I enjoyed this freedom to the max. But I lived a pretty low-key lifestyle for the first few semesters, only going out occasionally; it wasn't like seven dollars was going to get me far in that city. I would have done my first job even if it hadn't paid a cent, though, because my workplace was priceless, the most beautiful part of the entire Juilliard School.

The wonderfully catalogued library contained all the sheet music ever written, music for every instrument. From there, a staircase led to the room housing the record collection that spanned some ten thousand discs, including, of course, those of my greatest heroes, both violinists and conductors, records of Heifetz, Menuhin, Szeryng, Perlman, Oistrach, Kreisler and Furtwängler. In short, the entire universe of classical music, all on magnificent records.

You can imagine how perfect this place was for me. Someone would occasionally come in and return a CD, I would say 'thank you', check their name off, re-catalogue the CD and then have another leisurely half hour to continue my wanderings among the shelves, pull out a record, put on my headphones and immerse myself in the music. I was lucky with nearly everything I pulled out, and I felt like a guest at a three-Michelin-star restaurant having the head chef prepare every dish in the world in inimitable quality at my request. That's what I call a dream job. And if you get seven dollars an hour for it to boot ...

The problem was, of course, that seven dollars was too little to get by on. I started working as a waiter at weekends, at an iconic place called Underbar in Union Square. I'd set off there at 9 o'clock at night, would be ready to work from 10 p.m., serve drinks until 3 a.m., and then knock off. I was no mixologist, I'd poured a gin and tonic once at best, but this job was much more lucrative – firstly because of the telephone numbers you'd get passed to you on the sly, and secondly because New Yorkers were pretty generous with their tips; 15 to 20 per cent was standard, and if a group of guests got on well with you, you'd go home with 200 or 250 dollars in tips.

Was that enough, though? Still not quite. I began working at Urban Outfitters on 72nd Street. This is a shop chain for hip clothing, and warehouse sorting started at 6 a.m. As I was good at this, and punctual, I was promoted to a sales role within a few weeks, so I have Urban Outfitters to thank for a basic training in selling jeans. And even though I was never employee of the month, and never saw a big picture of Christian Bongartz up on the wall in appreciation of my services, I never gave my bosses any reason to fire me. The pay here was twelve, rather than seven, dollars an hour, so it was further improvement from a financial perspective.

Was that enough? To be honest, no, it still wasn't. What happened was, at Urban Outfitters, at the Underbar or sometimes even just on the streets of New York, I would occasionally have someone pass me a little card while saying: come by, you're a handsome boy, we'll find you a place to stay ... Modelling is certainly a big thing in New York, but I had long been sceptical of the industry as there's too much hustling involved. One day, though, a little group of young women assured me, 'This agency is credible. We have a great photographer who'll take a few nice photos of you, and the best bit is that we won't take more than a 30 per cent commission.'

And that modelling agency in downtown Manhattan did indeed hire me pretty regularly from my fourth to my sixth semester. So I went to the casting, sat around with fifty other guys, was called in, assessed, weighed, measured and asked for my telephone number. Then, one day, it happened: 'Come over, we think you're good, the fitting is on this day at this time.' Sometimes I did photo shoots, sometimes I was on the catwalk, and sometimes I modelled underwear, which saw me hop on stage in Calvin Klein boxer shorts. I did a lot of exercise at the time, increasingly veering away from the pizza and joining the ballerina queue at the salad bar, in part because my friends were all very body-conscious people – dancers and actors for whom every extra gram weighed them down. So I looked very presentable. And in terms of income, I would come away with a cheque for 500 dollars after two or three hours of shooting. After 2003 Fashion Week, I was indeed 5,000 dollars richer – which was of course a godsend for me.

As it would turn out, this wasn't even the end of my options, which brings me to the subject of nightlife. I would naturally go out with my aforementioned group of friends; 27th Street in Chelsea was the in place to go at the time as it was where Cain, Bed, Bungalow 8, Quo, all the popular nightclubs were, and my friends were generally an extrovert bunch. When you show up at a club with a crew like that, you'll get noticed sooner or later, and that's when you can get owners asking you, 'Do you want to work here on the weekend?' At first you think they mean waiting on tables, but no: 'Just do whatever you're doing here. Come with your friends – we prefer girls to boys – and have fun here with them.' Aha. And would we get paid for it? 'Yes. You guys being here livens the place up. That's worth 500 dollars to me. Plus free drinks.'

Five hundred dollars for the night? I couldn't believe my ears. It remained to be seen if they really paid, but what did we have to lose? If the drinks were free, it was worth a try. We were given the best table in the best part of the venue, and if the guy did end up coming through with the 500 dollars, I wasn't going to say no ... And that's how I became a promoter. Not exactly a profession, but a fantastic job.

From now on, I was responsible for creating good vibes. I started at Cain, directly opposite from Bungalow 8, and did what I would have done anyway: showed up with my crew, had a great night, awesome fun – and came away with 500 dollars. Or 1,000. You can't really go wrong when your friends are dancers and actors, because as soon as the first few bars of music started playing, the dancers would already be up on the tables; you didn't have to ask them twice. And then it would be more than just their classical-music classmate who would be watching on in open-mouthed awe.

Our presence was definitely worth it for the club owner. The clientele of these clubs had deep pockets, after all, and when they were out to have fun, they'd give their black American Express cards a workout. They'd pay a cool 500 dollars for a bottle of champagne, and would rarely stop at one – you would sometimes see rows of empty, half-empty and even unopened champagne bottles standing around on the tables as the sun started to come up. In short, the club owners used a formula of youthful exuberance and pretty girls in their early twenties to fill their venues with a very extravagant audience.

One night, I was sitting with my crew in Bungalow 8 when a guy wearing a baseball cap on a predominantly bald head came over to my table and said, 'Hey, is it okay to sit with you guys?' 'Yeah. My name is Christian. What's yours?' 'My name is Bruce.' As in Bruce Willis, with whom I then spent a fun evening, until he casually left, accompanied by two female dancers. You'd be constantly making acquaintances like that, seeing famous faces such as Colin Farrell, Paris Hilton, George Clooney, Keanu Reeves and the Olsen twins. The bouncers here were naturally ruthless. If they knew you, they would wave you through. If not – no chance. After all, celebrities have private lives too, and these play out at night at places like this in a totally chilled atmosphere, when things would happen that never made the headlines ... We were at the epicentre of New York's partying and pleasure scene, and, as bizarre as it may sound, I managed to finance the majority of my studies with the money I earned from being a promoter.

During this wonderful time, I fell in love with Layla. It was a harmonious relationship. Layla was a Slovenian model with an illustrious group of friends. While my gang represented art and culture, hers was all about living life to the fullest – it was the perfect mix.

My parents had announced they were going to be coming over for a visit. Layla had spent the night before in the bunk bed of my apparent prison cell at the residence, so she had only a very flimsy clubbing outfit to wear the next morning. As for me, I hadn't fully processed the fact that mum and dad would be on my doorstep that morning, and when they did arrive, Layla greeted them in a glittery little dress and high heels, with some makeup slapped on. This was the first time she met my parents, and it didn't go all that great. She told me off afterwards, saying 'Don't do that to me again!' But Layla came into my life during my laissez-faire phase, when I would just let things wash over me calmly.

When it came to our night-time club appearances, however, not only did we want to leave a good impression, but we had to, because, apart from the undeniable pleasure it gave us, the promoter's job was of course also a business. So we couldn't just spend the whole night sitting in a corner sucking on a straw; we had to put on some sort of a show, and Layla came up with the idea that I needed clothes that fitted the scene. So she became my stylist, which was commendable enough, and she can also take the credit for my long hair – because she was into guys with long hair. 'It'll look good on you,' she said, so I let my hair grow and gathered it into a rubber band. I've never had it cut short since.

So – thanks, Layla. But, as is the way on the nightlife scene, you don't see each other for two weeks, you meet up again, and hear the words, 'By the way, I've met someone else.' In Layla's case, this 'someone else' was a breathtakingly gorgeous Abercrombie & Fitch model with the body of a Greek god. I guess you can't say she'd made a bad choice this time.

You can find videos and photos for this chapter here.

A foretaste of crossover

In interviews, I'm often asked how I got where I am today. Perhaps the interviewers think there's a formula I devised for myself. There isn't. What there is, however, is my instinct that ultimately took me, via Israel and London, to the place that offered me the best opportunity for development – the city of New York and the Juilliard School. It was there, that atmosphere, that created the person who has now long been known as David Garrett.

The streets of New York are the best place to hatch future plans and dream big. Lots of conversations at the Juilliard School – with violinists, but also with actors and dancers – revolved around the question of what our dreams were. We were always looking ahead, and New York provided the telescope that

Out in New York City, 2004

brought our goals into view. It was also the city that gave us the confidence to achieve those goals.

And the Juilliard School was where, during the third semester, the initial spark for my major crossover project was ignited. Like so many other stories, this one, too, began in the melting pot of our school, between the salad bar and pizza counter. In other words, in the canteen.

As I have mentioned, that was where everyone got talking, and it became clear that dancers were always needing someone to provide the music for their school performances. Sure, they could get a band to play it, but why would you when you had so many good musicians all under one roof? I was up for it. 'What kind of music do you want?' I asked, suggesting the likes of Bach, Mozart and Mendelssohn. Yes, they needed some of that. But sometimes, they would say, 'I do contemporary dance and am a huge fan of Michael Jackson.' Or Led Zeppelin. Or someone would say, 'I have to dance three pieces; two classical and one contemporary – can you manage that?' So pop music, jazz, on the violin, maybe even rock? Sure, why not? Let's see if it sounds as good on my instrument as it does in its original form.

And so it began. I would spend my free time in the dance studio, watching the choreography, listening to the music piece and rewriting the music for the required four minutes of dancing in the exact rhythm and tempo for the violin. These little ballet performances would later see me playing live in a room of thirty or forty people – mostly classical stuff but also Michael Jackson, Led Zeppelin and Gershwin. The reactions were amazing; there would often be standing ovations not only for the dancers but also for me! Okay, I thought, it might not have been a Brahms or a Beethoven, but *Sweet Child of Mine* by Guns N' Roses didn't sound all that bad on my violin either.

The Juilliard School had two symphony orchestras of its own, consisting solely of students. I'd been part of one or the other since my first semester, and, even here in America, the audience we would look out at when performing on stage was an older demographic. But it was a different story when it came to dance and acting, which would attract a lot of young people, even though there would often be no difference between my 'dance music' and the symphony orchestras' repertoires. I once played a solo Bach sonata as background music for an actor's monologue, and had my doubts as to whether the young audience would like it, but even Bach was a hit.

So maybe young people weren't actually put off by classical music? Right from a young age, I had been told classical music was dying and audiences were dwindling. But now the penny was dropping for me. If twenty-year-olds come up to me excitedly after four minutes of listening to Johann Sebastian Bach, and say, 'Hey, what's the name of that piece? Write it down for me, I need to check it out', it means there's nothing wrong with the music. It means the average age of a concert's audience is probably more to do with the setting, the venue, maybe even the outfits. In the Juilliard School's symphony orchestras, for example, there were strict clothing rules: suit, bow tie, white shirt. But when it came to my performances for actors and dancers, it was just a case of 'come however you want, it doesn't matter at all. You can even go on stage nude if you want. As long as you're there on time and have your violin with you ...' So simply be less formal overall?

These were the very early days of something that would later grow into glorious, crazy awesomeness for me – my crossover project. But that would still be years away, and, for now, I would still often find myself wearing a suit and bow tie and sitting among the violinists in one of the Juilliard School's two orchestras.

The orchestral work was part of my training, for, even though many of the music students there aspired to be soloists, there was still a chance they would end up making their living as one of many in an orchestra. Now, orchestra musicians prepare for concerts differently to soloists: the latter practise for concerts on their own, whereas the former meet regularly for rehearsals with the whole orchestra, led by a conductor.

These orchestra rehearsals have their own rules. As a soloist, you can't imagine how tedious and arduous orchestra rehearsals can be, because, if even one instrument falters, everyone has to start again from the top. Orchestra rehearsals lasting four or five hours are thus tests of patience for all involved, and it does soloists no harm to experience this different way of working – not to mention the fact that it's also where they learn how to follow a conductor.

I, in any case, took orchestra rehearsals very seriously. I would get up early on the day, warm up, and run through my part from top to bottom – there weren't many others who would be as well prepared for a rehearsal as I was. But my ambition didn't stop there. My goal was to be right up there among the first violinists in the orchestra, as close to the conductor as possible.

You see, there's a difference between being a first or second violinist, because the standards for first violinists are higher, the technical challenges greater, plus there are solo interludes. So being a second violinist in the row behind them was not necessarily something to write home about, which is why the more ambitious among us aimed for a spot at the front. There was a set order in which people sat in the orchestra, determined by a process that avoided any favouritism: once a year, each of the students would play the same piece for a panel of professors, except they would be hidden behind a curtain, with only a number to identify them. Those who excelled could hope to score a spot at the front. Those who didn't would have to make do with the back seat.

My goal was to get pole position and I had almost achieved this in my second year, when I was second – not bad considering there were nearly a hundred candidates – and, from then on, sat right at the front during orchestra rehearsals, directly next to the first violinist – a great spot, a wonderful spot. But unfortunately I wouldn't be there for long ...

How come? Had I shown up unprepared? Had people noticed me being late? None of the above. The rehearsals started at nine. At five to nine, I was sitting in my seat chatting with the people around me. When the conductor gave the signal and briefly knocked on his stand with his stick, I took out my violin and was ready to go thirty seconds later – better prepared than virtually anyone else for the rehearsal. But my approach was not up to the Juilliard School's standards.

The orchestral attendant, who was responsible for the organizational side of things and thus for ensuring everything was just right, silently studied my behaviour with growing displeasure, before one day looking me in the eye and shouting, 'You need to be holding the violin by nine o'clock on the dot! Your behaviour is totally unprofessional, and we don't want to hear any of your yacking! If you keep this up, you won't be going anywhere!' This was all said pretty bluntly in front of the whole group.

I wanted the floor to swallow me up. Maybe he had mistaken my relaxed approach for a lack of concentration, but he could have gone about clarifying it more discreetly. I was fuming. A stream of curses surged through my head, but protesting loudly was out of the question. So I channelled my anger into the sheet music in front of me and scribbled pages' worth of abuse at that person down on paper – 'what a daft idiot', 'what a rotten thing to do', 'probably hasn't had sex in months ...' The guy sitting next to me might have thought I was overreacting a bit, but I was just in the mood to do it.

What I didn't realize, in my innocence, was that the sheet music wasn't thrown away after the concert. It would go back to the library for someone to carefully erase all the handwritten annotations. Mine weren't erased. Mine made it to the president of the Juilliard School, who promptly called me to his office. So off I went, unaware of what had happened. No sooner had I stepped through the door than I spotted my annotated sheet music in his hands. 'Did you write this?' Well, what could I say? That I had been acting on obsessive thoughts? That my work wasn't meant to be seen by anyone else? Especially not by him? I mean, he liked me. 'How stupid can you be?' he said, and ordering me to write a letter of apology to the vilified orchestral attendant. That was the extent of the consequences – nothing like I had experienced at the Royal College of Music in London – and the case was closed with that letter.

For the director – but not for the orchestral attendant. While he allowed me to keep playing behind the curtain at the annual auditions, I was disqualified from the actual process. His message was clear: you can play your heart out; I couldn't care less – you'll stay exactly where I've banished you: in the last row of the second violins! And so it was that for the rest of my studies I sat in the back row, with no prospect of ever playing my way out of those doldrums. To the orchestral people, at least, I remained a persona non grata. But that was okay, because, as I said, second violins have it a bit easier.

Even if you did something foolish, you got off lightly. Today, I realize that in New York, I was finally able to act my age. I no longer had to mimic the adults; I could act as old as I actually was, even though not everything I had the cheek to do met with the school management's approval. The triad of serious music, serious demeanours and serious table discussions from my Aachen days were finally a thing of the past. The levity and ease of my childhood years were coming back, and everything that had turned to stone within me during my late teenage years was given new life.

You can find videos and photos for this chapter here.

Getting the ball rolling

Of course, I would work towards something every day, but without setting a specific goal. I refused to commit to achieving a particular outcome. Who knows what could happen in the meantime and send you in a different direction? No, I wanted to keep surprising myself. Just the very idea of one day no longer being able to surprise myself gave me anxiety, so I was definitely in the right place when I found myself at the Night of the Proms in Antwerp in 2002.

Forty concerts in two months! And always with the same set-up: a symphony orchestra and a dozen rock bands such as Simple Minds ('Don't You Forget About Me') and Foreigner ('I Want to Know What Love Is') with a huge stage show, plus me – the only person covering the classical side of things, with

At the Juillard School graduation ceremony with Alexander

an abridged version of the third movement of Beethoven's violin concerto, *Csárdás* by Monti, and *Danse Macabre* by Saint-Saëns. Could it work? Playing classical music to 16,000 people in a hall the size of Berlin's former O2 Arena?

Of course the bands and I rehearsed with the orchestra beforehand, but what happened that first night is not something I would ever have expected in a million years. I was killing time in my small dressing room deep in the bowels of the building, as I wasn't on until later, and I suddenly felt a vibration. The first rock number was starting, and the noise that built up all around me was as if T-Rex from *Jurassic Park* was heading towards us – all we needed was a glass of water bobbing around on the table in time with his stomping. Then I heard fervent clapping and loud cheering, and thought: bloody hell. Soon you're going to be heading out there with your violin and playing Beethoven – it could end up being a massive flop. You'll probably have to duck as they throw beer cans and rotten eggs at you.

It was a sold-out hall, a rock audience, but there were no beers or eggs thrown. Perhaps it was also due to the fact that I didn't stand like a stiff statue on stage, that I moved around and, during the *Csárdás* even ... Wait, let me explain: after the first few rapid sections, this piece has a slow middle section, where the orchestra dies away and ultimately falls silent, while the violin reaches the highest notes it is capable of producing – a moment when everyone in the audience holds their breath and you can hear a pin drop – before continuing its initial rapid pace. And for that moment of utmost concentration, I got down on my knees. An absurd idea? I had come up with it back in New York, and had even talked to my brother about it. He had seemed a little disturbed at the thought, 'Dude, are you sure? Well ... give it a try.' I did, and, what can I say? The people actually enjoyed my knee drop, and, along with Simple Minds, I reckon it was me, with my violin and classical music, who got the greatest reception that day.

Going down on my knees hadn't affected my playing in any way, but the next day, people were saying, 'Did you see the violinist who played on his knees?' And the audience was made up of young music fans who liked to party. There would naturally have been other reasons that made my performance so memorable to the listeners. For one, I played the music with passion and joy, but also – the emotional palette of a Beethoven piece appeals to everything we humans can ever feel. So another similar experience to what I had found back at the Juilliard School with the dancers and actors: young people who were utterly crazy about classical music. And something gradually started brewing in my head that, despite these little nudges, probably still would never have evolved into my crossover project if I hadn't met Dutchman Franck van der Heijden in Antwerp.

The Night of the Proms is like a giant festival of music in Belgium – I had taken an entire semester off specifically for it. The same show would be performed forty times, the hall sold out for two whole months, and I had enough time to listen to the other artists and come up with my own ideas during the pieces. What did I find so amazing about this event? Clearly, the combination of symphony orchestra and rock band, and how perfectly they both meshed – the orchestra and the pieces by Simple Minds and Foreigner. The man who had written the arrangements for this Night of the Proms was its musical director, Franck van der Heijden himself.

At night, after the concert, we would usually all meet up in the hotel lobby. The work for the day was over, there was nothing left to be done, plus the guys from Simple Minds were hanging around, Bonnie Tyler was there, even Franck made an appearance, and that's how we began talking. Franck and I quickly realized we were kindred spirits and instinctively knew that we could get something going together. What, exactly? It was still difficult to say at that point – there was never any goal anyway – but I couldn't stop thinking about my success: what exactly was it about me that the people had liked? Because you never really know, even though you still try to figure it out. In any case, the response to my performance in Antwerp had left me extremely hopeful indeed.

'We need to do something together' – there may be no more commonly uttered phrase among artists than this one, and it generally never amounts to anything. But Franck and I were serious, and, in the summer of 2004, during the semester break, I was back at the wheel of my special 1996 Bon Jovi II-model VW Golf, driving from Aachen to Hilversum near Amsterdam, where Franck continues to live to this day. I would combine these trips with a detour to Rhoda, the girlfriend I had met in Antwerp – and it was another perfect combination indeed: a few days with Franck, a few days with Rhoda. Work and love in one; glorious times.

That's how the ball got rolling. Talk about an easy, downright effortless, start! The summer sunshine streaming into our living room in Aachen, me putting a tape recorder on the piano, pressing 'record', hitting the keys and playing the chords to the melodies I had in my head. I would then drive over to Franck with this tape and he would decide what had potential and what didn't, before we set about fleshing out my musical ideas. We soon ended up with four or five demo tapes of our own compositions, and I would listen to these at full volume on my drive back to Aachen. Not all the stuff was great, to be honest, but to me it was at the time.

Now, I'm an impatient person. I ideally prefer pieces to be finished yesterday. When you work at that speed, you're free in the evenings and still have half a weekend spare. Then Franck came to the party with his ideas: why not take well-known classical pieces and give them a contemporary arrangement, combining them with a jazz or rock band? I would then take over the solo part with my violin. Or take well-known rock numbers and treat them like a piece of classical music? As an old rock-n-roller, Franck would put on record after record – Toto, Metallica, Deep Purple – and I would sit there, violin at the ready, and improvise. Aha, this melody works on the violin. Or: I can think of a nice accompanying part to this melody. Or: No, this doesn't work at all. We recorded our initial attempts in Franck's recording studio – me on the violin, Franck on the keyboard or guitar – and if we liked the sound of an interplay, it meant a piece was guaranteed to work later on with a band or orchestra. That dream summer of 2004 was the time my crossover project was born, and some of those early attempts, such as *Eliza's Song*, *Serenade* and *Rock Toccata*, would later make it onto my first two albums.

Where would I be without Franck van der Heijden and his experience as a film-score composer and his visions? We've been inseparable ever since, which is why you'll hear more of Franck later on. But before I get back to the Juilliard School and Itzhak Perlman one last time, I just want to talk about the idea of a violinist playing the piano.

Why did I sit at the piano in Aachen when trying out music ideas? Why didn't I just use my violin? The reason is because the violin has only a very limited capacity to produce harmonies. Like the human voice, it is more of a melody instrument, meaning the violin sings much like a tenor or soprano sings a Verdi aria, and polyphony in this case requires more than one singer/violin. But a piano has the sound spectrum of an entire orchestra; you can produce any chord or harmony on it. No other instrument, apart from the organ, can do this.

When you're composing, the melody is one thing, and the violin will suffice for this. But then there are the harmonies, the foundation of any piece of music; only they can turn a pencil drawing (to use an art example) into a powerful, meaningful painting, and that's why all the great composers predominantly worked on the piano. Mozart was a very good violinist, but when it came to composing, he spent just as much time on the piano as Beethoven did, and Beethoven also played a bit of the violin. So it was no different for me and Franck. But the piano and I were never going to be best friends. Even after four years of piano lessons at Juilliard, it's still not really my thing, because playing the violin has meant my hands are used to a completely different kind of co-ordination.

But back to New York. After eight semesters, my studies were drawing to an end, and the fierce hopes I had started out with were no less fervent; on the contrary – now, having had this amazing training, the world of music would definitely be interested in me ... After my last lessons with Itzhak Perlman, however, we did have a serious conversation – a conversation I had asked for myself.

'Mr Perlman,' I said – hardly anyone spoke informally with him; even his long-time pianist Rohan de Silva never spoke to him on a first-name basis out of respect – 'Mr Perlman, I know I'm good, otherwise you wouldn't have spent so much time with me these last few years. But there's still one thought that keeps tormenting me. I'm afraid of overestimating myself; I'm scared I'm still not good enough for what's to come.'

Perlman considered this for a moment, before responding, 'No one, David, can know whether you'll have a successful career or not. Not even me – there are so many unforeseeable things that could happen. You certainly have the tools for achieving a successful career. But however your life may unfold, as long as you enjoy what you do, you'll never look back with bitterness. Do what's important to you, and do it with passion and love – whether it be playing in an orchestra or becoming a famous soloist. The worst thing would be for you to be doing things purely to please others. Don't do that. Please yourself.' And that piece of invaluable advice marked the end of the Perlman chapter.

You can find videos and photos for this chapter here.

There is no doubt:
violins are my life.

No matter how much I change, my love for the violin remains constant. Here I am with my dearly beloved Pressenda.

Going through some bold fashion choices in New York. A loud shirt or …

… my first colour-popping modelling shoot.

My personal highlights include playing Niccolò Paganini in the film *The Devil's Violinist* …

… and performing with the amazing Jonas Kaufmann to a sold-out stadium in Munich for the 2012 Champions League Final.

It was also a huge pleasure to sit on the famous couch of the *Wetten, dass …? (Wanna bet, that …?)* German television show with Thomas Gottschalk in 2009.

A pleasure so great, I did it again in 2011.

As part of my performance for Queen Elizabeth II's Diamond Jubilee, I had the honour of meeting her in person.

With Riccardo Chailly and the Orchestra Filarmonica della Scala outside Milan's cathedral.

It's good to work with someone who's your wingman: Jörg Kollenbroich with a violin-saving umbrella during an open-air concert.

One of the key things I strive to show people with my music is that classical and pop don't have to be mutually exclusive. I've won three pop ECHOs (this picture is from 2011) …

… as well as various classical ECHOs (this picture is from 2014). The Echo Music Prize was awarded to the most successful musicians each year until 2018.

In 2013 I received the Bambi Award, the oldest and most important media award in Germany.

In 2010 I was the recipient of the Golden Camera, an annual German film and television award.

2015

What a great moment!

I look forward to seeing you all again soon!

Daniel Kuhn and the black Amex

'Dear David, we've thought long and hard and have decided to end our co-operation with you. We no longer think you'll be able to achieve a successful career. Please understand our decision and don't hold it against us; we wish you all the best for the future and of course continue to keep our fingers crossed for you. But your journey from here on in will be without us.' Signed: Pamela Cronin.

I couldn't believe my eyes. Renowned agency Askonas Holt in London, my last hope, had just evaporated. The only one who had still been giving me work in the summer holidays – nothing earth-shattering, the odd 250 dollars here, 500 dollars there, but every little bit helped – and now this: no management, no record deal and no agency. Sure, I had disappeared into oblivion for four years, and, in the world of classical music, you don't get gigs just because you once performed well at a concert back in the dark ages. To outsiders, four years look like a time of stagnancy, a standstill, and, in this world, it meant 'go back to start', like in Monopoly. So had my father actually been right? Had the Juilliard School indeed been the biggest mistake for my career?

Now, David Garrett, the nobody, was sitting in his shoebox apartment on 42nd Street – a small living room, tiny kitchen, bed in the living room, all on the fourth floor of a 19th-century brick building in the New York district of Hell's Kitchen, where housing was still semi-affordable – even though rent still cost me 1,300 dollars, meaning I always had my eye out for the specials when at the supermarket. In other words, he was in a void, yet had still been taking comfort from the old American dream that anyone could become a millionaire, and then cold, hard reality had hit – studies complete, possibility of a new start, necessity for a new start, new start failed ...

And now? What would happen next? I was a better violinist than ever before, but hardly anyone around me seemed to know it. Fortunately, I had an understanding group of friends. Everyone was starting some kind of venture, everyone was dreaming of their great breakthrough, and, that night, I asked a few of them to come around for a drink, because there are moments when alcohol is the solution.

After spending four years in a student residence, these cute little digs between Central Park and the Hudson River had put me in high spirits. And as there was still a bit left over from my good-vibes job (and the Night of the Proms), and I was in fact still working as a promoter, I had made it clear, when my parents asked me about my future plans, that I intended to stay in New York – 'I'll manage somehow, I'll find my feet' – please not back to Aachen after four years in America. So now the ambitious Mr

Broke was forced to do some serious introspection: how, through what genius move, can I bring myself back into the conversation?

Jump on stage at 8 p.m. at Carnegie Hall and announce, 'I'm playing tonight'? Unfortunately it doesn't work that way. Play my violin on a street corner? I would have to play for years before someone able to give me a gig walked by. Look around for home concerts in the hope that there might be an important figure from New York's cultural scene in the audience? That's more like it, and I actually had a few contacts for this, the main one being Daniel Kuhn, a patron of the arts, at whose home I had already performed. While he didn't pay fees, he did provide food, prosecco and orange juice, and I recalled the audience being pretty attentive, the atmosphere almost intimate. I called Daniel. 'Listen, things are looking pretty bleak right now. I have no record deal, no agency, no idea what to do next. If you ever organize a concert night and need a musician, please give me a call.'

I fluctuated between hoping and worrying. You'll have to play twenty concerts, I thought to myself, before you're discovered by a big name from the music business who is willing to give you a gig – a passionate orchestral musician won't be much help to you. But Daniel Kuhn liked me, he was one of my fans, and I found myself playing more frequently at his place, which happened to be a stunning apartment in a skyscraper, with amazing views of one of the world's largest inner-city green spaces, Central Park. Things would kick off at 8 p.m., with five or ten people in attendance, all very nice, as were the accompanying snacks, but the outcome always left a lot to be desired. Some nights, I would go home with 20 dollars, other nights 50 or 100, a kind donation from one of the art-enthusiast guests, but when it came to getting the gigs I so craved – never a sniff.

So I had pocket money. I could still afford subway tickets and pizza. But, over time, my circle of friends dispersed, my promoter's job lost its shine, my appearances at Bungalow 8 and Cain became less and less frequent, and then D-Day came.

It was the depths of New York's winter, again. My situation had now reached crisis level. I wasn't able to pay my monthly rent; I was already getting knocks on my door and a furious voice asking 'So when's it coming?' – a familiar scene from Hollywood movies involving wretched characters in dire straits – and my food stock was down to emergency supplies. In other words, things were getting tight. I sat at home thinking 'Should I call Aachen? Should I ask my parents to book me a flight back to Germany?' For heaven's sake, no! That would be an admission of personal defeat. I refused to put myself through that, so I quickly rejected the idea.

And it was snowing outside, hard. The traffic was in chaos, and the usual crazies were out on Broadway in their cross-country skis. The next concert at Daniel Kuhn's place was due to be held that night, and New York had been buried in snow for the last few hours. But I needed money, the concert had to go ahead, even if I only came away with 50 dollars. So I grabbed my violin and practised my pieces, keeping an eye on the window – nope, it was still a grey sky speckled with white. It kept snowing incessantly, and evening drew nearer.

Setting off at 5 p.m., I took the subway, but also walked quite a bit of the way, and the first thing Daniel said to me when he opened the door was, 'Have you seen the weather today?' Yes. I looked around the music room. Everything was all prepared, Daniel Gortler, the pianist, looked ready to go, but no one was giving me any hope: 'I called a few people – they've all cancelled. There probably won't be anything happening today. But maybe it'll stop snowing and few brave souls will still venture over.'

I grew more and more anxious with every uneventful minute that passed. We spent the next three hours staring at the snowflakes outside the window. The snowfall was actually getting heavier; Central Park had turned into a winter wonderland, and the streets down below had fallen silent except for the odd taxi driver on his way home in his yellow cab. Friday night, and there wasn't a single guest to be seen. 'Let's just try again next week,' Daniel Kuhn suggested, and then I shared my predicament with pianist Daniel Gortler: 'I'm in dire straits. I'm about to throw in the towel. If only even two people were to come ... please, let's wait a bit longer.' But the clock struck 10 p.m., then 11 p.m., and it was still just us, my amiable host's patience finally running out. 'We'll postpone the concert to Monday,' he said, adding, 'Come on, David, it's not the end of the world.'

But it was! Daniel Gortler saw the disappointment in my eyes and offered to accompany me home. 'I can't let you go home alone in that state. I'll come with you. You live in Hell's Kitchen, right? That's twenty-five blocks away. We'll manage it.'

We set off. My desperation made me talkative. As we walked through the snowy New York landscape, I confided in him that I only had 12 dollars in my bank account.

'Maybe even just ten.'

'Impossible. I don't believe you.' He was obviously finding it difficult to reconcile my earlier successes with my current predicament.

'Wait. There's a bank over there. I'll get them to print out a bank statement to prove it to you.'

Next minute, I was walking into the bank, going over to the ATM and entering my credit card. The statement printed out and it was even worse than feared, showing a credit of just 7.95. If I went shopping the next day, they'd immediately freeze my account, because I had no overdraft allowance. Only 7.95 dollars ... I was already on my way out when I heard a beeping noise. I turned around and saw a black American

Express card sticking out of another ATM; someone must have accidentally left it there.

So what now? Leave it stuck there? I pulled it out of the slot, took it with me and showed it to Daniel, who had now seen from my bank statement that I wasn't exaggerating. 'Here,' I said, 'this Amex was sticking out of the ATM next to me. What should I do with it?' Daniel held it up to the light streaming out of the bank. 'Listen,' he said, 'this is what you do: buy yourself something to eat. Get a monthly subway ticket, then throw the card in a public post-box; the cardholder will get the money back from their insurance company.'

This would have saved me, but I had never stolen anything in my life, nor had I ever borrowed money without paying it back immediately. As a six-year-old, I had nicked the alms chest at a Swiss monastery and had copped a slap from my father, an experience I would never forget. But I hadn't been wanting to get richer from it; as a coin collector at the time, I simply had an interest in coins, and now I was supposed to do this with a stranger's credit card ...

But you shouldn't look a gift horse in the mouth, which is why, the next day, I did actually buy myself 250 dollars' worth of groceries and invest 150 dollars in a monthly subway pass, before inconspicuously tossing the credit card into a street-side post-box. This is common practice in New York, because everyone knows the mailman will take care of it – and I would scrape by for another four weeks. I didn't feel comfortable with what I had done, though.

Monday came around – the day of the postponed concert. The weather had settled, the streets were safe to walk again, and a respectable audience had gathered at Daniel Kuhn's place. Gil Shohat happened to be among them. We had never heard of each other – he knew just as little about me as I did about him – but, after the concert, he came over to me and introduced himself as the conductor of the Israel Chamber Orchestra. He had liked the way I had played – something you always love to hear – but didn't stop at compliments; he invited me to Israel. 'I'd love for you to play five concerts with us over the summer. We'd be prepared to pay you an advance fee.'

I might still have been without a record deal or agent – but I did now have an idea as to what my future would be.

My poor and penniless days were over. Thanks to Gil Shohat, thanks to Daniel Kuhn, and, last but not least, because of that beeping at the bank.

You can find videos and photos for this chapter here.

73

Flat-sharing with Alexander

Without the black American Express card, this book would never have been written. Because even Daniel Kuhn's promise to make up for the concert that didn't happen wouldn't have been enough to stop me from aborting my failed New York adventure and flying back to Germany that very Saturday – to a place where hardly anyone outside my own family had missed me. The German music industry had now certainly closed the David Garrett file; it wasn't wasting any more time with that lost son.

But my story doesn't end there. It continues, because Daniel Kuhn, cultured Jewish circles in New York and people in Israel took me under their wing, gave me opportunities to perform and helped me achieve success. On my concert tour in the summer of 2005, I was welcomed with open arms all across Israel, showered in spirited applause and accepted with genuine warmth and affection. I played in Tel Aviv, Jerusalem and Haifa, and as my name spread far and wide around the country, I had my first gig with the Israel Philharmonic Orchestra, and Gil Shohat from the Israel Chamber Orchestra booked me in for the following season. I was back as a classical musician, I was back in the game, and never again did I have any worries about paying my rent or stocking my fridge.

As I was now able to support myself in New York, I remained loyal to the music nights at Daniel Kuhn's place. Without running an actual agency – he was a psychologist by profession – he used his contacts to get me invitations to chamber concerts and concert performances, introduced me to people and continued to treat me to his snacks. In other words, life could go on. And it did, but before the Juilliard School fades from the pages of this book, I should probably summarize the most important things I learned from my studies:

First, you need to know what you're good at. You must be able to assess your capabilities. That's why I went to New York, because, at eighteen or nineteen, I no longer knew how good I was. Was I top or a flop? Could I match the best violinists of my generation, or was I just a short-lived footnote on the fringes of the international music scene? Your gut instinct won't help you; it has its own agenda that no one in real life is interested in. No, it's your head that needs to assess your strengths, and Juilliard did enable me to assess myself realistically.

Secondly, you need to know what you're not good at. This is where many people fail, because being a good violinist or a good pianist doesn't mean you're going to be equally good in other areas. So you need to know what your weaknesses are. Sure, you can work on them, and you can improve over time, but only once you acknowledge the third point, which is: you need to find people who are good in the areas you yourself are bad in.

So we move on now from my university experiences to the experiment that was the next few years. I wasn't going to be able to achieve this new start on my own, but who likes hearing others tell them what to do? How many consider it a sign of weakness to ask the people around them for advice? Obviously, it's the opposite that's true: respecting others' professionalism is a sign of strength, and confiding in good people is the greatest win for you. The difficulty lies in being able to recognize the genuinely good people.

Initially, I often turned to the wrong ones – yes-men, naysayers, all manner of pseudo-experts. Only over time did I manage to gather a team of colleagues who are truly great in their field, and who help me to keep improving. Believing in yourself is not enough. There will always be days when your faith in yourself shatters, and that's when I'm grateful for this handful of people who watch out for me, who tell me their opinion without sugar-coating it, and who bolster me up. One of these people is Alexander, my brother and new flatmate.

This was the next experiment I got myself involved in. Alexander was still in America, still a student in Boston, where I had occasionally visited him from New York. I had even performed to Harvard students on one of these visits. Every year on the 4th of July, American Independence Day, Tchaikovsky's *1812 Overture* is performed, and word of me being in town had got around the campus, so I found myself back in an orchestra playing Tchaikovsky as first violinist. You can't expect to have a keenly listening audience on a sunny summer's day in the park at Harvard University – there were constantly people moving around – but it was good nonetheless.

Now, having completed his law exam in the autumn of 2005, Alexander had accepted a job at a law firm in New York. We quickly agreed that, since we were both living in the same city, where the rents are obscenely high, why not live together? So we moved into a sixty-floor skyscraper on the corner of 54th Street and 8th Avenue. The on-site gym and pool added a hint of luxury to our lives, but the flat itself was barely larger than my old one in Hell's Kitchen: two shoebox-sized bedrooms and a tiny kitchen – all the furniture delivered from Ikea in Jersey and put together ourselves. I didn't want to be spending my nights on a little makeshift bed and insisted on having a queen-size one, but then the doors of the built-in wardrobe wouldn't open, so we took off the two wardrobe doors and shoved them in the basement, with a Yamaha keyboard squeezed into the kitchen. That's how insanely cramped it was.

My brother is the better cook out of the two of us. Back in the days when I would be on tour with my father, Alexander would have to stay at home with my mother and sister, sometimes cooking for them all, but in any case helping out in the kitchen, and he was familiar with how to run a household. I, on the other hand ... When I was at home, it would be a case of: dinner is ready, put down the violin, sit at the table and eat. That was the extent of my domestic duties. In other words, Alexander was the head of the household in our flat and 'sentenced' me to do the cleaning. That was probably the reason we stopped living together after two and a half years – or maybe it had something to do with the fact that I would occasionally have friends over? Our lifestyles were pretty different. My brother worked in the office from nine in the morning to six at night and would spend the weekend at home, not really appreciating rock 'n' roll until 3 a.m. 'Dude, that went on late last night. Do you have to make so much noise?' And yet I had been playing the music super softly ...

We did get on well, though. We liked the same movies, the same music, and you couldn't find a better life coach than Alexander. We were really close. But at the end of 2007, we felt it was a good idea to go our own ways again in terms of housing. It must be said, however, that I didn't actually spend that much time in New York during our flat-sharing days; I was increasingly on the road in Europe, in Hilversum and London, where the Old Brompton Hotel awaited me. But what exactly was I doing in London?

During the Night of the Proms in Antwerp, it hadn't just been Franck van der Heijden that I had met; I had also met Stewart Young, who was based in London and was the manager of Zucchero, the father of Italian blues, as well as other reputable artists. He had been impressed by the way I had rocked the hall with my violin, and had since been trying to get me into the business, only to eventually say, 'Listen, I don't have the time or strength to do all the work that needs to be done on this, but I can recommend someone.' That someone was Rick Blaskey in London. In 2005, I had the opportunity to meet him in Germany, and we arranged to catch up at a hotel in Düsseldorf.

So Rick was waiting in the lobby, all prepared to meet a classical violinist. When he saw me walk in, he immediately wondered what rock band was playing in Düsseldorf that week. Next minute, I was sitting with him and no further negotiations were necessary; it was love at first sight. No one would associate this guy with a violin, he thought. Nothing fits, but everything fits – a spectacular combination. In short, Rick was hooked. 'Okay,' he said. 'Let's do a deal.' He would later sum up his first impression of me in a single sentence: 'Seeing is believing.'

Rick Blaskey wasn't from the world of classical music, but he was convinced he had found a diamond, and was hell-bent on making sure the world found out about me. A new audience, a new concert style, and venues where no violinist has ever performed before – these were the ideas that were swirling around in his mind. And as I soon realized how important I was to Rick, I started spending a lot more time in London.

You can find videos and photos for this chapter here.

An old hotel in London

During those years, Rick was one of the people I could count on, along with Alexander and Franck van der Heijden. He lived in London, my home base was in New York, and when the phone rang at my house, it would sometimes be him, saying, 'David, come over, we want to introduce you to so and so.'

Hoping each time that this would be my opportunity to get closer to a record deal, I would jump on a plane. And, as I was still starting out, upscale accommodation in London was out of the question for me. My hotel standards back then were limited to two criteria: full of atmosphere and affordable – maybe with a good nightclub nearby too. After all, London is a bustling capital, and, as a twenty-six-year-old, you're not exactly averse to discovering new places. Rick suggested trying the Old Brompton Hotel.

The Old Brompton Hotel in London

And I wasn't disappointed. The Brompton turned out to be a typical old London hotel, which meant no lift, but instead narrow staircases covered in worn carpet, dim ceiling lighting in the corridors, pre-war beds with mattresses like hammocks, and a reception that was nothing but the absolute bare minimum: a table and key hooks on the rear wall. None of that bothered me; the place had charm, the price was good, and it was an easy walk to Boujis, one of the city's hippest nightclubs. That's where all the in people hung out, and, as I had learned how to deal with bouncers in New York, I was always able to get in even without a female companion. Arguing won't get you anywhere in these instances, but respect and politeness definitely will.

In short, the Old Brompton was my favourite hotel for a long time. After a while, the staff come to know you, which makes everything easier, and if you don't cause any reason for complaint, you get them on-side. But the Brompton wasn't exactly a medieval castle with massively thick walls. We're talking about a lightweight 19th-century construction here, and if the television was on in the room next door, I would be able to recount the whole programme word for word afterwards. But the situation was awkward for another reason: I liked to practise late at night. During the day, the telephone would constantly be ringing, plus there would be the regular meetings, the studio sessions, so it wouldn't be until evening that things calmed down, that I got time to myself, and therefore usually took to my violin.

So I would do some more practice. But this time I wouldn't call it practising; I wasn't just repeating the same bit x number of times, which no one else but me would appreciate. I would instead play a full violin concerto from start to finish in my room at a crazy hour. After the last note rang out, what would happen on the other side of the walls? An invisible audience would applaud and cheer from the rooms next-door: 'Thank you very much! Thank you and good night! I'll be back here tomorrow!' As you can see, it was a very nice hotel. Even the guests were my kind of people. I felt understood there.

But there was one person who didn't understand me, and that was Alexandra Bellington. She was about the same age as me, and I had fallen for her in New York. One day, Rick offered me a gig as part of a series of performances at the Royal Albert Hall. The plan was for it to be like the concert series they used to have in the 19th century, so a bit of everything: a tenor singing an aria, followed by a cellist and a soprano, then a clarinet concerto, before I came on stage with Sarasate's *Carmen Fantasy* and Paganini's *La Campanelle* – so a purely classical programme, on six consecutive nights. The Royal Albert Hall – the ultimate venue in England! I had been able to see this mighty rounded building through the high windows of the Royal College of Music – the goal that all of us students dreamed about, so close yet so far. Nearly all the big names have played there, from Robbie Williams to the Berlin Philharmonic, and they must all have been struck by a sense of awe the first time.

So naturally I asked Alexandra if she wanted to come along. It's worth mentioning here that Alexandra came from a well-off family. From good, indeed very good lineage, shall we say. But this hadn't been a factor up to now; Alexandra herself was very low-key about her family's posh lifestyle, which is why I had had no qualms at all in telling her beforehand that I knew a great hotel in London with a top location. How was I to know her concept of a great hotel was a little different to mine?

A few days later, our taxi pulled up outside the Old Brompton and we got out. She had her medium-sized suitcase with her, which, along with mine, I dragged up the narrow staircase with its worn carpet, deliberately ignoring her when she asked, 'Doesn't this place have an elevator?' I headed towards the junior suite I had had the foresight to book; it was perhaps five square metres larger than the Brompton's standard rooms. Right from the corridor, I could tell from Alexandra's shocked look that she had actually been asking those questions in earnest. Having arrived at our suite, I had set down both our suitcases, opened mine and was already putting my stuff into the cupboard when I saw her fiddling with the room phone. She was holding the handset and dialling a number. 'What's up?' I asked. 'Sorry, honey,' she said, trying to keep her composure, 'but I won't be spending the night here. If you're playing at the Royal Albert Hall, you deserve something better. Leave it to me.'

I was taken aback – partly because my masculinity had been a tiny bit offended, but also because I was always very reluctant to accept invitations even from very, very close friends. I put a lot of emphasis on paying my way, and was happy to do so. But when Alexandra said, 'pack your things up', it sounded pretty definite, so I carried the suitcases back down. A taxi stopped outside, we got in, and when it stopped again, we were outside the brightly lit entrance of Claridge's hotel. I vaguely recalled that Boris Becker used to stay here when he was playing at Wimbledon. Alexandra got the key from reception and led me to the presidential suite, where we would be staying next door to Bono from U2.

I don't even want to know how much a night at this place cost. But even apart from that, I wasn't comfortable with the whole thing. It went against every fibre of my being to be manoeuvred into a situation with barely no option of declining, but that's how it was; my predicament at the time didn't allow for a 'No, thank you.' So I went along with it for that one night. The next morning, however, my desire for independence won over, I packed up my things and disappeared, with the words 'no offence, but I prefer the Old Brompton'.

Don't look a gift horse ... yeah, I know. But big gifts make me uncomfortable. They make me feel obliged to be grateful, they force me to be obligated to someone, they cause me to be false and insincere. And I couldn't even offer to go fifty-fifty with her, because, as every classical musician knows, London pays miserably – it's considered the greatest honour just to be able to perform there at all. But I couldn't blame Alexandra for anything, even though she would still have taken it personally. She had handed me Claridge's on a platter and I had not only brusquely rejected it, but I had fled back to the Old Brompton! She must have thought me weird to say the least – but I was happy to be back dragging my little suitcase up the old narrow staircase and flinging myself on my old, saggy mattress in my trusty room.

A few months later, after a busy day of work, I decided to take a bath to relax, so I let the hot water run in my Old Brompton bathtub. I must have fallen asleep on the bed, because some time after, the phone rang, I woke up, picked up and heard the receptionist at the other end of the line ask, 'Have you left the bathwater running? It's dripping into the reception.' My room was on the fourth floor. I tore open the bathroom door to find myself ankle-deep in water. After that incident, I never showed my face at the Old Brompton again. It was just as well that I had to return to New York the next morning anyway, and I avoided my favourite hotel ever after. I didn't fancy my chances of being able to pay for three floors' worth of renovations at the Old Brompton totally out of my own pocket.

You can find videos and photos for this chapter here.

LIVE
MAGIC

Sixteen hours in economy class, middle seat

I admit the term 'crossover' didn't sound good when, in the mid-1990s, classical musicians started using their instruments outside the classical sphere. I think the reason for this was that these musicians weren't necessarily that good, and were looking for a line of work that would bring them financial success, a public profile and popularity. That's why I was initially wary of the crossover concept – the scene certainly hadn't produced anything earth-shattering up to that point.

But I felt sure I could do it better. I was confident I wouldn't be putting out any half-baked stuff. And, to this day, I actually feel vindicated by the bad reviews, because they picked up on a very different point – they never complained about the musical quality of my crossover pieces, they focused more on me: 'He's cashing in on his talent.' As if I was only about financial success.

While it may look like that, I see it as me using crossover to provide the greatest possible scope for my talent. It's not like I'm turning my back on classical music, and my skills as a classical violinist do not seem to have suffered from crossover at all – would top conductors and famous orchestras keep inviting me to perform with them otherwise? But no matter how enthusiastic I am about my crossover project, I know there will always be certain critics who give me the cold shoulder – not because they have something bad to say about my abilities, but rather because they see crossover as an affront to the fine art of violin-playing.

I don't think I need to take these reproaches too personally. I'm doing crossover at virtually the highest level, and, most importantly, my music is drawing people from many different backgrounds and of all ages to appreciate my instrument. Plus, crossover is often their first point of contact with classical music. Here is just one example of that.

Having completed two successful crossover tours in Mexico, I had an offer, in 2016, to play five recitals in a major theatre in Mexico City – that is, classical music evenings with no orchestra, just a violin and piano. All the concerts were sold out within twenty-four hours, and, every night, the event was projected on to a big screen outside for all those who hadn't been able to get a ticket. That sort of demand makes it pretty clear my crossover was significantly helping to promote classical music.

So it's not true that people buy tickets for crossover shows, but stay away when they see Beethoven, Mozart or Bach on the programme. When I perform a repertoire of Brahms sonatas in Germany, my audience is the same mix of three generations as it has been for my crossover tour through those same cities four months earlier. Whether this intergenerational appeal has to do with me as a person, or whether my listeners have discovered a fascination with the violin at a crossover concert, or whether my strategy of using this instrument in both fields is bearing fruit are questions that have no definitive answers.

But we're nowhere near that stage yet. I just wanted to explain my motives before my project really started to kick off with Rick Blaskey on-board.

And it really did. I sent Rick the demo tapes I had produced with Franck van der Heijden in Franck's studio in Hilversum. He liked them, so it was time to get the ball rolling. And Rick was the perfect guy for it, with tremendous experience in this area and the best possible contacts on London's producer scene – he had just finished celebrating his successes with Russell Watson, who had started out singing Elvis Presley and Neil Diamond songs in pubs and was now a respected tenor. When Rick called, people stayed on the line. He also thought creatively.

For example, *Duelling Banjos* from the movie *Deliverance* is one of his favourite pieces, a stunning lesson in the way music has the power to mesmerize: a boy of around thirteen with a banjo goes up against an adult guitar player in a music contest. The pair's little impromptu concert kicks off with simple melodies before escalating into a virtuoso duo. Rick brought this wonderful number up in conversation, and we turned it into a duel between the classical guitar and violin. And so it was that Rick's suggestion ended up on our first album as *Duelling Strings.*

But we still needed a record company. Rick knew about my contract with Deutsche Grammophon, which was part of Universal Music, so it made sense to knock on Universal Germany's door first; after all, I had spent my childhood and youth in Germany, and I would take Berlin over London as a place for producing my music in this case. So the head of the Jazz and Classical department there was probably going to be the right person to contact, and, after sending our demo tapes to Universal Germany, I met up with him at his Berlin office. To this day, I can remember, word for word, his answer to my question of whether he had heard our stuff: 'Yeah it's all very nice, but it wouldn't even sell ten CDs in Germany. It's not classical, it's not jazz, it's not pop, it's everything all at once, and please tell me exactly which section this sort of a CD would fit into at a Media-Markt or Saturn record store? Unfortunately, I have to decline. We're not interested.'

So my crossover plans were going to fail because of the way sections were sorted at German record stores? Disappointed, indeed totally crushed, I called Rick in London from Berlin. 'The guy has no idea,' he said – Rick never let anything get him down. So our next try was with Universal International in London, and, lo and behold – they were interested! They didn't have any problem with genre sections, they knew people would be able to find my stuff – and we got a contract! In other words: finally, in 2006, nearly three years after my first hopeless attempts in Franck's studio in Hilversum, my first crossover album was within striking distance!

And Universal didn't seem to want to waste any time. They selected fourteen pieces from our demo tapes and sent us straight to the recording studio. While everyone was pleased with the finished product, even Universal International didn't want to jump the gun. By that I mean that, even in London, they weren't prepared to take any risks, which is why they were hesitant to cough up the entire budget there and then. Before investing huge sums in advertising on the major sales markets of the US, Germany and United Kingdom, they started with a test run in Southeast Asia – which is not unusual when dealing with a newcomer's work. Pretty much all music companies follow the same approach of pulling a new artist out of the hat in a few markets that don't require giant advertising budgets, and then, if the artist proves a hit, they venture onto the big markets.

Southeast Asia? I knew, in principle, what was in store for me; I had gained experience in promoting my classical albums right from a young age. But this time it was a completely different type of music and a different type of audience, and I was excited to see what was going to happen.

The first thing was economy class – sixteen hours of being packed like sardines, legs bunched up; and not just once, but something like thirty times, on flights to Singapore, Taiwan or Hong Kong. When you're 1.91 metres tall, it's certainly not fun, but the road to success is arduous and paved with hardship. 'What are you doing all the time in Asia?' my concerned mother wanted to know. 'What are you doing to yourself with all that flying?' But my gut instinct told me the same thing Rick Blaskey did: if I can conquer these East Asian markets, it will open doors for me in Europe.

Once there, it was a case of giving interviews from morning until night, to everyone from a school students' gazette to the news broadcasts. My mini performances in the shopping malls of Taipei, Singapore and Hong Kong were more exciting. Each one of these gigantic centres had a little stage for such purposes, where I could set myself up prominently and, after a brief interview, get going on my violin, sometimes accompanied by a pianist, sometimes by a guitarist – during the daytime, in the main traffic areas, where all the wide arcades converged, perhaps even with a café nearby, which people could look down on from the upper levels.

The architecture of these places would often be reminiscent of old opera houses, except that they were state-of-the-art, with a glass dome over an open area in the middle of the mall, so that customers could look down on me as if from the row seating of a concert hall. If no accompanist were available, I worked with backing tracks, meaning that the music, apart from the violin part, came out of a loudspeaker, the same way street musicians do it. One sound technician was enough for this kind of show, though they didn't always totally understand their craft. The results were consequently not always brilliant, but the response was overwhelming, and my CD was instantly made available for sale at the nearest record store.

Long story short: I was a hit. In Singapore, in Taiwan, this type of music got people excited everywhere – but Hong Kong outdid them all. That was where shopping-mall musician David Garrett really triumphed. By the end of my half-hour performances, I would have attracted an audience of at least 2,000 people, who applauded me kindly and fervently. And even better: our album made it to #3 on the Hong Kong pop charts!

Unbelievable. On the other side of the world, I had managed to take my music from zero straight into the hearts of the people and the highest echelons of the charts! I was famous in Southeast Asia! But I had also worked incredibly hard for this success, had done non-stop radio and television appearances, collaborated with local musicians and had rigorously followed the #1 rule of promotion, which was: visibility, visibility, visibility – though I did have it easier in that, being a full-grown German with long hair playing the violin in Asia, I was always going to be a subject of curiosity right from the start.

I want to end this story with a little anecdote. Was it in Taiwan, was it in Singapore? I can't remember exactly. But I can still visualize that imposing Asian street market that sold everything from washing machines to toothpicks, all with brand names, but at a fraction of the original price. A few years ago, I was strolling through it late one night with my tour manager Jörg, all the stalls with their bright lights, and what did I find? A whole stack of David Garrett CDs and DVDs, none in their original packaging, all pirated copies, but I couldn't have been less annoyed. On the contrary, I was over the moon. It's quite a feat to have your product sold among fake Rolex watches and piles of mangos at a Southeast Asian black market!

You can find videos and photos for this chapter here.

Support act for Jools Holland's England tour

No bassist, no drummer ... on our first tour of the UK in 2007, we didn't even have a full band organized. Whatever – it was time for our breakthrough in Europe! It didn't necessarily look like it at the time, because, technically, we were travelling the highways and country roads of England as a support act for Jools Holland, the pianist and bandleader whose mix of jazz and pop was popular among English audiences at the time.

So we weren't the headline act. But things were picking up, because news of my success in Hong Kong had made its way to London, and Universal International was now taking on the local market: *Virtuoso*, my first crossover album, had been released in England and the usual promo tour of concerts, talk-show appearances and breakfast-TV chats was in full swing. I was never too

Cover photo of my first album, Virtuoso, *2007*

fond of that last one though, because it meant getting up at 4.50 a.m., setting off at 5.15 a.m. without having any breakfast, only to then wait for what felt like an eternity at the broadcaster for your appearance slot, despite them having made you rush beforehand ... Whatever; breakfast-TV was all part of it.

The posters advertised us as 'David Garrett', with the rest of the band missing out. But I guess you can't really call two accompanying musicians a proper band. As we had to manage on a very modest budget, our little gang always drove behind Jools Holland in a rented van, putting in appearances at four or five cities in a row. Inside our van was our guitarist, the wonderful Giorgio Serci, and Rick Blaskey and me, as well as John Haywood, our driver and keyboarder, whom I want to say a few words about.

John wasn't just an amazing pianist; he was also a producer, songwriter and arranger. For example, he was the one who arranged Metallica's *Nothing Else Matters* for *Virtuoso*, which we recorded in a tiny studio in conditions I will never forget. His microphone wasn't exactly the best, and, to fight the icy cold of that English winter's day, John had brought an electric fan heater that blew a warm breeze around our legs. He had to turn the machine off before each recording, otherwise its comforting drone would have been heard in the background. But I didn't care about any of that. I hadn't been bothered by the fact that John's recording studio was essentially a cramped, makeshift shack, because we had the right chemistry between us – he was also starting out in his career and was similarly working towards a big goal. To me, that was more important.

During these exciting early days, everything was pretty chaotic and improvised at the best of times. At night, Giorgio, John and I would have to go on stage and perform our short programme of four or five numbers with minimal instrumentation, namely just a keyboard, classical guitar and violin. But we were sorely missing a drummer for the *Carmen Fantasy*. During the rehearsal, we realized that the percussion elements were essential here, so I made a spur-of-the-moment decision to play this part myself, fastening a rattle to my right foot with some tape. And that's exactly how I performed it that night. We told our audience that this odd set-up was because our drummer was unfortunately unable to make it due to unforeseen circumstances. I then placed my hand-held microphone on the ground and set the rhythm with my foot rattle. Sure, it's not what you'd call professional, and our performance as Jools Holland's support act was very basic indeed, but the improvised *Carmen Fantasy* turned out a treat.

I had known since Southeast Asia that the road to fame was paved with curious, sometimes even thorny, incidents. And it doesn't always go smoothly later on either, but, in the early days, you sometimes bring mishaps on yourself, if nothing else because you're still not totally serious about the whole thing – as was the case towards the end of our barnstorming England tour, on our trip back to London from Manchester.

As I was still in the phase of sowing my wild oats, I had worked out beforehand that it took three hours to get from Manchester to London. So if we ended our performance in Manchester at around 8.20 p.m. and packed up our equipment quickly, we would get into London around midnight – and I could still meet up with a London girlfriend in the early hours ...

So I was itching to get there. Speed limits? Pffft – 'John, put your foot down!' I had somehow managed to make John twitchy, which is usually not even possible; I was standing behind him, oozing impatience, when we eventually had to refuel on the M1. Okay, no problem, on we continued afterwards – except that, a few minutes later, the engine of our fully loaded van sputtered to a halt. John veered left to get off the motorway. So there we were. What had happened? 'Didn't I tell you it was a diesel?' Yes, I had, but John had obviously made a mistake, being in the rush that we were. And the breakdown service took its time. A mechanic arrived after one and a half hours, hitched us up and slowly towed us to the nearest garage, where our fuel tank had to be drained before it could be refilled with diesel. So, instead of arriving in London in time for my midnight rendezvous, we didn't get there until 6 a.m. I flung myself on the bed at the Old Brompton and fell straight to sleep. It just hadn't been meant to be.

Fortunately, none of these efforts were in vain. *Virtuoso* sold well in the UK, much to the delight of everyone involved, and you would have thought the German market – in a new state of optimism – would have keenly followed suit. But that wasn't the case. Neither my third place on the Hong Kong charts, nor the sales success in the UK, had made any impression on Universal Germany; they probably still didn't want to know about me because of the genre sections at Media-Markt and Saturn. In hindsight, it was a huge stroke of luck, because when companies release things against their will, they work with only a small budget, they assign the project to people who haven't been in the business long, and the sales department shows little interest in the record. But it worked out a different way; in the meantime, the tireless Rick Blaskey had got hold of someone in Germany who wanted to release my album through his company, and a meeting in Berlin was arranged. So I flew over.

You can find videos and photos for this chapter here.

Breakthrough

The company was DEAG. Peter Schwenkow, its boss, was already sitting at the conference-room table with Rick Blaskey and André Selleneit, also from DEAG, when I walked through the door, hair long, wearing my usual jeans, boots, T-shirt and bandana à la Axl Rose from Guns N' Roses. And, for whatever reason, the DEAG representatives took a real shine to my look. Sure, I'd overdone it a little bit, but it was pretty much how I dressed normally anyway – I was hell-bent on only wearing clothes I felt comfortable in. I don't have the most pleasant memories of suits, and, having been bitten once, I now put comfort ahead of all else.

In any case, Peter Schwenkow thought I was cool, as did André Selleneit. They were also able to get something going with my

On the way to the stage

music, after which everything suddenly started to move pretty fast. As Universal held the rights, DEAG had to sign a contract with Universal Germany, so both companies' lawyers got together and agreed that DEAG could sell my next three CDs in Germany, Austria and Switzerland. My next three CDs? They were obviously putting a lot of trust in me. Certainly a wonderful outcome, and we then went through the same process in Germany as we had done in England.

Actually, no, it was a lot better. DEAG had got it into their heads that they wanted to go really big with their Garrett launch, and they had the right people to do it. For example, I got to know Elke Krüger, who had been a specialist in TV promotion for thirty years. André Selleneit, who I quickly made friends with, told me he had sent her two photos of me with no comment, and Elke had called back seconds later saying, 'Cool guy. I'll take him on. What does he do anyway?' Is that really what happened? You don't question good stories. In any case, Elke thought my music was just as cool as I was, and got to work.

I have her to thank for television appearances on talk shows, in magazines, on all possible platforms, such as *TV Total*, a very popular, prime-time talk show with Stefan Raab – which was really amazing. Someone else I'll be talking about in the next chapter, namely Tobias Weigold, had the particularly fortuitous idea of getting me to play on the ARD show *Titel, Thesen, Temperamente*. The name meant nothing to me – perhaps, given I lived in New York, that was understandable – but I now had experience in television productions, and I pretty much knew what to expect; they'll talk to me about my childhood, ask me about the Juilliard School, and then discover that this David Garrett, who had now matured into his own person, was in the process of kicking off a brand-new project ... That's basically how the interviews worked in New York too. And because DEAG were fully behind me, they had the foresight to stock all German record stores with *Virtuoso* before our segment on *Titel, Thesen, Temperamente* was aired – contrary to expectations, there did appear to be room in the right genre sections of German record stores after all. But DEAG went even further, additionally organizing a concert tour of five major German cities – Berlin, Hamburg, Frankfurt, Cologne and Munich, where they rented smaller halls, rooms with capacity for 400–500 people.

I couldn't believe my ears, because, this time, we wouldn't be touring as a support act. We wouldn't be leaving the stage after half an hour to make way for the star of the show. We were the stars of the show – with a totally unconventional programme: a violinist who stood on stage for nearly two hours, sometimes playing classical music, sometimes crossover, sometimes jazz, and that violinist was going to be me.

I was acutely aware this tour could end up being the career springboard I had so desperately yearned for. But it was just as well that it was still a little while away, because we didn't yet have a set list long enough to fill an entire show. We didn't yet have a full band either, even though Ben Bryant had now joined us as a drummer. Things got even more intense after my segment in *Titel, Thesen, Temperamente* aired, because, the week after, I got a call from an elated André Selleneit, whose words I can still hear in my head to this day. 'David,' he said joyously down the telephone line, 'we can't keep up with our CD production! Your records are selling like hotcakes – we're churning them out night and day! And the tickets to your concerts are being snapped up just as quickly. Would you mind if we moved your performances to larger halls? The ones we had planned are already nearly sold out!' Unbelievable. Rick Blaskey was on cloud nine, and I was gobsmacked. How was this possible? Even today, it never ceases to amaze me when I think about it.

So larger halls it was. Peter Schwenkow now had his sights on an audience capacity of 1,200. But the eleven CD tracks we had on our set list so far weren't going to be enough to get us through a ninety-minute concert; we'd run dry halfway through. The longer I thought about our first Germany tour, the more I realized that I was breaking completely new ground, and the gamble I was taking.

I spent weeks racking my brains in New York over what other pieces we could perform live on stage. There needed to be a couple of virtuoso compositions in there that would wow even those who weren't fans of classical music; pop pieces also needed to be in there, but perfectly arranged so that they didn't just appeal to rock or jazz enthusiasts. In any case, I had to captivate my audience – it would be a nightmare scenario if people started leaving after ten minutes ... Constantly gripped by the fear of messing up this great opportunity, I spent my days tinkering away at the programme, and half the night honing my hosting texts.

Because one thing was certain: I wanted to do what I had done in Hong Kong and in all my performances in Southeast Asia, which was talk a bit between pieces. I would engage with the audience and draw on my repertoire of anecdotes about composers and musicians to combat the preconceived notion that classical music is tedious and heavy-going. In other words, a balancing act, because the texts couldn't be too funny. I wasn't there to be a comedian, after all. I also had to be careful not to alienate the seasoned classical music fans with my nonchalance – while still avoiding dry, overly technical introductions. Just as well I was still living with Alexander at the time.

He helped me prepare my first speech notes – sometimes a little tale from my life, sometimes a few words about the composer, sometimes interesting facts about the violin, and maybe even the odd amusing story Perlman had told me. 'Sit down,' I would tell my brother, 'I'll read out what I'm thinking of saying.' And

Alexander would be a tremendous help. 'That's way too long,' he would say, or, 'What's so funny about that? People will never, ever get the joke.' Was he right? We would see. The upcoming concert tour was really going to be a case of jumping in at the deep end, but one thing was clear: I had been preparing the basic framework of my crossover programme, spending those weeks essentially working out *the matrix* for performances to come – provided this first experiment worked.

The tour began, still without a bassist, who somehow ended up being the one that got away. But the drummer was more important to me, because I didn't want to be performing with a foot rattle this time. What kind of audience were we expecting anyway? At this point, we didn't even know who had been buying my records. Would the seats primarily be filled with staunch classical music-lovers wanting to crucify me? Rock fans? Violin students? And then came the big surprise: at my first crossover concert in Germany, I looked out and saw young faces! What a relief. When I stepped on stage, the atmosphere was reminiscent of Antwerp 2002, and it stayed like that the whole night. The audience in every city really got into it, the exuberant *joie de vivre* from the Night of the Proms was back, and, after one concert when André Selleneit was in the audience with his wife, he said to me, 'Surely there's another violinist playing along behind the stage? It's impossible for all those sounds to be coming out of one single instrument!' But they were.

And then there was the hosting bit ... Just like I had done when giving presentations at the Juilliard School, I had a piece of paper with keywords on it placed discreetly on the floor; a glance down and I would know what to say next. But not always. 'Actually it's Rachmaninoff up now,' John Haywood whispered to me after I had cheerily announced we were about to play Debussy. So there'd be the odd mix-up in the sideshow, but also in other areas.

'Listen,' I had told my guys, 'I don't want to be standing in the spotlight the whole time. I'll go off stage every so often to freshen up while you play your solos.' So at the first concert, I announced, 'I'm a bit sweaty, I'm just going to change quickly, but enjoy my band in the meantime', left the stage, got to my green room, only to find it locked – and who had the key in his pocket? Mr John Haywood. So I had to go back on stage in my sweaty shirt, wait for my band to finish playing, briefly explain the situation to the audience, and step out again, key in hand. It all added a bit of hilarity.

You can never plan for these kinds of comedic interludes, and I was lucky to have musicians who were able to handle the comical situations just as smoothly as I could. Of course I had the odd blunder. Of course there have been some audience reactions that have prompted me to remove certain things from my speeches because even my brother had been off the mark. But we still impressed on that first German tour. Had it been because of the ease with which we had brought our programme of classical and pop pieces to the stage? I'm convinced this ease has the power to loosen tension and undo stomach knots, and that is perhaps the reason for our success.

In any case, a memorable incident occurred a few months later during my first classical concert at Leipzig's Gewandhaus. Quite a few people in the audience had already seen me perform my crossover programme on my first tour. After the break, I returned to the stage and was playing the first movement of Brahms' second sonata when, after the applause at the end, a woman stood up in the room. I was tuning my violin and naturally noticed someone had got up out of their seat – aha, I thought, looks like someone wants to leave. I was wrong. The woman stayed at her seat and called out to me, 'Mr Garrett! Mr Garrett! You've been playing for over an hour now and still haven't said anything!'

She had obviously assumed that I would be telling little stories even during my classical concerts. Just picture it: the Gewandhaus, a classical music audience, great pieces by great composers and a suitably rapt and attentive silence ... never had I experienced such a situation, and, for a few seconds, I froze. Were people upset? You can't just ignore an interjection like that and keep playing; that would definitely not be on. So I looked at my pianist and then turned to the audience, 'If you like, I can tell you a bit about the pieces still left to play.'

Thunderous applause. That woman probably hadn't been the only one who had found my silence strange. I then performed the next few pieces, the last one being by Kreisler (yes, that same artist from Chapter 2), before ending the concert with one of my favourite anecdotes. It goes like this: after a concert, a woman goes up to Kreisler backstage, shakes his hand, praises him on his playing and adds, 'And your Stradivarius! I've never heard such a magnificent instrument!' At which Kreisler takes out his violin, inspects it carefully from all sides, even puts his ear to it, and finally looks at his admirer with feigned bemusement. 'I'm sorry, madam,' he says, 'but I don't hear anything.'

Since then, I've given little introductions before each piece even in my classical concerts, and it's a presentation style that's always been very well received.

You can find videos and photos for this chapter here.

E 18 St

La Grotta

When I think back to the years after finishing university, it's like I'm watching a movie I've previously seen at the cinema. When did it happen – ten years ago? Fifteen years ago? I can barely remember the order of events now, because days, weeks and months blend into one big haze of images and memories.

After 2004, I had fallen into a hole, worked my way out of it, doggedly pursued a goal, flown back and forth constantly between New York, London, Berlin and Southeast Asia, played in shopping centres, then on stages in the UK with a small crew, and finally got exactly where I wanted to be – in front of packed houses in Germany. After all, I was from Germany, had enjoyed my first successes there, and wanted to rebuild my profile in my country. In terms of emotional intensity, I had never experienced anything like it before. Today, it sometimes seems as if these were all out-of-body experiences – or, to put it less dramatically, as if I had been watching myself up on stage from the first row of the audience.

And it didn't stop, because, after a six-month concert tour, I'd be back wondering: what should we do next? It's a question I keep asking myself even today. I work, come up with new ideas, compose and produce music, release a new album, go on tour, look at my team's exhausted faces and say, 'Okay, guys, what's next? What should we do now?' Because there's always another tour to plan, and I would suddenly find myself back at another awards show, accepting a prize for 300,000 records sold, or playing in front of 40,000 people in London's Hyde Park.

Having gained a new audience was the best thing about this success for me. Many people had never listened to classical music before, and being able to convey this music's *joie de vivre* in a normal concert hall would have been hard, because, at that sort of venue, everyone's usually very serious, almost funereal. It's possible these young people come to my concerts partly because of me, but then I prove to them that they've really come for the music – so that, on the way home, they don't say, 'That Garrett guy was great', but rather, 'Beethoven was great!' And that's the moment when it's worth remembering that crossover makes up only one part of my life.

It's not that I wanted to give up classical music – on the contrary! – but, after Juilliard, I no longer had a manager around to reliably arrange gigs for me. At that time, I needed to get help quickly, and, in the autumn of 2005, it came: I met Yvonne and Tobias Weigold from Weigold & Böhm International Artists & Tours at the Hotel München Palace in Munich – to audition, just like old times. Obviously I was no stranger to them, but, in this industry, you need to be able to prove yourself as an artist in a live performance, because people want to convince themselves of your skills with their own ears. Apart from that, Weigold & Böhm naturally also wanted to get an idea of David Garrett as a person. They only knew me from my early days as being part of a 'twin-pack', with my father having generally always been in tow. They wanted to know what I was like now, how had I developed as a person. Was I decent and approachable or had New York turned me into a prima donna? And so it was that I performed a one-hour concert for my new managers in a suite at the Hotel München Palace before signing the contract with them. I was in good hands with Rick Blaskey; he had long proved that. And, over the next few years, it would become clear that I was just as lucky to have Yvonne and Tobias Weigold – unlike Rick, their agency continues to manage me even today.

But I have nothing against Rick; I'll talk about how we parted ways later on. In the meantime, he tirelessly lobbied for me, negotiating new fees before every tour, because audience numbers were skyrocketing and, in addition to Germany, Austria and Switzerland, we were also starting to perform in the UK, the US and Italy. I gradually started earning more and more, to the point where I eventually had quite a sizeable amount in my account, prompting me to consider, for the first time ever, what best do to with that money.

Now, I have an utter aversion to paying rent – just the word alone brings back nightmarish memories of my destitute days in Hell's Kitchen. I definitely needed my own four walls, my retreat and sanctuary, my place to chill out, and I didn't want that to be in London or Berlin; I wanted it to be in New York, where I had already been living. Where exactly? Chelsea, my girlfriend at the time, loved Gramercy Park in southern

Manhattan, a district with historic buildings and 19th-century character, and it was her taste that sealed the deal: I bought my first-ever home in the form of Apartment 6a on Park Avenue South in Gramercy Park. Not a bad way to start. I was on cloud nine.

Was my success going to my head? I was indeed hell-bent on having my first home perfectly appointed – if you can, why not – so I headed to Armani Casa. This shop no longer exists, but, at the time, Armani made a lot of money out of me, and I loved the look of my finished place. I had 110 square metres of space, enough for two televisions and two sofas, all in a gorgeous district – it would have been a luxury anywhere, let alone in New York. There was only one down side to the apartment, and it struck everyone who set foot in it. Only its proud owner was oblivious to it: the rooms were dark and gloomy, constantly in shade.

You obviously pay a higher price per square metre for light-filled rooms compared to those whose windows look out onto a backyard that never sees the light of day. When buying the property, I had focused only on the location and size, and had considered the internal courtyard a forgivable flaw. Eventually, however, I realized how right my brother had been when, during his first visit, he had commented dryly, 'You won't need to draw the curtains here if you ever want to sleep in.' To cap it all off, I had opted for dark walls. At the Armani shop, I had succumbed to the charm of an all-grey Asian wallpaper, but when you stick this wallpaper on every wall, it soaks up every last bit of light. After the student residence, the shoebox in Hell's Kitchen and the shared place with my brother, I obviously hadn't quite found my style. I christened my dream home 'La Grotta' and started looking around for another place three years later. Someone who doesn't go into an office, who stays at home and practises the violin – in other words, someone who doesn't just come home to sleep – needs bright spaces more than anyone!

So I went to the other extreme. My next apartment was as white as the Taj Mahal, with pale sandstone floors, snow-white walls and light-filled rooms. It was a loft, much larger than La Grotta, and located in the up-and-coming district of Chelsea, which saw me back near the Hudson River. And I also liked Chelsea for its bars and nightlife; it was an entertainment district. However, while I would have almost ended up a depressive in the gloominess of La Grotta, its opposite was equally unsatisfactory in terms of feeling homely. On good days, my new home almost had a Mediterranean vibe, but on others, it was just white, and I eventually got sick of it. I'd had enough of the style overkill; I yearned for a real home, so I did what I'd actually started to make into an enjoyable habit: I began looking for a new place to live. I'll save the result for a later chapter, but I'll just say another few words about my curious hobby.

'Open houses' are kind of like a custom in New York City. If someone's selling a property, they'll open it on the weekend for any prospective buyers, serve you coffee, sometimes even some cake, and give you a sheet of the property details, before allowing you to explore the place at your leisure. There are, of course, always quite a few mere curious passers-by among the serious prospective buyers, and I won't deny I've often been one of them. I'm a big fan of open houses, partly also because I have a penchant for architecture. Well before I was ever in a position to buy, I would spend a sunny Saturday on my bike, riding all over, enjoying a cup of coffee, looking around, then moving on to the next place, just to dream. It's how I managed to see at least 150 New York apartments, maybe even 200, and suffer the odd blow myself – as you have seen, despite having had considerable experience in this field, I hadn't always acted on the most reliable of instincts. I did hit the jackpot with my third New York pad, but more on that later. Right now, I think it's time for another love story.

You can find videos and photos for this chapter here.

Love over money

My relationship with Mascha started off as crazily as it ended (and I recounted that end way back in Chapter 1). I had just met the stunning, vivacious, infinitely loveable Mascha in a New York nightclub and we were already sitting in the bedroom of my shared flat, whose cramped size turned out to be an advantage here. My brother was already asleep, and Mascha had only just come up 'for a quick nightcap', but, as is always the way with love at first sight, Mascha stayed over. The next day, I woke up madly in love, and, after having a joint 'flatmates brunch', she suggested going for a walk around the city.

I need to provide a little backstory here before I go on. The week before, I had performed a concert to a sold-out venue in São Paulo, and the repertoire had included Tchaikovsky's *Violin*

Concerto in D Major, which I had rehearsed many years prior as one of Bron's students in Lübeck. After the concert, I had been paid a fee of 10,000 dollars, in packs of 100-dollar notes. This was a huge amount for me; never before had I been paid so handsomely for a concert.

Back in New York, I placed this bundle of notes in a strongbox – no one was going to break in here – and stowed it away on a shelf so that it wasn't instantly visible. That first morning on our walk around the city, Mascha and I ended up near Central Park's little zoo. It's an area where there are lots of inviting clothes shops. Mascha's interest was promptly piqued, and, in the good mood that I was, I paid for a dress that she liked. Now it was my turn to look for some clothes. We continued on, browsing here and there. I slipped on a pair of jeans, tried on a jacket, found a few T-shirts, and was about to pay for my purchases when Mascha placed a hand on my arm. 'You treated me, so now I'll pay for you,' she said. Now, 500 dollars is not exactly a small amount, and I had never had a woman pay for my clothes before, but okay. She casually pulled out five 100-dollar notes, and I felt like I had found the dream woman par excellence – gorgeous, but also an amazing personality and character. Definitely the love of my life. While you may not be able to say that categorically after only twenty-four hours, my euphoria wasn't going to be diminished by any little nagging thoughts at that moment.

We said goodbye. When I got home, I picked up my violin and started practising something. In the meantime, I decided I would take my money to the bank after all, and opened the strongbox. It was almost empty. Of the 10,000 dollars, 8,000 were missing. My heart stopped. Surely not Mascha? To be on the safe side, I asked my brother – but no, he hadn't taken it. 'Did you have anything to do with it?' I asked Mascha the next day, but she fiercely denied it. So who had taken it?

Now, money is not that important to me. I part with it easily and am generally pretty laid back about financial matters overall. So I didn't see my suspicions as a reason to end the relationship; love meant more to me than money. I then played in Brazil for 2,000 dollars – not a bad fee either. But still ... it was still weird.

In any case, our relationship was getting off to a peculiar start. Well-meaning peers would probably say, 'Get out; she's dodgy.' But I would not be put off. There are some people who somehow manage to change your energy when you're around them. Principles you normally stick to strictly suddenly end up becoming secondary. You become bewitched and ignore that you might just be on very slippery ground but even that seems amazing to you. I definitely felt attracted to Mascha like a flower to the sun. I enjoyed the sense of lightness and ease being with her, and it took me a long time to realize that too much sun eventually damages a flower. Mascha was both sunshine and a very slippery slope all rolled into one.

I did things with her I never would have done otherwise. For example, she worked as a model at Fashion Week in Paris. I was busy in New York, but during the week she was away, I had been booked to play a concert in Zurich. One day before, I was standing at the airport counter and changed my mind at the last minute – actually no, no ticket to Zurich, thank you. I missed Mascha so much that I made the romantic decision to quickly stop by Paris before performing in Zurich in the evening. I didn't pause for even a moment to consider how I would get from Paris to Zurich.

I arrived in Paris at 9 a.m. Soon after, my management called in the form of Rick's deputy, Jamie Corby. 'We're here at the gate in Zurich, but you're not there.'

'I'm in Paris. I had to see my girlfriend.'

'But you know you've got a concert tonight, right?'

Yes. But I was so obsessed. Mascha could have completely bankrupted me the day before, but I would still be standing with her, holding hands, under the Eiffel Tower. At 7 p.m., I took the latest possible train to Zurich and still fortunately managed to make it in time for the concert. Things could so easily have gone completely wrong ...

So something was already brewing. This behaviour was not like me. With Mascha, gone were the days of *mind over matter*; this relationship was heart over mind right from the start. Mascha had her flaws, but who didn't? One time, I couldn't find my credit card. 'I've been looking for my credit card for the last two hours,' I said as Mascha walked through the door. She looked at me blankly, but, out of the corner of my eye, I noticed her slip a credit card under the bed. 'Hey, it's down there!' Aha. Was this further evidence against her for what happened on that first night? While I was at least growing more suspicious, my feelings didn't change. All she had to do was smile at me and everything would be forgotten; we'd be back in each other's arms. While checking the account statement for that day later on, what did I see? A pair of shoes, makeup and other not exactly cheap bits and pieces. Nevertheless, the two years we spent together were among the best of my life.

And then came the end.

My second crossover album, *Encore*, not only saw a repeat of *Virtuoso*'s success, but sales nearly doubled, with half a million records sold. Peter Schwenkow from DEAG and I had different opinions on what the album should be called – Schwenkow found the term *encore* absurd, and I countered this by saying that even Eminem had brought out an album with that title, but whatever – the French call out 'encore' at the end of a concert because they want more, and that's exactly what I didn't want to deprive my fans of after *Virtuoso*. I was over the moon that my 'encore' had appealed to even more fans than the first album.

Rock Symphonies was to follow as the third album. The recordings were planned for fall 2009, at the Electric Lady Studio in New

York. You can just imagine how tense I was – the things that go through your head! Would we be able to top the success of *Encore*? Or had we already peaked and were instead on the downward decline? Would I have anything new to offer, and would it meet with people's approval?

Fluctuating as I was between hope and worry, my emotional state was both unstable and buzzing with joy, because I had two weeks of intense work in my favourite studio ahead of me. With its psychedelically painted walls and crazy atmosphere, the Electric Lady has a mysterious power that is no doubt partly the result of its history: its founder Jimi Hendrix, along with Led Zeppelin, AC/DC, U2 and countless other legends have all left their mark here, and there couldn't have been a greater inspiration for this long-haired violinist than that imaginary line of ancestors ... And enter Mascha with her insatiable lust for life.

I should have said no. There always seems to be a strong shot of carelessness mixed in with any wild *joie de vivre*. Mascha embodied both. And me? I wanted it all – only to then wake up with a heavy moral hangover. Anyone who wants everything, loses everything. At some point, you have to choose between ease and the hard-earned success that lies in the beauty of your music, regardless of financial gain. This dawned on me the morning after, and I chose music. Mascha was unfortunately the wrong one for me, even though she had been the right one.

You can find videos and photos for this chapter here.

Johann Sebastian Bach to the rescue

My drummer Jeff Lipstein, who is as great a person as he is a musician, likes to tell a story I can't even remember happening. Let me preface it by saying that, when we played in large halls, everything was amplified; every instrument, including the drums, had a microphone.

Whether this was on the third or fourth German tour, it doesn't matter – in any case, all the amplifier equipment crashed in the middle of the concert. In the space of a second, we suddenly lost sound, and all you could hear was the soft beating of the drums. So what do you do? Sit around on stage and shout 'we – have – a – technical – problem!' into the auditorium?

No. I'm of the opinion that every situation can be saved. Plus, I don't like having emotional breaks in a show, and I try to think

With German Chancellor Angela Merkel during President Obama's visit to Berlin, 2013

of all sorts of ways to prevent anything that could possibly kill the vibe. Thinking quickly, I temporarily sent my band off stage, indicated to the light technician to direct the spotlight onto me, took a few steps into the audience, and played some solo pieces by Johann Sebastian Bach – for the next ten minutes, even though, to me, it seemed more like thirty before the technicians fixed the problem and my band were able to come back on stage.

Bach has come to my rescue in so many critical situations! Fortunately, I have a strategy that comprises two things; what most people probably don't realize is that, even during a crossover tour, I always practise as if I'm preparing for a Beethoven concerto, going slowly through a Paganini *Caprice* and playing a Bach solo. Except for the complicated bits that tend to arise during a crossover concert, my rehearsals have a purely classical repertoire. In other words, every day is a classical music day for me.

When mishaps like the one I just mentioned occur, your heart is of course initially in your mouth. No one is able to tell you how long it's going to be before the problem is fixed – it could end up being an hour or more – and it's reassuring for me to know that, by playing classical music, I still have a few cards up my sleeve. My repertoire is long enough to last a technical outage spanning a week or more, and I always start with Bach, because he wrote the best music for solo violin – high-energy, rhythmical, sometimes downright dance pieces with familiar harmonies, and, no matter whether it's kids, teenagers or older adults in the audience, Bach always speaks straight to the heart. And while we're talking about the emotional nature of classical music, I just want to say something about emotions from my personal perspective, a musician's perspective.

Sure, I'm an extremely emotional person, but one who places utmost emphasis on order and structure. Starting with my own home, I've always liked having tidy surroundings; I detest chaos, and find the thought of losing control terrifying. Perhaps that's also because I'm a musician, for music is the opposite of chaos; music is structure. No one can make music from internal chaos, and when I, as a musician, want to bring out the strongest emotions in my audience, that's precisely when I myself need to be able to control my own emotions. If I were to indulge in emotional outbursts on stage, I would trigger the opposite reactions, namely consternation, irritation and disconcertment.

And that's why you practise every day for hours. Not just to improve your playing, but also to train yourself to control all the emotions a piece of music may trigger for you. The audience doesn't need this control. They're allowed to get swept away and stirred up. I, however, have to restrain myself. As an artist, you're kind of like a conductor of feelings, but if you give free rein to your own emotions, the audience stops feeling anything; art becomes chaos, and the music's impact fizzles out.

By the way, it's not just about playing during a concert; listening is just as important, especially if you're a solo violinist playing with an orchestra. After all, making music is never only a case of playing notes and hitting keys; soloists are required to pay close attention to the other instruments in the orchestra to keep in dialogue with them and sometimes pick up on a mood, before again elevating the counterpart – never as a virtuoso statement in isolation, but rather as an emotional reaction to what has already rung out from other parts of the orchestra.

There are countless ways to vary a musical phrase – but this isn't chosen at the whim of the soloist. It should instead be a response, an answer, and, in this case, I, as the violinist, would be reacting to the oboe, clarinet and flute, engaging with their emotions as if in a conversation, or countering them with my own vibe. Played in this way, in dialogue with all other instruments, is how music lives.

I hardly need to emphasize here that, to this day, I remain utterly committed to classical music. Of course, I also put all my heart into crossover; never have I gone on stage for a crossover performance just to make my life easier. I leave the stage no less exhausted than after two and a half hours of playing classical music. But when I read comments on Facebook or elsewhere constantly begging me to 'come back to classical', all I can really say is that I have never been unfaithful to classical music.

My third album, *Classic Romance*, is proof of this. In 2008, I went into the studio with conductor Andrew Litton and recorded romantic pieces (in the broadest sense of the word) by the likes of Mendelssohn, Dvořák and others. Litton knew me from my early days and was himself somewhat dubious initially as to whether I would still be taken seriously as a classical violinist. So I offered to play for him. I did, but, barely a page into playing, he waved me off, keeping his words short and sweet: 'I look forward to it.' How pleased he must have been when more than 200,000 copies of *Classic Romance* were sold! Two thousand would have been a decent outcome for me, 5,000 would have seen me pop the champagne – but 200,000? It was unheard-of success – and yet, one year later, in 2010, it would be easily surpassed by the crossover recording *Rock Symphonies*, the album that had prompted my split from Mascha.

Six hundred thousand CDs sold, #1 on the Official Charts – no one could have even dared to dream of such numbers. It was inconceivable for a violinist to be #1. At the German Echo Awards ceremony, I went all out with my performance look – eyeliner, hair loose and no shirt under my black jacket (official reason: I couldn't find the right coloured T-shirt to match). 'It looks horrifying; you can't do that!' my appalled record company protested. But, in my mind, I could.

So, at that time, I was earnestly tinkering away at my crossover house of cards that, these days, is soaring to positively dizzying heights, and, even in those years, I would catch myself thinking, 'Who knows how long this success will last.' I vaguely remember playing my first crossover album for my father, and him promptly warning me of having excessively high hopes. In his view, crossover was a short-lived thing, and even I felt a little uneasy about it, but the reality is that *Rock Symphonies* received the Echo Award for best rock-pop album in its first year of release – a surreal experience for someone who had grown up in the classical music industry. The other award-winners – all old hands, veterans of the pop scene – must have been rubbing their eyes and adjusting their spectacles when they saw that long-haired violinist standing up to get his Echo.

And the halls got bigger with every tour. Suddenly, 3,000 seats were no longer enough; it had to be 5,000, then 10,000. By 2009, I was playing at the Lanxess Arena in Cologne, in 2011 at Berlin's Mercedes-Benz Arena, and, in 2012, opera singer Jonas Kaufmann and I opened the Champions League final between FC Bayern Munich and Chelsea at Munich's Allianz Arena to a fired-up crowd of 80,000 – a huge, huge spectacle. During my first performances as a support act in England, I'd had to compromise on my perfectionism – foot rattle, anyone? – but now I could let rip, and wouldn't be satisfied just with big screens at the large halls; I also insisted on having a head-mounted camera so people could see my left hand from my perspective during *Flight of the Bumblebee* and everyone in the audience could witness this feat of finger acrobatics.

What was the highlight of this seemingly endless series of performances? My concert for Obama? Or my performance for the Queen? Both were amazing, but the circumstances were so different, as were their respective vibes – and my own reactions.

Obama made life easy for you. In 2013, he was due to come to Berlin, and the chancellery asked me to provide the music for this state visit. Of course, anyone would be delighted to do this, but what do you play for the president of the United States? I indirectly managed to learn of his penchant for Bruce Springsteen, and opted for *Born in the USA*, a piece that stirs you to your core and is not as melancholy as his equally popular *Streets of Philadelphia*.

Obama came. I could see him sitting next to Angela Merkel from my stage in front of the Brandenburg Gate. It was a glorious summer's day and he obviously enjoyed my performance. Afterwards, one of the security guards tapped me on the shoulder to tell me President Obama wanted to say hi. Well, it can't get better than that. I followed him into the embassy and, soon after, Barack Obama was standing in front of me – tall, relaxed and extremely friendly. He thanked me, confirmed I had got his music taste just right, and asked if I wanted to take a photo with him. Of course I did, but I had barely grabbed my phone from my pocket when all the bodyguards immediately reached for their guns. That remained the only incident, and the resulting photo shows me standing between Germany's then-chancellor and the then-president of the United States of America. I still like looking at it.

And now to the Queen. She didn't make my life as easy, which is why the story of my encounter with her is a little more detailed.

In 2012, Rick Blaskey had managed to get me on the events programme for the Queen's Diamond Jubilee, and he had listed the venue as Windsor Castle. I started to get a bit nervous even on the way there, and what happened thereafter can best be described as a play in three acts.

Act 1: All the artists performing that day – the men in dinner jackets, as required – were directed into one of the castle's halls and lined up in a long row as instructed. We hung around waiting, then a door opened, the Queen entered the room and started inspecting the line of artists, extending a gloved hand to each of them. Prince Philip followed behind her with slight smile on his face. I was one of the last in line, so had time to observe the others – it took an age for her to shake forty people's hands. What did the others do? Did the men bow, did the women make a curtsy, did they reverentially mutter some fittingly flowery phrase or did they just silently lower the eyes? Even though it was the same procedure for each person, I watched on entranced, and every step closer that the Queen got, the more anxious I became. My palms grew sweaty and I started shaking a bit, imagining myself leaving my body and watching the whole thing from above. We'd all seen her on television, but seeing her in person was an experience that's difficult to put into words. It was as if the entire glorious history of Great Britain were packed into this one woman; you saw her less as a person and more as an institution. Eventually, it was my turn, she was finally standing in front of me and ... I have no idea what I said. Hopefully nothing stupid.

But I do remember the words I exchanged with Prince Philip. 'You're from Germany?' he asked. 'Yes, I grew up in Aachen.' To which he instantly replied, 'Aachen? That's famous for show jumping, isn't it?' That was the end of our conversation, and we were then ushered into an even larger room where Act 2 began.

There was a table of muffins and sandwiches in the centre of the room, but no one dared take one. Was it even appropriate to eat here? Was that not a bit too boorish? Were you allowed to get caught with your mouth full in this distinguished setting? What if the Queen came back right now? No, better not to. My stomach was one big knot anyway, I wouldn't even be able to get a single bite down, and it looked like everyone else felt similarly; no one touched the food.

Act 3. The concert began in the late afternoon. A riding arena, a vast dressage ground, had been set up in Windsor Castle's giant internal courtyard, and rising up behind it was the stage where orchestras and bands took turns playing. The royal family had gathered in the royal box on the other side of the arena, and the weather was glorious – all the participants were certainly glad of the sunshine, because only the royal box was under cover. Eventually it was my turn to perform, and I played a five-minute-long version of *Duelling Banjos* with horses constantly passing back and forth between me and the Queen – had she even been listening? And the crazy thing is: these horses moved to the beat of every piece. Their steps were in sync with the music. The animals and riders must have been practising for weeks prior; it definitely wasn't an improvisation. And I just stood there and thought, 'Four years ago you couldn't even scrape money together for your rent, now the Queen of England's horses are dancing to your violin.'

But it was only afterwards that I was able to enjoy the spectacle of that afternoon. Until then, I dutifully followed an elaborate protocol, allowing people to usher me here and there, following instructions and making sure I didn't make any embarrassing slip-ups. It wasn't until I shut the hotel door behind me that night that I thought, 'WTF! Did that really just happen?' But the grin on my face in the mirror told me: 'Yeah, man. It was all real.'

You can find videos and photos for this chapter here.

New York, New York

Boldness’ would also be a fitting title for this passage, because, between 2010 and 2013, I pretty much ran riot in New York. As I write this, I find myself occasionally shaking my head, and perhaps readers will shake theirs too, but let’s not forget: the success my music achieved was huge, and I was not prepared for it.

Success changes you, because it changes your whole life. Not that I would have lost touch with reality; I’d been fortunate to have spent my childhood as a classical musician, obeying the laws of discipline and self-control. After that, it’s very unlikely you’ll end up getting swept away by the tumults of life, never to be seen again. But what can happen is it can completely knock your socks off. In other words, you’re young, you’re bursting with energy, your career is going great, you’re working like mad, you’re

In the Audi R8 GT ... Just because you can, doesn’t mean you should!

striking a balance between the moral and the immoral, and if there's an opportunity to party, you go hard, following the motto of 'I deserve it.'

At least that's what you tell yourself. In any case, once I left the airport in New York, I never slept. Screw the jetlag; the nightlife was beckoning – let's see what it had to offer this time. I would often be there for only five days before flying to somewhere like Moscow or Milan for a performance. It was quite a dash, but that was my life now: work to the limit, party to the limit. There was less and less time for making acquaintances, and no time at all to get to know someone better; the 'quick shots' mounted up, and I hardly saw my parents either.

I would sleep in late, work for three or four hours, and then spend the nights doing the rounds with my promoter friends. In some clubs, I didn't even have to pay for drinks – they were free. Most of my money went towards an expensive habit of mine: parking my car directly outside the club entrances. Wait a minute ...

What car? Correct. I hadn't had a car in New York up to that point. No sensible person drives a car in New York. You pay 800 or 900 dollars a month for the garage space alone, and there is no parking anywhere; if you're feeling suicidal, take your bike out at night, otherwise walk or use the subway. But Audi had now come up with the idea of parking an R8 GT outside the door for me – a pretty fancy vehicle that had become all the rage in the US following its appearance in the *Iron Man* movie starring Robert Downey Jr. In short, an eye-catcher, an attention-grabber. After a year, they would replace it with a new model for free, and I confess I felt like a million bucks in that set of wheels – apart from the fact that I'm not the most skilled of drivers.

So this R8 was actually wasted on me, but it definitely turned heads – including my own. And, at the time, I enjoyed attracting attention, which is not an easy thing to do in the epicentre of exhibitionism that is New York. One time, I met up with a girlfriend from my early promoter days. She still remembered me as that guy who lived in a tiny flat overlooking a rear courtyard, and couldn't believe her eyes when I roared up in my R8 – 'Did you win the lottery?' Yes, kind of. And because everyone had to know how fate had smiled upon me ...

It was my first R8 and my last year in La Grotta. There was a hip club three blocks from my flat, and, two blocks in the opposite direction on the same street, my car was waiting for me in a garage. What did I do? Having barely arrived back in New York, I walked to the garage, took the car out and drove the five blocks back in the opposite direction. That would have been ridiculous enough. But to top it off, I couldn't resist parking my R8 right next to the entrance to the club for everyone to see. A pure ego trip. Seeing and being seen ... In any case, if you greased the bouncer's palm well, he would move the little red traffic cone aside so you could park right outside the club in the spaces reserved for the wealthier guests, for those who arrived in R8s. And now David Garrett had arrived – *Hey, rock star, come on in ...*

And then? It was as if you'd turned on a torch in a jungle at night – correctly assuming there's an opportunity to suck something dry here, hundreds of mosquitoes gather in the beam of your light. In other words, anyone who flaunts his wealth attracts people whose intentions are not always pure. I didn't care. I lapped it up for three years, even though I was the one pulling out the credit card at the end of the night at clubs like Provocateur. Countless people at my table must have been excited to be around me only because they knew I wasn't the stingy type. But you can also spend money on rubbish in life; perhaps that's how you learn to tell the difference between sense and nonsense. As I have already mentioned, money didn't mean all that much to me anyway. At the same time, however, I did also live quite inexpensively, because money makes money – my clothes would automatically be posted to me without me even asking for them, the car would magically be at my door whenever I wanted it, and the odd watch would suddenly also somehow fall into my lap.

In those days, I made friends and drank to these friendships so quickly that none of it was serious. It was during this time that I met Sharon in a club. She was sitting at my table and was stunning. I only saw her sporadically, and you couldn't exactly call it a deep and meaningful relationship, but we got on well, even though she was a bit trying. You see, she had set her standards based on what I could provide, and her mood quickly soured if I didn't go all out the way she had envisaged.

After about a year, we realized we hadn't taken a holiday together. Whoever suggested it, I don't remember, but, in any case, Sharon chose the Maldives, and I booked us two and a half weeks there. Shortly before our departure, it occurred to me that I didn't actually know Sharon that well ... And here's my advice for any parents out there: if your child falls in love with someone they can't resist, pay for them to spend a two-week holiday in the Maldives. If it really is true love, they'll get through it and you'll just have to accept it. It is much more likely, however, that they'll end up having massive fights, because in the Maldives, they're at each other's mercy; there's no escape.

So we flew over and landed on a tiny, gorgeous private island – a bungalow just for the two of us, a small pool out the front, and the whole day to do nothing but swim and snorkel. But the mood soon soured, because the combination of these two holidaymakers together was far from a happy one.

From my side: I had brought my violin here too. You see, a day in the Maldives is endless; I swear it's longer than twenty-four hours. Despite having intended to stay away from the violin for a few days, I was playing it the very first day to fight the boredom. Even after three hours of practising, it still felt like I had the whole day ahead of me. I admit I do get bored easily. I was missing music. My head was abuzz with thoughts of my upcoming projects, and those thoughts didn't stop just because I was in the Maldives. The quieter things around me got, the louder my inner voice became, ordering me back to the violin, back to the desk, back to the telephone. Perhaps that's why I haven't taken more than six extended holidays as an adult.

Sharon saw things differently. Let's put it like this: I have no issue with people having a quiet glass or two to drink during the day, but if someone's already raging drunk by 2 p.m. ... I mean, I had imagined this holiday to be a bit more romantic. On the fifth night, we were sitting outside under a sky full of stars – it felt like you could just reach out and grab one – and Sharon was smashed. I eventually made the comment, 'Do you really have to be like this?', to which Sharon slurred, 'When I look at you, I realize how much I miss my ex.' It was like something out of a mediocre Hollywood movie. I wasn't resentful, but it was clear that we were done. I booked her a flight back to New York the next day.

I myself had no reason to return immediately. Of the now thirty-one people on the island, split over sixteen bungalows, I was the only one who was single, and no one flies to the Maldives just to sit by themselves at a dinner table set for two, staring at their phone. Hurt and sad, I nevertheless wallowed in this loneliness until the two and a half weeks were up.

Now all I need to do is explain my breakup with my R8. My testimonial deal with Audi had been going for five years now, but I had hardly been in New York, because I was now spending nearly half my time doing promotional work. Shortly before the annual model replacement, my tour manager Jörg visited me in New York. He wanted to know what my latest R8 looked like. I had a think. 'Black,' I replied, 'a gorgeous coupé.' At that moment, an employee drove my car out of the garage, revealing a red convertible covered in a thick layer of dust. The milometer showed 36 miles – the exact distance between the Audi dealership in New Jersey and my garage. I obviously hadn't driven the car a single time in the last year, and the price for the garage space had now increased to 1,200 dollars a month.

Jörg, the voice of reason that he was, summed up the situation by saying, 'Do you really think the people at Audi won't notice that the total mileage is only 72 miles? And do you think you're still the right person for a testimonial deal?' He was right, and Audi and I went our separate ways. That R8 had been an awesome toy for four years, but it now represented a past I look back on with mixed feelings. I had lived it up. I had also made a few mistakes – occasionally these had been enjoyable little transgressions, but often I had found myself thinking 'for God's sake!' That last year, my magnificent R8 was replaced with a conventional taxi, and that's the way things would stay.

You can find videos and photos for this chapter here.

On tour in Europe and the US

My fifth album, *Legacy*, was released in 2011. It was a CD of classical pieces, and I'm not sure Universal, my record company, was too thrilled about another foray into classical music – isn't Beethoven too serious, after all? But I was determined to take my audience with me on a musical adventure, and, this time, I wanted to head into the lofty peaks of classical music. So I went to London's Abbey Road Studios with Ion Marin and the Royal Philharmonic Orchestra, combining Beethoven's *Violin Concerto in D Major* with famous pieces by Fritz Kreisler, my great idol when it came to violin compositions and arrangements.

Contrary to all expectations – including my own! – *Legacy* sold more than 400,000 copies; only The Three Tenors had ever achieved anything similar in the classical music genre. How

Before my concert in Los Angeles, 2014

can I explain that sort of sales success? It could have been that many people were curious and wondering what Garrett would do next. So had word got around that I was always coming out with surprises? If so, it was definitely the perfect idea to head back to the studio that same year, but this time to record the next crossover album. It was to be called *Music*, purely and simply, because I wanted it to encompass all styles, pieces from all over the world, as well as stuff I had written myself. It was precisely this mix that made it exciting, not just for the listeners, but also for me, because you can never predict how the repertoire for that kind of album will evolve.

So I was on tour in South America and suddenly woke up to completely new musical influences. In a Mexican restaurant, for example, I noticed a guitarist was playing *Tico Tico*, a blisteringly quick, dynamic melody that everyone has probably heard at some point. As someone always open to collecting new ideas, I immediately took a few notes, which is always my general approach; whenever something piques my interest, I grab my notebook. I can't actually fall asleep when I have an unaddressed idea floating around in my head. So, even late at night, I will turn my light back on, put my contact lenses in and jot the idea down straight away in my notebook. Then I'm able to rest and finally fall asleep, until the next idea comes ten minutes later – so on goes the light again ...

The reward for my sleepless nights, the *Music* album, ended up selling a whopping 600,000 copies. It was unbelievable.

The thoroughly pleasing side effect of this productivity was that I won awards quite often. In a nutshell: a total of nine Echoes in classical and pop, a Golden Camera, a Bambi and various other cultural and music awards. The main effect, however, was of course the concerts that followed. I was now touring on three continents, and my memories of these performances are pretty blurry. When you lead such an unsettled lifestyle, you end up in a kind of delirium, and when you wake from it, all you can recall are the highlights, much like the fragments of a dream. I want to mention a couple of these highlights.

Back in 2008, even before I started doing concerts in the States, people had started to hear about me there. Specifically, the clothing company Banana Republic, which was basically omnipresent at the time, had contracted me to work with three other musicians on a major advertising campaign. The four of us were the faces of Banana Republic, and anyone entering one of their shops would see me smiling back at them with my violin, wearing my Banana Republic outfit – at around 3,000 outlets.

Our activities in the US kicked off properly soon after. And the person to get it all going was none other than Oprah Winfrey, whose show had more viewers than any other in the US. In other words, if you're able to perform on her show, you've made it, and I jumped for joy when I was invited to play. For me, it was the jackpot, and even Rick Blaskey had high expectations for the American market. Unfortunately, we would soon get a reality check. My band and I had to play forty concerts in forty-five days – an extremely exhausting schedule, especially in the early days when we were still going everywhere by tour bus, from South Carolina to Texas, from Houston to North Dakota, back to New York and on to Boston, Philadelphia and Chicago, and from there possibly to the west coast.

Not that I have anything against tour buses. Ours had a comfortable bedroom at the back with a king-size bed, and its atmosphere was perfectly decent too, but it was totally ill-equipped to handle potholes. The band guys were kind enough to let me have the bedroom while they made do with the bunk beds in the middle, but my nice big bed was directly above the rear axle and there's certainly no shortage of potholes on American country roads – indeed one was enough to jolt me awake. After doing two US tours this way, we made the joint decision that, while we would be happy to continue using the bus during the day, night travel would have to be by air.

So we would then book the cheapest flights, with the bus waiting for us at the airport the next morning. As is common in the US, these domestic flights rarely had a business class, and it was often even impossible to reserve seats, so boarding could end up being a bit interesting – everyone would storm the plane, ticket in hand, and claw their way to a seat in order to nab a free overhead locker for their carry-on luggage. So there we would be, four guys with a guitar, bass and violin, each of us stressing about not being able to stow our instruments away. Musical instruments are hand luggage, of course, and every protesting stewardess soon falls silent when told how much a violin is worth – or when politely asked, 'So you have seven-figure insurance? Because then I'll just quickly note down your name and address in case something happens to my violin in the cargo hold ...' I had this conversation many times, always getting my way, but guitarists and bassists are naturally also hesitant to part with their instruments. So boarding was always a test of our assertiveness.

Now, when young guys spend weeks in each other's pockets, a lot of shenanigans go down. One time, John had been lucky enough to score an aisle seat, while I had the window, and the pair of us were hell-bent on defending the middle seat against any would-be occupant in the hope of getting some extra space and leg room. Necessity is the mother of invention, and I took out my constant companion, my travel pillow, placing it incongruously on the middle seat, kitting it out with a jacket, sweatpants, a hat and shoes, even fastening its seatbelt and putting sunglasses on it. So there he sat, our middle-seat passenger, a fully-fledged member of human society, albeit a little lifeless. But why hadn't the plane started taxiing? It had been half an hour already.

A baffled stewardess was hurrying up and down the aisle. 'Is there a problem with the plane?' I asked her. 'No,' she said, 'but there's too many people. We're missing a seat and we can't fit the last passenger in.' A super awkward moment. Jörg pointed to our fake passenger – 'Are you guys paying for your friend over there?' At which point the penny dropped for the stewardess. The crew were less than amused, and the other passengers didn't exactly side with us either, so we were careful not to keep laughing about the disguised travel pillow. It probably wasn't our best idea, even though such clownery could easily be justified after a tiring and rather monotonous tour.

We would spend two months every year for the next four years leading this life of alternating between American highways and airspace. Then we were done. I had expected more from the US. The investment had been huge for rather disappointing return, and travelling across that large country was so tiring and stressful that, afterwards, I would be completely drained and only a shadow of myself at subsequent concerts elsewhere around the world. Plus I was also afraid that, if people started recognizing me on the street in the States too, I wouldn't have any privacy any more.

For years I have preferred touring Germany, Austria and Switzerland in a caravan. I don't like being driven down the Autobahn in a car at 120 miles an hour; the caravan's speed of 70 is more than enough for me, and I can even have an espresso as I travel.

In the early days, however, we would often travel by minivan – usually for many hours at a time. You want to make the most of every minute of this downtime, which is why I would have these vans' rear seats taken out, sit cross-legged on the floor, take out my sheet music and start practising during the trip – just the way I had done as a child. Back then, my father and I drove around in our VW Kombi, and I would sit cross-legged on the floor at the back, playing, while he shouted his corrections and comments back at me from the driver's seat. It all seems a bit weird now. In those days, we definitely could have done without those extra shifts. But now in the minivan, the time constraints we were under made these ventures unavoidable.

My radius broadened after 2010. My tour schedule started including cities in Latin America, as well as others in Italy, Northern and Eastern Europe, Russia and East Asia. Obviously, the more diverse the cities you visit, the more diverse your experiences are, for example in Mexico City ...

As I soon discovered during the sound check, the venue was a giant arena. It could hold 14,000 people, and I started to feel very worried; as there had been hardly any advertising beforehand, I would probably be playing to rows of empty seats. The plan for the concert was that I would slowly make my way through the audience from behind and head towards the stage, playing my violin the whole time. It had worked well in Germany, where people turned around to look at me, following my entrance with their gaze and giving me friendly applause. That was it. But in Mexico City, there was suddenly talk of six bodyguards that the organizer wanted to assign us. How come? Surely it would be enough just for my tour manager Jörg to stick close behind me like usual – if someone really decided to leap up, he would simply have to give the hand signal and the person would sit back down. And now six security guards? Okay. 'If you say so ...'

The concert began, and the venue was packed to the rafters – it was sold out! I came in and started playing, and hundreds of people jumped up and rushed towards me; the security guards had to surround me like a politician on his way through a press pack, and I thought to myself, 'Is all this commotion a good sign or is something brewing here?' Seconds later, I found out: I was experiencing the Mexican version of a warm reception.

My performance in Moscow also comes to mind. There were 4,000 people in the hall at the Kremlin. I started playing, looked out at poker faces and received only tentative applause after the first piece. This tepid response persisted the whole night, and, afterwards, I asked my tour manager 'What did I do wrong today? Was my playing a bit rough?' He just shrugged his shoulders. I later found out that there had been a high-ranking politician in the audience, which had been reason enough for everyone else to keep themselves in check. And to think I had been crapping myself. Whenever something doesn't go as expected, my first thought is always that it's my mistake, my failure.

Back in Mexico City, I eventually managed to stagger my way to the stage once the spotlight temporarily lost me in the pandemonium. Then, during the concert, there was a moment of irritation when I started hearing singing in my earpieces. What was going on? Had Franck incorporated a choir into this piece? I took out the right ear plug to discover it was the entire hall singing along! 140,000 people were blaring out *Living on a Prayer* by Bon Jovi! I have never experienced anything like it; it's not even something I could ever have dreamed of, but, in Mexico, you clearly need to be prepared for the most effusive of receptions.

It was the same later on in Argentina and Brazil. Six security guards? Sure, bring them on, good idea, if nothing else for all the hands that try to grab you and even reach for your violin. At a subsequent concert in Japan, I told my guys, 'Don't worry, it'll be different here.' After all, I was familiar with the local customs from previous trips; the Japanese were quiet fans, giving only brief applauses between pieces. No sooner do they start clapping than they stop. But they make up for it at the end by showering you with flowers and fruit baskets with ruby-red apples the size of pumpkins. Latin Americans, meanwhile, climb onto their seats and are very vocal in their enthusiasm – the artist must never be left in any doubt that they are fiercely adored. As a musician, you soar through concerts like that. You ride the wave of the audience's fervour, and, afterwards in the green room, you sit around with your band in silence, just staring at each other because sometimes you are simply lost for words.

You can find videos and photos for this chapter here.

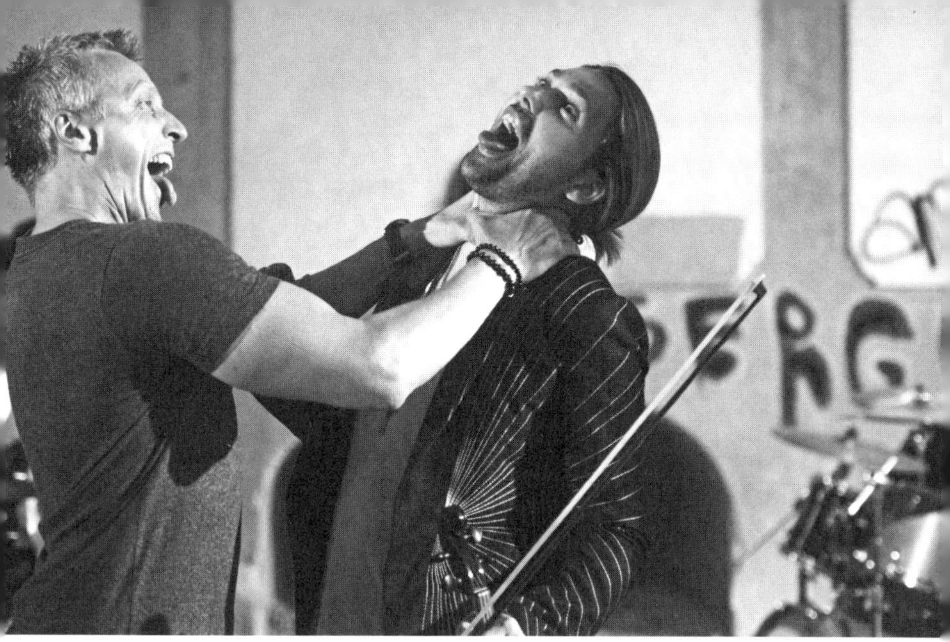

The loneliness of a violin soloist

Jörg Kollenbroich joined us in 2010 as tour manager. His predecessor had had a very specific trait in that he had never been on time. If we were due to leave at 8 a.m., he would generally appear much later, and of course that was not on. Jörg, on the other hand, turned out to be the human embodiment of a Swiss clock. I was delighted, because, with my whirling brain, I sometimes forgot the time. I would soon discover we were the perfect fit in every respect.

The first episode with Jörg that I remember was me waking up in my hotel room and Jörg, who had a second key, coming in with a cup of coffee for me. Next minute, he'd barely set eyes on my open suitcase when I heard, 'That's just pure chaos. I'll show you how to pack a suitcase.' And he bent over my suitcase to calmly give me my first lesson in tidiness, while I watched on, mug in hand.

Mind you, I'm anything but messy. I don't even have a cleaner; I do my own cleaning, because no one knows the dirty corners of my apartment the way I do. I need an orderly, clearly structured environment to work in, otherwise I end up having thoughts of my unmade bed flitting around in my head while I'm trying to practise. But Jörg quickly made me feel like a slob.

His second asset is that he can't keep his mouth shut. I consider this a good thing, because I don't like yes-men and people repeating my opinions. I want to have people around me who talk freely and openly. Now, however, we're at the stage where Jörg doesn't even have to say anything – I'll just look at him, he'll look at me, and I'll instantly know I've messed up.

And his third asset is something that brings me back to Rick Blaskey in London.

I owe Rick a lot. When the British royal family hired me to perform at the Queen's Jubilee, I might have been the one playing the violin, but it was Rick who had done all the groundwork. When it came to professionalism, creativity and assertiveness, he was definitely one of the best. But there was one thing that displeased me: as time went on, I felt he was withdrawing more and more; for me, work was building up, yet it was very difficult to get a hold of him, especially on weekends. No matter whether I was having problems in Southeast Asia or small-town Nebraska, after 6 p.m. on a Friday, my calls to him would often go unanswered. After one such weekend of failing to get help from him, I finally called him on the Monday morning and expressed my anger, 'Rick, you can't just be virtually uncontactable on weekends.' To which he simply responded, 'David, I also do have a life.'

So did I ... But I knew him. There were two things that were as important, if not more important, to him than our partnership:

his family, of course, but also his football club, Sheffield Wednesday.

Now Sheffield Wednesday is the club in the British football League that never learned to win. For him, as a Sheffield Wednesday fan, his club's games were so important that my weekend problems had to wait.

These days, I understand him. It's just that, during those years, I didn't have any public holidays or weekends, and had constant glitches and mishaps in some shape or form. Being able to contact him directly in London would have been worth its weight in gold – but what really sealed our split was the fact that he hardly ever left London, while I was relentlessly jetting all over the world.

I would have liked him to be there more, like he was at the start – and not just to help me in emergencies. I needed someone I could share my joy with, savour my triumphs with and review the day's events with over a beer. Because joy you're forced to keep to yourself soon implodes and gives way to an inexplicable melancholy; only when you share your joy with someone you trust does it then settle nicely in your soul. Sure, that was too much to ask of someone who had a wife and child, but I did miss that company after a concert. And Rick knew it. In any case, he opened our final conversation by saying, 'I'm pretty sure I know what this is about.' Perhaps he hadn't been totally wrong when he had told me he could do more for me, like initiate new projects, from his desk in London. But I wouldn't be swayed. And that was the end of the Rick Blaskey chapter.

Now came the question of who could replace Rick. Jörg and I had become best friends in the years after 2010; he downright indulged me with his attentiveness, reliability and straightforward manner. I had had a good experience with my classics manager Tobias Weigold, the embodiment of German thoroughness, a pillar I could rely on. With Jörg Kollenbroich, I'd also had a good experience. Plus he was footloose and willing to travel the whole world with me, but – would he also be able to talk to record companies and negotiate crossover contracts? He has now long proven he could, because, since 2015, he has not only been my tour manager, but also Rick Blaskey's replacement, in other words, my manager for all things crossover.

Travelling has been much more fun for me since. Jörg and I normally spend 250 days a year together, and this can lead to episodes that would unfortunately never have been possible with Rick – like at Moscow's Red Square in 2015.

At the time, I was not happy with the videos for our *Explosive* album. We were due to travel to Russia, and I had painted this picture in my head of David Garrett and his violin standing under the famous onion domes of Red Square, playing *Babushka*, a tune from that album, filmed by Jörg on his little action camera. What we hadn't imagined was the large number of police and special law enforcement officers in the square, security staff whose job was to make sure tourists behaved appropriately and to prevent any mischief. So we were forced to play cat and mouse with the guards. Were they looking in our direction? No? Then off we'd go – me playing and Jörg filming. Fifteen seconds later, a security guard would smell a rat; I'd pack up my violin, Jörg would shove the camera into his pocket, we'd disappear into the crowd, suddenly reappear somewhere else, and start the whole spiel again: me playing the violin, Jörg filming, guard getting suspicious, us hightailing it. And so it was, rinse and repeat at least twenty times until we finally had a video of the full *Babushka* piece, complete with onion domes – a stunt reminiscent of a perfectly synchronized museum burglary, or *Ocean's Eleven* in Red Square.

But I'm even more grateful for the void Jörg fills after my performances. Whether I'm doing a concert to 10,000 people in Rio de

Janeiro or playing in a small German town, the curtain drops and I'm no longer alone in the hotel lift, no longer trudging down the corridor on my own, no longer mindlessly staring around my empty hotel room, no. I instead head around the block with Jörg, sit down with him somewhere, have a nightcap and chat a bit – they're small things but they have a huge bearing on how happy I feel after a concert. Away from the stage, it used to be too quiet all around me; now there was a voice, an ear, a face, and suddenly I was able to rest easy at night, because I had been able to finish the day sitting around, enjoying some jokes and philosophizing with Jörg.

To give my readers an idea of what my travel regime has become over time, in other words, what was in store for someone who said they were willing to travel with me, I'm going to dedicate a chapter listing all my performance venues. It's admittedly going to be an experimental chapter, containing (almost) nothing but names of cities. You can skip it if you want. But you can also read it, because a lot of the things that happened during that restless period are just a colourful blur in my head, and, after reading the next few pages, you'll certainly understand why.

You can find videos and photos for this chapter here.

My tour schedule, 2009 to 2019

This list of concert locations shows only the places where I've performed concerts. It doesn't include television appearances or interviews, of which there were probably twice as many, nor does it include studio sessions, trips to and from, meetings and talks, private concerts, charity concerts, photo shoots, the daily two to three hours of practice, writing pieces, producing demo tapes, trips home, or those few remaining sacred hours of privacy relegated to the late evening.

It starts in 2009: Cologne (Lanxess Arena, the largest hall in Germany). Munich. Leipzig. Berlin. Münster. Stuttgart. Zurich. Mannheim. Bremerhaven. Kempten. Frankfurt. Hamburg. Cologne. Zurich. Bologna. Como. Bergen. Munich. Regensburg. Stuttgart. Pirmasens. Ludwigshafen. Moscow. Hong Kong. New

A shot from one of our concerts around the world – the Waldbühne in Berlin

York. Braunschweig a.k.a. Brunswick (Hong Kong – New York – Brunswick in five days!). Viersen. Kiev. Potsdam. Mannheim. Aachen. Vienna. Nuremberg. Hanover. Hamburg. Bamberg. Freiberg. Karlsruhe. Leipzig. Brunswick. Düsseldorf. Bremen. Cologne. Echternach. London. Saarbrücken. Niedernhausen. Berlin. Halle/Westfalen. Berlin. Saarbrücken. Dresden. Potsdam. Shmf (no idea what that is). Essen. Ludwigsburg. Zurich. Salem. Regensburg. Munich. Freiburg. Fayetteville (USA). Glanville (USA, but everyone knows that). Trenton. Harrisburg. Pittsburgh. Pirmasens. Bonn. Brunswick. Zurich. Orlando. Fort Myers. Fort Lauderdale. Houston. Los Angeles. Kansas City. St. Louis. Chicago. New York. Alexandria. Indianapolis. Boston. Munich. Weimar. Hamburg. Bremerhaven. Kassel. Cologne. Erfurt. Magdeburg. Stuttgart. Mannheim. Wetzlar. Hanover. Munich. Passau. Münster. Berlin. Baton Rouge (capital of Louisiana). Boston. Seattle. Portland. Reno (awful city). Zurich. Chicago. Saint Paul. Albany. Concord. Montclair. Harrisburg. North Bethesda. Charlotte. Nashville. Clearwater. Fort Lauderdale. Dallas. Vienna. Essen. Wuppertal. Düsseldorf. Duisburg. Karlsruhe. Heilbronn. Würzburg. Bielefeld. Bochum. Halle an der Saale. Leipzig. Dresden. (Keeping up?) Berlin. Wiltz. Venice. Cologne. Bremen. Leipzig. Mannheim. Oberhausen. Cologne. Frankfurt. Berlin. Hamburg. Düsseldorf. Stuttgart. Zwickau. Leipzig. Rostock. Bremen. Nuremberg. Hanover. Dortmund. Frankfurt. Munich. Vienna. Basel. Seattle. Portland. Sacramento. Los Angeles. San Diego. Little Rock. Omaha. Minneapolis. Madison. Chicago. Boston. Wallingford. New York (a nice concert; Perlman was in the audience). Montreal. Pittsburgh. Alexandria. Jacksonville. Miami. Orlando. Fort Pierce. Leipzig. Bremen. Hamburg. Baden-Baden. Frankfurt. Munich. Hanover. Bad Segeberg. Hamburg. Cologne. Oberhausen. Bremen. Cologne. Stuttgart. Wiesbaden. Salem. Ludwigslust.

Vienna (with the Vienna Symphony Orchestra, Brahms' violin concerto. I had of course been practising in the back on the floor of our van beforehand). Munich. Bad Kissingen. Dresden. Halle/Westfalen. Mannheim. Verbier. Amsterdam. Frankfurt. Bucharest. Bad Wörishofen (with the children's orchestra comprising the winners of the *Jugend musiziert* competition. I always loved that. You could work with that orchestra – the young people were over the moon that I was there, which is why I'll always have wonderful memories of Bad Wörishofen). Helsinki. Copenhagen. Oslo. Stockholm. Paris. Milan. Verona. London. San Diego. Los Angeles. Rome. Sacramento. Seattle. Chicago. Pittsburgh. Morristown. Washington. New York (Perlman was there again). Shanghai. Tainan. Taipei. Vienna. Hamburg. Dortmund. Munich. Nuremberg. Leipzig. Hanover. Halle/Westfalen. Zurich. Frankfurt. Berlin. Hamburg. Düsseldorf. Stuttgart. Leipzig. Munich. Cologne. Milan (classical, Paganini concerto). Luxembourg. Leipzig. Nuremberg. Basel. Oberhausen. Hamburg. Cologne. Berlin. Frankfurt. Munich. Innsbruck. Mannheim. Stuttgart. Erfurt. Bremen. Stuttgart. Cologne. Magdeburg. Halle/Westfalen. Berlin. Chemnitz. Nuremberg. Düsseldorf. Hamburg. Lucerne. Linz. Mannheim. Bad Segeberg. Würzburg. Munich. Erfurt. Berlin. Leipzig. Dresden. Ludwigslust. Zurich. Aspach. Bayreuth. Kassel. Mönchengladbach. Hanover. Münster. (Can you now see how there are many nights I don't even remember?) Hanover. Munich. Zwickau. Bad Kissingen. (I'm not just copying and pasting the same page of the tour schedule!) Wiesbaden. Ingolstadt. Regensburg. Nuremberg. Basel. Bad Wörishofen. Hamburg (Laeiszhalle). Schloss Elmau. Jerusalem. Tel Aviv. Jerusalem. Tel Aviv. Haifa. St Louis. Kansas City. Dallas. Houston. Portland. Seattle. San Jose. Sacramento. Anaheim. Santa Fe. San Diego. Mexico City. Naples. Genoa. Minneapolis. Milwaukee. Chicago. New York. Pittsburgh. Wallingford. Worcester. Atlanta.

St Petersburg (Florida). Schloss Elmau. Stuttgart. Hanover. Berlin. Salzburg. Kempten. Munich. Düsseldorf. Frankfurt. Lucerne. Ulm. Lübeck. Vienna. Mannheim. Cologne. Nuremberg. Pingtung (Taiwan). Taipei. Seoul. Busan (South Korea). Tokyo. Osaka. Bad Kissingen. Frankfurt. Mannheim. Stuttgart. Nuremberg. Berlin. Brunswick. Leipzig. Hamburg. Hanover. Halle/Westfalen. Munich. Zurich. Cologne. Dortmund. Düsseldorf. Innsbruck. Vienna. Mexico City. Guadalajara. Monterrey. Moscow. Turin. Naples. Frankfurt. Hamburg. Halle an der Saale. Heilbronn. Paris. Essen. Lucerne. Nuremberg. Kassel. Berlin. Lyon. Luxembourg. Vienna. Munich. Salzburg. Lucerne. (Now you can understand why I'm quite happy not to have a big following in some countries.) Ulm. Freiburg. Bad Kissingen. Cologne. Istanbul. Milan. Mönchengladbach. Magdeburg. Schwarzenberg. Forchheim. Baden-Baden. Berlin. Bolzano. Kempten. Graz. Buenos Aires. Porto Alegre. Curitiba. São Paulo. Rio de Janeiro. Brasilia. Milan (two days after performing in Brasilia). Florence. Verona. Rome. Moscow. St Petersburg. Bucharest. Prague. Bad Wörishofen. Düsseldorf. Mexico City. Monterrey. Guadalajara. Mérida. Toronto. Tel Aviv. Haifa. Tel Aviv (with the Israel Philharmonic Orchestra). Frankfurt (Alte Oper). Genoa. Cremona. Interlaken. Saarbrücken. Nuremberg. Munich. Strasbourg. Mannheim. Stuttgart. Berlin. Dresden. Hamburg. Moscow. Essen. Hamburg. Paris. Freiburg. Bonn. Rome. Bad Kissingen. Brunswick. Leipzig. Mannheim. Nuremberg. Dortmund. Bremen. Hamburg. Berlin. Halle/Westfalen. Cologne. Munich. Vienna. Zurich. Stuttgart. Frankfurt. Łódź. Minsk. Moscow. St Petersburg. Kiev. Odessa. Tel Aviv. Mexico City (five concerts). Turin. Piacenza. Basel. Lucerne. Karlsruhe. Kempten. Munich. Bregenz. Pavia. Padua. Kiel. Vienna. Munich. Freiburg. Frankfurt. (Can you even begin to imagine the travelling time involved with all this? The number of miles racked up?) Berlin. Erfurt. Munich (pack bag, head to airport, check in, fly, check out, collect bag, head to hotel ...). Basel. Rüsselsheim. Sindelfingen. Liechtenstein. Reggio Calabria. Aachen. Bucharest. Bad Wörishofen. Krakow. Warsaw. Gdansk. Hamburg. Oslo. Stavanger (on the *Queen Mary II* cruise ship, where I did three concerts in five days). Hamburg. Tel Aviv. São Paulo. Buenos Aires. Santiago de Chile. Vilnius. Riga. Tallinn. Bucharest. Sofia. Kiev. St Petersburg. Moscow. Budapest. Ljubljana. Zagreb. Rome. Florence. Milan. Bolzano. Mérida. Mexico City. Guadalajara. Monterrey. Chemnitz. Erfurt. Berlin. Dortmund. Oberhausen. Cologne. Zurich. Stuttgart. Hanover. Brunswick. Leipzig. Bremen. Schwerin. Kiel. Hamburg. Mannheim. Frankfurt. Munich. Vienna. Magdeburg. Tbilisi (a gorgeous city, amazing concert, but you don't get to see much of Tbilisi in one and a half days). Verona. Caserta (in southern Italy). Tel Aviv. Istanbul. Skopje. Prague. Krakow. Łódź. Gdansk. Vilnius. Riga. Tallinn. Minsk. Another stint on the *Queen Mary II*.

We've now reached 2019. 2020 didn't happen due to the COVID-19 pandemic. There were no accidents on any of these trips. There was the odd time when my plane had to abort a landing or where an engine failed, but that was it; I've never been in any serious danger.

But this lifestyle isn't exactly free from risk; you can never discount potential embarrassment, after all. Because there comes a point where you can't even remember where you are, and you can practise reading out the name of the city you're in twenty times backstage – 'We're in Fayetteville, we're in Fayetteville ...' – but then you go on stage, play the first piece, pick up the microphone and think, 'Bloody hell – where am I again?'

This sort of embarrassing episode once happened to me at a major venue: the Tempodrom in Berlin. The concert began with me descending the long staircase down to the stage. As I walked,

I played *Pirates of the Caribbean*, and it wasn't entirely easy to feel my way down the steps against the glaring spotlight. But I made it safely to the edge of the stage and shouted into the microphone, 'it's a great night here at the Tempodrom in Munich! I'm happy to …' The rapturous euphoria in the hall suddenly switched to an ominous unease. Had I said the wrong thing? In any case, something definitely wasn't right, and, as I kept talking, I tried to go back over what I had said at the start. I realized then what I'd said in the very first sentence – and my heart stopped. 'Oh man. Did I just mix up Berlin and Munich?' Yep, I had, and, despite my apologies, the vibe didn't get going again for another two or three pieces.

Ever since that day, I've had a sheet of paper on the floor next to my microphone showing the name of the city I'm in so I don't say Halle an der Saale when I'm in Paris, or Moscow when I'm in Chicago.

You can find videos and photos for this chapter here.

Violin crash in London

I always choose my hotels carefully. In the early days, I naturally took whatever I could get. The Old Brompton had been a stroke of luck, but I didn't want to rely on that later on. Over the past thirteen years, I have spent way more of my life in hotels than within my own four walls, and I soon discovered that a hotel's vibe affects my mood and my entire attitude towards life. Some artists just need a bed and clean towel, having little concern for anything else, but I have my preferences, and if I particularly like a hotel, I tell Jörg, 'I'd like to stay at this hotel again next time.' Or even that specific room.

A sense of friendliness is very important to me. It could be a small hotel with incredibly nice staff, or it could be an established health resort, or indeed even a modern hotel where I like the way the light streams into the room. Jörg sometimes shakes his head, because that sort of thing doesn't mean anything to him – all he cares about is having fresh linen and an on-site gym – but I like hotels that act as sources of inspiration.

So much of my life has been spent on all the other tedious things that travel involves, and the travel itself is rarely fun either. When I do eventually get to my destination, it needs to feel like coming home – and there are some very nice hotels! Sometimes it's the stunning location, other times the cosy atmosphere, and sometimes it might just be the mattress that I find amazing, the pillow I'm able to sleep deeply on, or the bed linen that triggers feelings of happiness.

But enough of the travel stuff already. It's been a while since I mentioned my pet subject, namely the violin, and there's still a lot left to say about it – about my own violins, but also about the history of the violin, about the great violin-makers of history, for example, or the most famous violin virtuosos. But we'll start with what I experienced with my own violin at the end of my wunderkind era.

The Stradivarius loaned to me (and which I had not been allowed to use in Israel at the crucial moment) had been returned to the Talbot family before I went to London. In New York, I played on cheaper instruments; only before concerts would I sometimes seek out a dealer to borrow a really good violin. I rubbed along like this until, in 2006, I was able to afford a Guadagnini, an instrument crafted by violin-maker Giovanni Battista Guadagnini in 1772 and purchased legitimately at one of my father's auctions. It cost 200,000 euros – which was actually a bargain, because even twice that amount wouldn't have been considered expensive for that violin, though for me it was a lot of money. In December 2009, I finally managed to pay off my Guadagnini, feeling a weight off my shoulders. Barely two weeks later, on Christmas Eve, I was to perform Mendelssohn's *Violin Concerto in D Minor* in London's Barbican Hall.

The circumstances could hardly have been better. The Barbican Centre is a modern arts centre with an awesome concert hall. My parents had travelled from Aachen for the occasion, and the applause that followed my performance was everything I could have wanted. Once the concert was over, I slung the violin over my shoulders – being proud of this acquisition of mine, I had had a furrier line the case with green leather, and had attached two straps so I could carry the violin around with me comfortably like a backpack. All in high spirits, we made our way to the underground car park where my parents had left their car.

It was raining, of course – we were in London, after all – and I slipped on the top step of the concrete staircase leading down to the car park and slid down the rain-drenched steps, unable to stop, before thudding onto my back at the bottom. In other words, I had landed on my Guadagnini. I picked myself up, not wasting a second worrying about myself, and yanked off the case. While the violin wasn't the pile of shards I had feared, the top of it had cracked in more than one place, from front to back. In other words, I had just destroyed about a third of the purchase price.

What an awful night. My Guadagnini would eventually be restored at considerable expense, but what drama to suddenly plunge from euphoria to deep grief ... I myself hadn't broken anything; I didn't even have any bruises – the violin case had well and truly cushioned my fall and absorbed the impact, but the shocking sight of the splintered, cracked violin top had imprinted itself so firmly in my brain that I couldn't stop seeing it. Even after it had been restored, that violin continued to be tainted for me, and my love for it evaporated. It simply was no longer my violin.

Thank God my insurance company covered the restoration costs. Violins can be very valuable – good-quality 18th-century

Cremonese violins can be worth millions – and, no matter how careful you are, you can never rule out the possibility of them getting damaged, which is why it's a no-brainer to get these instruments insured. It's a different story for bows. I never insured my bows. What could happen to them? Big mistake. A bow has broken on me twice – both times on stage.

One of these had been my greatest treasure; it was all that remained of my concert income from my wunderkind days by the time I moved to the States – a bow made by famous French bow-maker Nicolas Maline, worth around 40,000 euros, with a gold and ivory trim. This precious object had been sacred to me at the time; it was my emergency reserve, my life insurance, and it was this very bow that snapped at the tip during a Juilliard School concert. Thereafter, I was on my own, so to speak, and so was all the more grateful for any job that came my way.

Three years after the accident in London, my father called me and mentioned a Stradivarius. 'I've had my eye on this violin for years. It's privately owned and it looks like there's now a possibility of buying it – do you want to see it?' Oh I wanted to see it, all right. I was on the lookout for a replacement, but merely having a look will of course never suffice in such cases; you also need to play the instrument, because being a Stradivarius doesn't necessarily mean it will sound fantastic. But the fact that it had been made in 1716 was promising. That was the time Stradivari was at the peak of his craft, and the Messiah Stradivarius, the most famous of all violins made by the Cremonese master, was also produced that same year.

I remembered a ten-year-old me playing the Stradivarius that was now apparently up for sale. The family who owned it had a huge instrument collection, and, as my father had long been on good terms with them, we had occasionally been invited to their home. I now happened to be in the area and arranged a time to meet the owner – 'Would you mind coming to my hotel and kindly bringing the violin along with you?' I was excited, and pondered the fact that, even though the stated price was seven figures, this was at the lower end of what you would expect to pay for a Stradivarius. Why? It either had a flaw or I was the luckiest little devil on the planet.

There was a knock at my hotel room door. I let the owner in and was itching to just grab the violin case straight out of her hands, but I had to keep my composure and engage in small talk. Finally the conversation came around to the object of my desire, and I opened the case. The instrument was stunning! It was beautifully preserved and, once I had played a few bars on it, there was no doubt that I was indeed that lucky little devil! It was love at first note, and it annoyed me that, for the time being, I had to hand this magnificent object back. But I wasn't Tarisio; I didn't have any varnished flea-market violin in my cupboard that I could have given to the owner as a swap.

My father was kind enough to take charge of the negotiations, and the agreed price ended up being a little less than that originally set. The instrument's former owner would later often attend my concerts, and was happy to listen to me playing on 'her' Stradivarius. I've generally used it at all my classical concerts ever since, but never at a crossover concert.

There are two reasons for this. Stradivariuses are, in principle, designed to be played in great halls, because their sound has the necessary carry. In crossover performances, however, I work with a microphone and have a pickup on the violin, so the full benefits of the Stradivarius get lost. And besides, it would be irresponsible to use it outside concert halls, because, in crossover performances, I'm constantly moving – and, incidentally, I can't be sure that everywhere I go in the world will be as reserved as a certain audience in Moscow had been. In other words, the risk of crashing to the floor with your Stradivarius or getting caught up in a crush of Mexican enthusiasm is just too high.

You'll have already noticed throughout this book that it doesn't take much to get me raving about violins. You can see it in my face; I can't help it. That's why I've always tried pretty much everything I can to get my hands on great violins – I've held truly legendary models of this instrument, and have even been able to play on some of them. I never tire of learning about the history of violin-making and about the genius craftsmen whose workshops have produced the finest violins ever known. For this reason, I'm going to dedicate the next passage to delving deeper into the world of violins and violin-makers.

You can find videos and photos for this chapter here.

Guarneri, Stradivari & co.

Niccolò Paganini had an entire collection of unusual violins. One of them was a 1743 Guarneri del Gesù, which is today displayed at Genoa's Palazzo Tursi and, as a tourist attraction, is encased in bulletproof glass. If it were ever put on the market, which no one thinks will happen, it would sell for little less than 80 million euros – just as a ballpark figure. Even a 'normal' Guarneri today goes for a cool eight-figure sum; indeed a particularly fine model recently sold for 22 million euros. While top-class Stradivariuses may be a little cheaper, they'll still set you back 14 or 15 million.

But this difference doesn't have anything to do with quality. It is because Antonio Stradivari (1644–1737) lived an amazingly long life, reaching the age of ninety-three, and must have

What an honour! In Genoa with Niccolò Paganini's famous violin: 'Il Cannone', 1743, crafted by Guarneri del Gesù

made thousands of violins together with his sons – even today, the number of instruments produced by his workshop is 1,200. Giuseppe Guarneri del Gesù (1698–1744), on the other hand, died at the age of forty-six and, unlike Stradivari, had been constantly plagued by money worries. So he couldn't afford any employees and therefore produced much fewer violins in his short life – only around 200 have been preserved.

Apart from the quality aspect, this is why the prices of his violins today are so mind-blowingly high. Collectors naturally become interested when top-quality artworks exist in such limited numbers and cannot be reproduced, so these types of violins always hold their value.

A few years ago, I did a concert in Genoa. I couldn't get Paganini's Guarneri out of my mind; just once in my life, I wanted to touch it, to hold it in my hands, so I asked the museum if I could do this as an exception. The director's generosity exceeded even my expectations – he was actually prepared to let me perform my concert on that violin! Guarded by four security officers, it was brought to the concert hall that night and I did indeed play on that instrument, which UNESCO includes on its list of Intangible Cultural Heritage. While I didn't do it with sweaty hands, I certainly had tears in my eyes and a smile on my face – was this insanity or ecstasy? Probably both. After all, Paganini's Guarneri is the ultimate violin, and playing on it is the ultimate experience.

I've read a lot over the years, and now know the locations of every instrument I'm passionate about. If, for example, I'm performing in Prague, I'll ask my management beforehand to call the Czech National Museum: 'Please ask the director if I can come around and look at the Prince of Orange. It's a Guarneri from 1744, the year of his death, and unfortunately usually locked away, so not even put on display, but perhaps they'll make an exception to let me have a look.' And it doesn't usually just end up being a look. I'll probably also be able to touch it, naturally with the greatest of respect, if not awe.

And then there's Cremona, the centre of more than just Italian violin-making. It is home to the most exclusive violin museum in the world, with an absolutely stunning chamber music hall that has witnessed 500 years of violin-making. And, once again, I couldn't resist. When I performed Brahms' *Violin Concerto in D Major* there a few years ago, I of course once again got my management to ask the question, and the museum directors were kind enough to lay all the violins I liked on a large table – half a dozen Stradivariuses, two Guarneris and four Amatis. After this overdose of beauty and perfection, I was in seventh heaven during the concert that followed.

I'd just like to say a few words here about Andrea Amati (1505–1577). While he didn't reach the same level of fame as the other two did, he certainly was just as important. If Cremona is the birthplace of the modern violin (as well as the modern cello and the modern viola), then Amati is its inventor. Very rarely in human history has a man-made object been developed not gradually, step by step, but rather launched into the world in its complete basic form virtually overnight, yet this is exactly the feat Amati achieved, with the violin's design only having been modified very slightly ever since.

There were predecessors. Even back in the Middle Ages, there had been slender, pear-shaped instruments in the form of bandsmen's fiddles and rebecs. But Amati set new, higher standards for his instruments, selected his wood more carefully, made changes to the shape, stretched the top more by making it more convex, used higher quality paint and varnish and better adapted his violins' dimensions to the human body. Plus, a young Antonio Stradivari studied under Amati's grandson Nicola in his workshop, establishing a direct link from the inventor of the modern violin to the manufacturer of what are currently the most highly prized violins (apart from Guarneri's).

Until well into the 19th century, the instruments produced by Nicola Amati were no less coveted than Stradivari's. Then, however, the violin was discovered as a solo instrument and suddenly had to meet new requirements. The focus increasingly shifted to the volume of the sound and its ability to carry, because violin virtuosos like Paganini (1782–1840) filled large concert halls, and you had to be able to clearly hear a soloist's playing even in the last rows. It was in this aspect that the Stradivari and Guarneri del Gesù violins very much outdid Amati's, and even Paganini naturally played on instruments made by the former two. He eventually established the violin as a solo instrument, taking violin-playing to never-before-seen heights of virtuosity, and his mastery in turn had an impact on violin-making, which is why I briefly wanted to discuss his importance.

On an electric guitar, Jimi Hendrix was the zenith of feeling and emotion; on the violin, Paganini reached the summit of what was technically possible. Much to my regret, there are no sound recordings available of him playing (and unfortunately not even a photo either), which is why some people today have doubts over whether he did actually play everything as cleanly as believed. I would counter this by saying that anyone who writes music with such a high degree of difficulty must also be able to play it brilliantly, because the mere fact that Paganini trusted his fingers to be able to perform such acrobatics is enough to redefine violin-playing.

It can therefore be said, without exaggeration, that the violin would never have achieved such prominence in the Romantic and Late Romantic period without Paganini – the focus would have instead been entirely on the piano. It was only thanks to Paganini and his vast cosmos of technical capabilities and impossibilities that the violin was elevated to equal ranking as a solo instrument. Admittedly, he did not get anywhere close to Beethoven or Brahms as a composer – indeed, his orchestral arrangements weren't even written by him – but all the violin parts are his own original work, and their level of genius is unparalleled. Even the best violins would prove to be unfit for this degree of virtuosity; even Stradivariuses and Guarneris needed to be adjusted to accommodate this. But before I get to that point, we need to look at how violin-making developed after Amati.

A century after the modern violin was invented, when a number of violin-makers were by now working in Cremona, Antonio Stradivari appeared on the scene. He would make a name for himself even back then. It was his love of experimentation that saw him produce different creations throughout different phases of his life. Every Stradivarius deserves the label of 'magnificent', but Stradivari's best period, his 'Golden Period', was between 1700 and 1719, by which time he had already been making violins for fifty years. It was during this time that the Stradivariuses most coveted today were created, with such top craftsmanship and so perfect in terms of their dimensions, that, to this day, they are the blueprint that every violin-maker follows. Paganini himself wouldn't have been able to complain about the volume of these violins, but there was one aspect in which even a Stradivarius was no longer up with the times: as was the case with all other violins, its neck was too short for a virtuoso violin soloist.

The neck is the bit where you hold the violin. It's what the fingerboard is attached to and what the strings stretch across. It also contains the pegbox, whose pegs are used to tune the instrument, and ends in the usually rather artistically carved scroll. At the start of the 19th century, this neck was replaced on virtually all violins, including those made by the big names. In other words, once the pegbox and scroll had been carefully sawn off, the original neck with the fingerboard was taken off and substituted with a new, more elongated neck with a longer fingerboard, before the scroll and pegbox were then also put back on. Why? Because violin virtuosos like Giovanni Battista Viotti and Giuseppe Tartini had been advancing into increasingly higher pitches since the mid-18th century, even before Paganini took virtuosity to the next level. So the pitch range gradually broadened, but the length of the neck and fingerboard on conventional baroque violins meant fingering for the high pitches was no longer possible, and the aforementioned adjustments became unavoidable. Incidentally, the piano went through a similar development; it originally only encompassed two octaves in the form of the harpsichord, and only by expanding the keyboard at both ends did it become the modern piano with its five or six octaves.

This neck extension does not in any way affect a violin's value. The most important thing on a string instrument is its body and scroll – not the neck. If anyone should discover an old violin with the original neck among the rubble of an abandoned Italian villa, I would congratulate them on their find, but unfortunately they wouldn't be able to play a contemporary repertoire on it. That's why even a Guarneri worth 22 million euros won't have an original neck.

The reason I've been focusing on Cremona when talking about the history of violin-making is because of those three big names – Amati, Guarneri and Stradivari. There were of course many other centres of violin-making; in Germany, for example, the small Bavarian town of Mittenwald, and elsewhere in Italy, cities such as Venice, Genoa, Turin and Milan. I hold the Venetian violin-makers in just as high esteem as I do their Cremonese counterparts – Montagnana, Santo Serafin, Goffriller and Gobetti, just to name a few. But Cremona's unique concentration of outstanding violin-makers is simply extraordinary, raising the question: why Cremona?

The general consensus is that the forests nearby produced wood that was more suitable than any other when it came to making violins. Is this true? While there are plenty of books around that seek to uncover Cremona's secret, a definitive explanation is yet to be found. As is always the case in life, there were probably multiple factors at play.

There is no question that the Cremonese violin-makers had struck it extremely lucky in terms of their choice of wood. Their decision to opt for spruce and maple remains exemplary to this day; we still use spruce wood for the top plate and maple wood for the back plate, ribs (side pieces) and scroll. But does that provide enough of an explanation? Definitely not, and this is where the next lot of experts will bring in the wood's priming. Not the paint, mind you. I'm not talking about the colour our eyes see, but rather the undercoat, which is made from a whole mix of components. You see, what's fascinating is that, when you use actual paint on a violin made by one of the 18th-century Cremonese masters, and this paint corrodes from sweat and wears away from prolonged use, you don't see grey underneath like you do on French or German violins – you instead see a shimmer of gold, a shiny yellow. How come? What did Stradivarius and co use to make up their primer?

To this day, we still don't know; the formulas haven't been preserved. Their secret was fiercely guarded in Cremona much like the way a Michelin Star chef guards the recipe of his or her famous dish. Because, as you can imagine, the competition was intense. There was hardly a street in the small town of Cremona that didn't have a violin-making workshop on it; everyone was fighting for their survival, and no one was exactly going to be shouting their special formula from the rooftops.

It is possible that this primer may be another reason for the sound quality of the Cremonese violins. Then there's the fact that the actual paint applied on top of the golden primer is itself breathtakingly, inimitably beautiful. Even the masters of modern-day violin-making can, at best, only hope to approximate the hues a Stradivarius produces when it glints in the sun. For centuries, people have been trying to copy these shades, but the results only look just like that – a copy. Was there something in that paint that made the wood breathe particularly well?

What we do know is that many factors came into play: the fabulous choice of wood, the primer applied on top, the sublime paint and tremendous skill – that unique dexterity that saw violin-making become an art form in Cremona. And let's also not forget the trained ear – because how do you tell if the top and bottom plates are the right thickness before the strings have been fitted, indeed before the violin has even been put together? By measuring, but also by tapping. Through constant light tapping, because the resonance ultimately tells you whether the wood has been processed to a thickness that will later generate a glorious sound.

Okay, enough already about the violin-makers, but one last word about the violins: what's actually the difference between a Stradivarius and a Guarneri? I've been fortunate to have experienced this difference myself, and would describe it like this: the sound of a Stradivarius is perfectly balanced. It is magnificent, even a little otherworldly, or should I say, divine. If there's one thing this sound is lacking, it's the darker side of life, because, on a Stradivarius, it's only ever sunshine, never blizzards, never storms, not even a grey sky. A Guarneri, on the other hand ...

Even as a child, I had been moved and overjoyed to play a Guarneri. I had had the opportunity to do so when visiting establishments such as violin dealers, and its sound had never failed to stir something deep within me. Because what is music, after all? Pure emotion. It is joy and sadness, it is happiness and tragedy, it is life in all its richness, and, in my opinion, a Stradivarius doesn't delve as deeply into the gloom of sorrow and suffering as a Guarneri does.

You can find videos and photos for this chapter here.

Why I don't recommend stealing a Stradivarius

No matter how perfect a violin may be, it is not capable of producing anything on its own. It needs a matching part in order to fulfil its function and become a musical instrument. I'm of course talking about the bow, which is needed to produce the sound in the first place, but also plays a key part in determining the type of sound the violin makes – reason enough for me to say a few words about bows.

Sometimes you could be forgiven for thinking violinists only have left hands. And it's true that the left hands do so much that the right hands are rarely mentioned. In reality, what the right arm, the bowing arm, does may look somewhat less sophisticated, but is not necessarily any less virtuoso than what's required of the left hand. The characteristic nature of the sound is actually

Pretty much best friends: my violin and I recording the Encore *album*

largely determined by the bowing – by the speed, pressure and articulation with which a violinist uses the bow. So both hands are involved in producing an individual sound – the right no less so than the left.

The habitual bowing movements, the up and down bows, are an art in themselves, because listeners should not be able to hear the switch from up to down; this needs to happen seamlessly and inaudibly. I also need to hit the individual strings, move from one to the other, play two, sometimes even three or all four strings, at the same time, then jump back to just one string – all this is extremely delicate, high-precision work requiring utmost flair and finesse. Or there's the legato, a prolonged, even sound in which the right hand needs to remain stoically calm, while the left may be letting off an explosion of sounds; but the right also needs to be able to manage a spiccato, in which the bow hops across the strings in staccato-like motions, producing each note as an individual sound. In other words, the right hand must operate totally independently from the left to perform all kinds of movements, displaying absolute precision in doing so. Is it any wonder French violin experts have a saying that, '*Le violin c'est l'archet*' – it's the bow that makes the violin.

It's not the case that all great violinists are equally good with both the right and left hands; they're essentially like footballers, who almost always have a preferred foot for kicking goals. Examples of violinists who were virtuosos with both hands include Jascha Heifetz and Nathan Milstein, though there are violinists for whom the bow is more of an aid just to produce the sounds, and whose skills all lie in their left hand. Isaac Stern had a very quirky bowing motion. While Heifetz seemed to surf across the strings with lots of quick movements, Stern virtually kneaded every note into the string by splaying his fingers a little and placing his elbow lower down. But for pretty much all violinists, including me, the bow is not a foreign body, it's not a piece of wood strung with horsehair; it's an extension of my right arm, with nerves running through it, capable of sensing and feeling, and connected directly to my head. In other words, I use the bow to feel just as I would my arm or hand.

Now, the bow has a history of its own, though the protagonists are not the same as those involved in developing the violin. If Cremona is the capital of the modern violin, Paris is the capital of the modern bow, and François Tourte (1747–1835) was the man who, between 1800 and 1830, used experiments and intuition to develop the bow design we see today.

What did Tourte change? Essentially, three things. Baroque bows were slightly convex, curving outwards, making them a little less taut, whereas François Tourte's new bows were concave, curving slightly inwards with greater tensioning, enabling greater pressure to be applied to the strings. Tourte also produced longer bows that allowed a note to be prolonged, that is to say, vibrate for longer. And thirdly, he was able to create perfectly balanced bows that were more pleasant and effortless to use. As with the violin itself, all these changes naturally served to make for increasingly virtuoso playing.

Good bows also have a substantial price tag: an excellent product crafted by François Tourte will cost you 250,000 euros or more. That's a lot of money, but when you see the qualities of a really good bow ... What makes it so valuable is primarily its perfectly struck balance. It also makes a violin's sound richer and bigger, and broadens the range of articulation. The way a violin and bow work together is similar to that of a palette and brush in painting: the violin is what provides the colour, so it's the palette, while the bow – like the brush – determines the articulation options. It's the element that dictates how dynamic you want your finished product to be. So the bow doesn't just produce the note; it also influences the outcome, the sound, the music.

I have never been obsessed with great bows in the same way I have been with the magnificent feats achieved by the master violin-makers. There are bows costing 3,000 euros that more than suffice for me. I know that Isaac Stern used a different bow for every sonata, but that's getting into the territory of private indulgence or, as far as I'm concerned, private knowledge. A single bow is enough for me, and it can be quite run-of-the-mill, as long as it is well balanced.

Back to my Stradivarius, which is what got me onto this tangent of violin-making history in the first place. Given its value, you might be wondering if I lived in constant fear of it being stolen. The answer is no. It would be the silliest thing a thief could possibly do, because it would be extremely difficult to sell a stolen Stradivarius to customers. Every single Stradivarius is documented like Leonardo's *Mona Lisa* or Munch's *The Scream*. So the risk of having your cover blown is way too high for any would-be robber, and the possible monetary gain for anyone who did still attempt it would likely be laughable, considering the risk involved. There is only one plausible reason for stealing a Stradivarius, and here's a little story about it from the 1930s.

Famous Polish violinist Bronisław Huberman, who had taught Ida Haendel, had two old violins – a Stradivarius and a Guarneri. While doing a concert at Carnegie Hall, he left the Stradivarius in its case in his green room, only to find no trace of it afterwards, until some time in the 1970s, when an amateur musician who had spent his life playing in the cafés of New York died. His modest estate naturally included a violin, but it wasn't his – it was the missing Stradivarius! It had obviously spent decades enjoying being played on in cafés and bars. So the thief had caved to his temptation and acted out of passion to fulfil a dream – not because he had been wanting to make money out of the violin. To my knowledge, Huberman's Stradivarius is the only one that has ever managed to stay lost for so many years.

This brings me closer to my more recent memories, only to jump back to the 19th century, because, in those years between 2011 and 2013, my life would revolve more around Paganini than it ever had before – as the lead role in a film by British director Bernard Rose, entitled *The Devil's Violinist*. And, as is so often the way in such cases, it all started out totally innocuously.

Christian Angermann is a long-time friend. One day, he called me from Cannes. 'David', he said, 'I'm here at the film festival. Do you want to come along?' I sure did, and I soon found myself spending the evening with people from the movie business. The inevitable question soon came up: 'So what do you do?' I told them a bit about me, mentioning classical music, crossover, the violin and eventually Paganini. The mention of this name piqued their interest; they wanted to know more about him, and I seized the opportunity to share my knowledge: a difficult youth as a wunderkind, who rose up from absolute poverty to become the highly acclaimed star of concert halls, while also suffering brutal blows in his love life, increasing loneliness and an early, agonizing death – I delivered the whole spiel with quite a bit of passion, though I thought nothing of it at the time.

A few weeks later, I got a call from Christian. 'No idea what you said in Cannes, but it's certainly fascinated someone. They've pitched the story to a director in the US, and he wants to make a film out of it.' Aha. You have all these conversations that amount to nothing, yet a casual chat on a summer's night in France was going to result in a movie? I let Christian know I wasn't an actor, though I would be able to manage the music scenes pretty well. In other words, I was interested, but also for another reason. You see, I was familiar with older Paganini films, including those with

Klaus Kinski, and, even as a child, I had been annoyed at the way actors on screen went about handling violins – they were all a mess, left hand not co-ordinating with the right; every violin scene just looked impossible, which wouldn't be the case if I were involved. Plus, I had long been dreaming of writing film scores, and if I now had the opportunity to do so ...

'Sounds good overall,' I told Christian. 'Let's meet up with the producer.'

You can find videos and photos for this chapter here.

The Devil's Violinist

By the time director Bernard Rose uttered the words, 'I've prepared a little scene, because I want to know how you are in front of the camera' at our meeting, I had realized he was serious about it.

It would have been nice to have known; it's not like I had made a mad scramble for the lead role. But, in a film like the one he was describing to me, the focus had to be on Paganini's unique virtuosity; it needed to be a genuine musical film, and, even if I do say so myself, I was the perfect person to play Paganini. Of course they then wanted to know if choosing me would be a massive mistake, particularly as the film was going to be in English – so we did some test takes, and it didn't look like anyone thought I had been a total disaster afterwards, because

Shooting the Paganini film The Devil's Violinist *with Andrea Deck*

the preparations continued, and the whole project gradually took shape.

What else could I contribute? My knowledge of Paganini, for one thing. We spent weeks mulling over the script, trying to work out which episodes of his life had been fateful for him, what the highlights were, what the low points were, and which concert scenes we would include. Sometimes we would come up with absurd ideas, such as doing the entire film in Italian, but I didn't feel confident enough to do that. Plus – ninety minutes of subtitles? So we stuck with doing the whole thing in English.

I was also able to ensure historical accuracy, at least for the musical instruments. Since 1920, there had been a shift towards stringing violins with steel music wire; in Paganini's day, however, people were still playing on gut strings – this naturally had to be taken into account, and the orchestral instruments also needed to be relatively true to the originals. But the greatest appeal about this project for me was the score. There had been some highly dramatic scenes in Paganini's life, often after concerts, when the enraptured audience rushed towards him, as if out of their minds – those sorts of moments needed stirring music, and that's exactly what Franck van der Heijden and I delivered. So this movie actually saw two of my dreams come true: I was able to slip into my idol's shoes and compose a film score, which is something I had wanted to do since my days of studying composition under Eric Ewazen at the Juilliard School.

But of course writing the film score, playing the violin parts and taking on the lead role was a gargantuan task. While I enjoyed the thought that no acting student from my year group at the Juilliard School had as yet managed to play the lead role in a film, I was a bit worried that, as a complete layman, I was going to be upstaged by my actor colleagues. Because they were all experienced pros: Jared Harris, for instance, had worked with Steven Spielberg and was now playing the bad guy, the demonic manipulator, as Paganini's manager Urbani. Plus there was Andrea Deck as Paganini's lover, and Joely Richardson as journalist Ethel Langham. And to think director Bernard Rose then asked me not to take any acting classes!

Now I like to prepare things meticulously. I can't rest easy when I know I'm jumping in the deep end of something, so I ignored my director's request and entrusted myself to Harold Guskin, who had taught several famous actors and had written a book with the promising title of *How to Stop Acting*. He lived directly opposite me in New York, and I had twelve acting lessons with him.

What did he say when I sat down with him, looking anything but relaxed, at that first lesson? 'Read the script out loud. But not your part; all the other parts. And just don't act!' In other words, get acquainted with the whole script and learn the plot inside out so you can react spontaneously during shooting. Acting was clearly just like music: even as a musician, you can only react to the other voices in the orchestra if you're familiar with the full score. Later on, when shooting, I did indeed notice that no one stuck rigidly to the script. Anyone who has the whole story in the back of their mind during each scene can always vary their script in front of the camera. After my experiences with Harold Guskin, I, too, was eventually able to cultivate this controlled spontaneity. But I still had to learn my part by heart, of course.

I certainly couldn't call myself an actor after all of this, though I was calmer and more confident. The fact I ended up doing at least a half-decent job on screen, however, was also thanks to my actor colleagues; they all made me look good, helped me shine and got the best out of me. But my preparations didn't just stop with Guskin's classes.

We know from pictures that Paganini was extremely skinny, basically skin and bones, and, being the ambitious person that I am, I set about losing eight kilos before shooting began. So halve my portions? No. Go on a diet? Sure, we'll cut out sugar and carbs for two months. Exercise? Absolutely, as much as possible. Athletic Jörg now had to come to New York, so he could actively make sure I took my training programme seriously. We would do a daily run through Central Park and also go to the gym every day. We spent two days wondering why we couldn't see any women using the equipment, and, on the third day, we found out that the David Barton Gym on 23rd Street was the #1 gay gym in New York – something that proved very beneficial, because those chiselled bodies hugely motivated me; the pair of us looked pretty flabby by comparison.

Then came the first day of shooting. It was a disaster. We started in the evening, and the director told me dryly to 'just do it'. The scene wasn't in the script at all. I had to improvise, which was something I hadn't learned with Harold Guskin, and I'm not a just-do-it kind of guy – which my director discovered relatively quickly. Fortunately, that scene didn't make it into the film, but from the second day onwards, we went by the script and my nerves gradually settled.

And I actually found my performances in front of the camera less taxing than the boredom and endless waiting. I had thought everyone would be constantly moving around on set, that every scene, every shot, would be repeated again and again, but no – of the eight hours on set, I would generally only be in front of the camera for half of them. Most of the time was spent sitting around, and, as I didn't want to waste any of it, I practised backstage, much to the chagrin of my actor colleagues, who were forced to listen to my études and scales during their breaks. The costume fittings brought a bit of variety to the everyday shooting routine. My wardrobe consisted of at least eight different outfits that had been replicated based on the hordes of paintings and drawings of Paganini and were specially tailored to me. Paganini certainly hadn't been unpretentious, and appears to have invested quite a lot in his clothing.

In general, the aim was to be as true to the original main protagonist as possible, which meant that our Paganini was a lonely, isolated person whose success only made him lonelier. Because, as a famous figure, you've constantly got lots of people wanting a piece of you, while you're thinking they're there for affection or friendship. Those experiences are painful and, over time, you grow wary, raise your guard, withdraw and eventually don't want to have anything to do with anyone. It's not hard to find elements of desperation in Paganini's life, and his demise in Nice in 1840 was agonizing indeed: syphilis, bone decay in the lower jaw, haemorrhage and death. But he had had to stop performing quite a long time before due to his many health problems.

The film doesn't go too deeply into this end; we wanted to focus more on his early days, Paganini as a child being taught by his father. You can imagine how ruthlessly this father went about developing his son into a genius to escape the poverty the family lived in. Paganini did indeed go on to become an extremely wealthy man, but he ended up losing a lot of it through gambling. He also had little luck as a co-owner of a casino in Paris, because his own business partners pulled a fast one on him. So Paganini is ultimately a tragic figure – rich, sick and lonely.

But the film understandably concentrates on his most amazing performances and virtuoso pieces. He enjoyed another particularly great success in London towards the end of his career, which earned him the most rousing applause ever heard at the time: while playing, he cut through one string after another until only the lowest one, the G string, remained, and he played his piece to the end on this one string. He had apparently used a razor blade to do this, but this explanation never sat right with me. If you didn't want to stop the piece three times for the three cuts, you would have to constantly have all five fingers on the bow, and, as far as we know, Paganini did not stop in between. So maybe it wasn't a razor blade after all. Maybe he did the cuts similar to the way I did it in the film – wearing a ring with an embedded blade on my forefinger.

All the London scenes were shot in a giant hall at Bavaria Film GmbH studios in Munich. Three entire streetscapes from 19th-century London had been set up there, and, while it was glorious summer weather outside, we were inside braving a London winter – except in peak-summer heat. I was sweating – even when I was allowed to take off my black fur coat – but so too were the extras, and they especially needed to be kept happy. They weren't pros, they weren't cut out to take the stress and strain of a film production, and then this happened: we were planning to shoot Paganini's amazing London performance in a Vienna concert hall when a technical fault occurred in the stage lighting. The shoot had to be stopped, and the mood of hundreds of extras visibly deteriorated. Now what? Risk our extras going on strike? No.

I had got myself a copy of Paganini's Guarneri del Gesù specially for this film, so I took it and performed a solo concert for them, a whole ninety minutes, with Bach's *Chaconne*, which I had played as an encore to an aghast audience at Munich's Gasteig as a thirteen-year-old, and loads of Paganini *Caprices*, until the technician finally gave us the green light. Even I don't just casually do this sort of thing, but it would not have been at all ideal to have extras who had lost all interest after two hours of waiting around when the next thing we had to shoot was an ecstatic concert audience.

It was an elaborate production. The landscape shots were filmed in Italy, while Vienna provided the urban backdrop for all the sets not shot in the studio. One time, we even had to go to Regensburg for indoor shots inside Thurn und Taxis Palace. To this day, I consider myself lucky to have had actor colleagues who took me under their wing, came over to me during their breaks and went through the script again with me. On top of that, I was fortunate to have had a director in Bernard Rose who did not torment his actors to the point of tears, only to then smile evilly and exclaim, 'Now we can shoot!' I wasn't an actor by profession, after all. A lot of it was learning by doing, but it was all a great experience, and when the film hit cinemas with the title of *The Devil's Violinist* in 2013, I was in the audience for the premiere. I wasn't totally comfortable about seeing my face enlarged to 4 x 4 metres on the big screen – I would have preferred to watch with one eye shut – but I still love the music scenes even today.

There's also a postlude to this story.

Paganini had long black hair to match his slightly demonic aura. He had actually cultivated this image – no way in hell would he have acted more innocent than his fans liked. So, before we started shooting, we had to decide whether I would dye my hair black or wear a wig.

In my opinion, you can always tell when someone is wearing a wig, so I told them to dye my hair black. But I did take the hairdresser aside beforehand to ask if there would be a problem restoring my hair to its original condition afterwards. 'No, no,' he assured me, 'I'll be able to do it in no more than three hours. I'm an expert in this field.' OK, if that's the case then ... So my hair was constantly redyed black throughout the shoot, and, on the final day of filming, the hairdresser headed over. I wanted to fly to the States the next day, so he got to work right away. He fiddled around with his tools and then I sat there, head in foil, a real sight for sore eyes.

Half an hour passed and I realized that, normally, the hairdresser keeps lifting up the foil to check how things are looking. I mean, you do the same with a cake when it's in the oven; it's not like keeping an eye on things ever does any harm. But the hairdresser just sat there, playing on his phone or flicking through a magazine, the picture of confidence. What an expert he must be to act so nonchalantly about a task as important as restoring my original hair colour! At that moment, I admired him, but I soon started to get suspicious. He could just as easily turn out to be a dud. I began to worry that his confidence was just a sign of complete incompetence and blatant arrogance ...

Long story short: when he took off the foil, half my hair was still hanging inside it and the rest no longer looked like hair. It looked more like apple sauce. My hair had dissolved and chemically rebonded itself – something for my old chemistry teacher, Mr Edel, who I'm sure would be able to explain the process to me now. But even without his help, I could tell something had gone seriously wrong; you didn't need to be a hair connoisseur to realize that. And the hairdresser? He offered a half-hearted apology but deflected any responsibility for the disaster: 'Here's a conditioner; use it for a whole week.' When I woke up the next morning and touched my hair, it made a crinkly noise like the sound of dry straw that had been exposed to intense sunlight for an entire week – and it felt like it too.

There was no use complaining; the damage had been done, so I went to see a hairdresser I knew in New York. He reacted with a mix of humour, which I couldn't appreciate at the time, and horror. 'It takes at least six weeks to turn dyed black hair back to blonde!' And it did. To think my expert had believed he could manage it in three hours! If I ever need to have black hair again, I'll be opting for a wig.

You can find videos and photos for this chapter here.

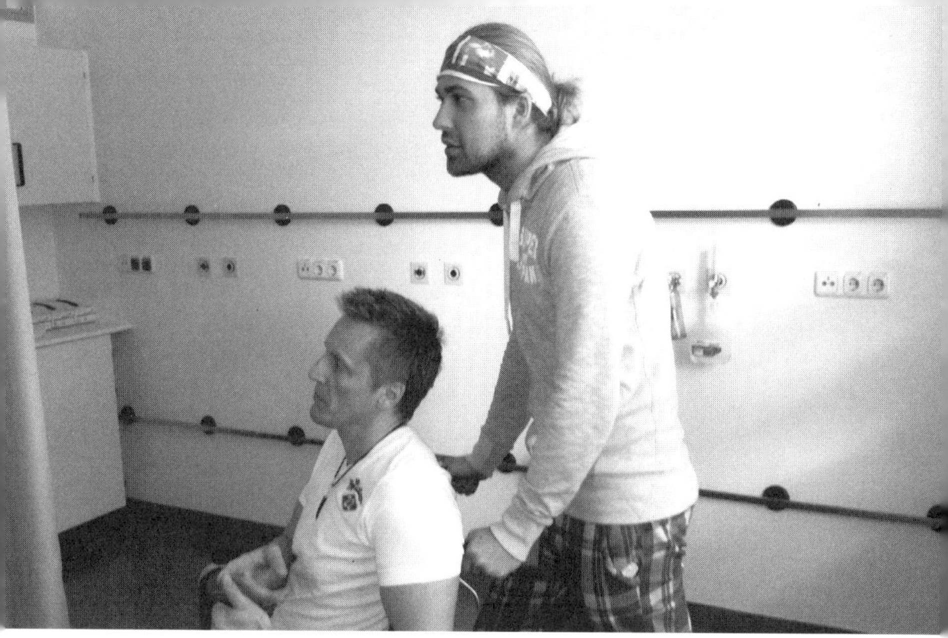

'What's Mr Garrett like?'

What else is there to say about my hair? At the most, that I generally tie it up when on stage, because long hair can tickle and annoy you when it moves. During virtuoso parts in particular, it dances all around my face, sometimes even getting in my eyes. But if it starts dancing on the strings and gets caught between the string and the bow, that can trigger a chain reaction: the hair grease sticks to the bow, the rosin on the bow strings loses its effectiveness and the violin gets quieter and quieter ... a nightmare! So, while I sometimes undo it for photo shoots, I tie it up when it's time to really play, even though there may be some fans who want to see me perform a concert with my long hair flowing. Readers of this book now know why they never will.

And speaking of fans: it is occasionally quite nice to be known outside your hometown. Let me give you one example: when it comes to exercise, Jörg is as ambitious about it as I am about music. I barely have to suggest some kind of physical activity and he'll say, 'No problem, I'll smash you.' And he pretty much always does. In other words, I'm better at violin and he's better at sports. With one exception: badminton.

You see, my brother Alexander and I often used to play badminton in our garden at home, whereas Jörg wasn't as experienced in this sport. One day, on a tour in Germany, we had an afternoon free, so we rented a badminton court, played a match and Jörg didn't know what had hit him; he never stood a chance of winning. But Jörg isn't a quitter. Every time he lost a set, he insisted on playing another; after the eighth set came a ninth, and then it happened: I heard a bang from his direction, like wood hitting metal. Jörg was lying on the ground, seemingly totally exhausted. So, once and for all, I could proclaim to be the best at badminton. But it wasn't exhaustion at all – he had torn his Achilles tendon, and our next concert was that night.

I took him to the hospital and, as much as I otherwise like being incognito, I didn't want to be on this particular occasion. At that moment, I wanted to be David Garrett to everyone at that hospital, so I took off my cap, let my hair out and, fortunately, luck was on our side: 'Hey, Mr Garrett! Can we take a photo?' For once, no. I needed Jörg badly; he was responsible for organizing everything and for the security side of things. 'No, we need to see a doctor as soon as possible' – and they actually did move quickly for us; Jörg was given a single room and operated on that same afternoon. As a thank you, I gave everyone involved free tickets to my concert that night.

As no other beds were free, he was moved to the maternity ward after his operation, and the nurses bringing his food sat on the edge of his bed asking him, 'So, Mr Kollenbroich, what's Mr Garrett like?' Yes, Jörg sure was a popular patient, but not for long – he was back working for me a few days later, temporarily on crutches. I'm telling this story to demonstrate that my long hair continues to be worth its weight in gold, and fame isn't always a bad thing. It does make some things easier, though normally I'm the last person to use my profile to gain privileges; it actually goes against every fibre of my being. We never played badminton again, by the way. Not that I ever asked Jörg to anyway.

But because of the world we live in, fame can also make your life very difficult. Which brings me to the next thing I want to talk about: the book you're holding right now is the first I've ever written. I need to emphasize this, because there are already two books out there about me. I sometimes get young people handing me one of those books, asking me to sign 'my book' – and I have to stop myself from telling them I didn't actually write that book, that I was never even asked about it, and that both of them are just a collation of interviews cobbled together and unimaginatively combined with things you can find on my Wikipedia profile. The law allows this, but both books are utter drivel and, for me at least, not at all enjoyable to read.

But I can live with that. What's less pleasant is the obsessive adoration from certain groups of fans. The following story happened in 2011.

As I was performing in Cologne so often at the time, I would stay at the same hotel and would hold my room there even if I were playing in another nearby city, such as Düsseldorf or Bonn, the following nights. That year, I had to spend the second day in Dortmund, after which we left the greater Cologne region. Weeks later, Birgit Korwitz, who runs my social media channels, sent me pictures of the inside of my Cologne hotel room; detailed photos of my open suitcase, my bed, my toiletries bag, my violin case and my underwear. How was that possible?

As it turned out, one of my hard-core fans, a young woman, had found out where I always stayed in Cologne, had applied for a housemaid's job there, had been hired and had gained access to my room while I was performing in Dortmund. She had also used the opportunity to let a few fellow female fans in, rifled through my suitcase, taken the aforementioned photos and then posted them in her community, her online fan group. David Garrett's personal items in David Garrett's hotel room must have been super-hot property in those circles.

I have to say, it still sends a shiver down my spine to think about this invasion of my privacy. Something like that is clearly taking things too far, but it's unfortunately not an isolated incident. For example, I could also have done without the young woman who managed to get onto my property in Mallorca when I wasn't there and post photos of herself lying by my swimming pool. That is trespassing, a matter for the police, but I'm wary of giving her the attention she probably seeks. So let her show off her photos if she wants, as long as she doesn't cause any harm at my end.

Those are two rather mild stories; there have been more extreme incidents too. What all these types of experience have in common is the utter brazenness of some people. One time, I was queuing up for boarding at the airport and, because I've learned to keep an eye on what's going on around me, I noticed a young man approaching me from behind. Seconds later, he thrust his phone into the hands of the guy in front of me and said, 'Take a photo of me and Garrett!', wrapping his arm around my shoulders. Sometimes I feel like I'm the Eiffel Tower – that anyone can just photograph me without asking.

Often I also just have to smile. I was sitting at an airport gate in my slightly sweaty travel clothes once when I saw someone trying to secretly take a photo of me. As if I wouldn't notice them intensely squinting at their phone in their lap! In such cases, I usually go over to the person and say, 'Do me a favour and delete the picture you just took. We'll take a proper photo now.' In a nutshell, ninety-eight per cent of fan encounters are enjoyable, but that last two per cent are appalling – people absolutely losing it like in the heydays of the Beatles or the Rolling Stones. But, as they can't always be avoided, they seem to be the ones who make the headlines. Here's the most extreme case I've experienced in my forty-one years.

There are people you would prefer never to have met. One of them put me in a situation, in 2016, where I was suddenly exposed to a very unpleasant report about my private life. I don't even need to explain how I felt. But for those interested in details ... I gave one interview to a major German newspaper on this matter, and then never said another word about it. Even now, I want to keep things the way J. K. Rowling did in her he-who-cannot-be-named incarnation of evil in her Harry Potter books.

The whole thing rocked me to my core. What I found most distressing, however, wasn't the negative headlines, nor was it the financial side of things; it was my own reaction to the incident. But let me start with the positive: I was forced to do an about-face, to rethink everything: how did I want my life to be in future? Which people did I want to have around me? And what more could I now expect from New York's nightlife? I had learned to separate the wheat from the chaff among my friendship group. And I eventually found myself standing in a New York club wondering, what am I actually doing here? And what are the other people doing here? That's when I broke off my relationship with that world. Since then, I've also stopped doing at-home interviews. I can no longer handle having television crews in my private spaces. I'll keep talking about my life, but I'll protect what's sacred to me. Sucker punches bring you back down to earth and, after a fall, you reassess things – they're beneficial experiences.

What I do continue to find devastating, however, is that those incidents have made me overcautious. Once bitten, I've been constantly on my guard ever since. I've held my tongue in every interview and talk show, and, at every public appearance, I've told myself: don't make any rash comments – any phrase can be taken out of context, used against you and intentionally misconstrued. And it was the right thing to exercise extreme caution. It was the right thing to take everything literally. But there's now very little left of the fun-loving David Garrett. Toeing the line was the order of the day, and it's meant audiences now see me only as a boring pussyfooter. This book is the first time I'm letting my guard down and loosening that grip of caution. It's been ages since I've spoken so openly. And, in doing so, I'm wiping the slate clean.

You can find videos and photos for this chapter here.

Tour craziness

For nine whole years, I had felt like a New Yorker, only heading to Germany for work as a visitor. Whenever I wanted to go there, I had to catch a plane and factor in ten hours of travel time. Then there'd be concert tours around Germany, and I'd often be commuting between London and Berlin. I have to admit my mother was right when she said, 'You need a base in Berlin.'

And, in 2009, it happened. I found accommodation in a fantastic location right on the Spree River, and soon discovered Berlin was an incredibly amazing city. Just like New York, it offers everything you expect of a metropolis, and Bergmannkiez, with its stunning architecture, traditional little cafés and awesome record stores, became my favourite neighbourhood.

Touring with the Israel Philharmonic Orchestra and Zubin Mehta

You see, I love vinyl records. I grew up with them, after all, and I can still hear the scratching of the needle before the music starts, and my father's voice warning me, 'Don't let the tonearm fall!' I find it the height of cultured sophistication to be able to look through your record collection, pick one out, place the black vinyl carefully on the turntable and, with a trained eye, put the tonearm into position. The Beatles' *White Album* is a favourite of mine to enjoy over a Sunday coffee.

Vinyl records are perfect for a bit of quiet leisure time, and what I particularly like about them is that, even if a piece doesn't appeal to you straight away, you'll still listen to it through to the end because it's too much of a hassle to find the next piece on the record. You just keep it playing while you potter around in the kitchen or read a book – and you may actually find yourself eventually warming to it. These little surprises – such as disliked tracks ultimately becoming your favourites – are something you can only get from vinyl records.

I now love Berlin just as much as I do New York. When my parents separated in 2010, I had a think and decided to let my mother have that first Berlin apartment, while I myself moved into a new apartment in a lovely old building in the Kreuzberg district. The New Yorker in me insisted on having a large living room with open-plan kitchen, because I loved the spaciousness of New York lofts and also because the piano fitted without cramping the room too much. I could now rehearse a recital within my own four walls, with the pianist on the Steinway and me with my Stradivarius clamped under my chin. Besides, I like locking the door behind me and completely forgetting about the outside world.

And that was a rare enough occurrence. After the Paganini movie, I swapped the film studio for the sound studio to record *Garrett vs Paganini*, a classical album containing the music from our film. But, as there was still room for other tracks, it also included pieces by other composers, works that had some connection to Paganini – whether it be that the composer had inspired him, like Domenico Scarlatti, or that the composers themselves had been influenced by Paganini, as in the case of Tchaikovsky or Rachmaninoff. Anyone familiar with the album will know it also has two other songs – opera melodies sung in Italian – that continue to bring back happy memories for me to this day.

Like so many other tracks, *Ma dove sei* came into being in Franck's recording studio in Hilversum. I had come up with the melody, and we worked together to test out the harmonies on the piano, before eventually both feeling that Italian lyrics would complement it perfectly. So? 'Why don't we ask Andrea Bocelli?' I always aim for the stars first; if I only end up with the moon, that's fine too, but this time I was in luck – a few weeks later, world-famous tenor Andrea Bocelli emailed me his recording without hesitation, without any negotiations, without even asking for royalties.

He had sung *Time to Say Goodbye* at German boxer Henry Maske's last fight. And there I was now sitting in Los Angeles with his producer David Foster, playing *Ma dove sei* for him. 'Who wrote that?' Foster asked. Err, me. He looked at me. 'That's the most beautiful piece I've heard since *Time to Say Goodbye* by Andrea Bocelli.' A compliment from David Foster, who has enough gold and platinum records to fill his house from cellar to attic, counts for double – at the very least. Afterwards, in my hotel room, it was all I could do to stop myself double-somersaulting for joy.

The lyrics, by the way, had been written by one of Franck's Italian friends, who had also sung the preliminary demo version for Bocelli. I myself can't write lyrics. I'm the most untalented person under the sun in that field. So I was fortunate that even *Io ti penso amore*, the second vocal track on *Garrett vs. Paganini*, had ready-made lyrics – Bernard Rose, the director of our Paganini film, had written them after being inspired by one of Goethe's poems.

The music of *Io ti penso amore* is essentially the second movement of Paganini's *Concerto No. 2*. When we were rewriting this movement into an aria, I had Nicole Scherzinger's voice in my head. Years earlier, I had been given the opportunity to hear her sing a piece by Andrew Lloyd Webber in London, and it was now precisely her tone, her timbre, that I had in mind. What can I say? A few weeks later, I was at Abbey Road Studios with Nicole Scherzinger, and the recording brought me to tears. Joy is not a powerful enough word to describe how I felt. When two things, your own work and an amazing external vocal, perfectly complement each other, you experience moments of being completely overwhelmed. That's what bliss feels like.

The next highlight was a concert tour of Israel. Being invited by Zubin Mehta to tour with the Israel Philharmonic Orchestra is like being asked by Scorsese or Tarantino to play the lead role in one of their films. We performed in various Israeli cities over seven days, and the eighth concert gave rise to the album *Timeless*, with Brahms' *Violin Concerto in D Major* and Max Bruch's *Violin Concerto in G Minor*. It's unbelievable enough that this CD also made it to #1 on the classical charts, but what's even more unbelievable is that it also made it into the top ten on the rock and pop charts.

And while we're talking about recordings: one year later, in 2015, I had accumulated enough ideas for another crossover record. The result was called *Explosive* – a title that would sadly prove to be fatally in synch with the times. Horrific terrorist attacks rocked Paris and other cities, and my record company found the connotations between my music and those attacks a bit awkward. But I stuck with *Explosive* – if people did make such associations, then my music would be the humane, life-affirming antidote. Hardly anyone noticed that most of the tracks were self-compositions that I had snuck in. But, in any case, *Explosive* went to #4 on the German charts.

I'd also like to mention another – pretty serious – highlight: the years 2015 and 2016 were when my crazy touring reached its peak. Let's take a random week as an example: on the Monday there would be a two-hour recital, on the Tuesday another city, another country – a crossover event; on the Friday we'd be somewhere else – a Brahms concerto – and on the Sunday, once again somewhere else – the next crossover event. So I'd arrive in Asia in the morning, play a concert that night, quickly set my alarm for 8 a.m. before going to bed, then head back to Munich in the morning. I'd arrive there after fourteen hours of flying, practise from 6 a.m. until 10 a.m. the next day, then sleep from 10 a.m. to 5 p.m. before heading to the Gasteig, stepping out on stage and playing Mendelssohn's violin concerto. In other words, I was getting more and more performance requests, because there are no language barriers when it comes to the violin; it will be understood just as easily in Scandinavia as it is in Mexico or Australia. The only countries I hadn't yet ventured to in Europe were Spain, the Netherlands and Portugal – which was fine by me: if those three countries also started showing interest, I'd definitely go insane.

But then I'd suddenly be playing in Zagreb – where no one could have known me because I'd never been there before! Or in Sofia, Kiev, Moscow – where I had never done a single radio interview or television appearance beforehand! Up to that point, the approach had always been to spend the month before a concert being seen or heard in all the media. That's what everyone did, and I was no different.

But then the internet came into play. Bulgaria was completely new territory for me, but all 8,000 people in the audience in Sofia knew me. How? Very simple: an artist's promo tool these days sits in the hands of anyone who owns a smartphone. Fans in Germany post a video online, which can be seen all over the world, and suddenly I'll get international attention without even knowing. Suddenly I'll be performing in countries such as Georgia or Kazakhstan which I've previously known hardly anything about.

In 2015, however, my heart started to make its displeasure known in the form of minor irregularities. Fortunately, I had good people around me, and they were the voice of reason when they told me, 'Put your violin down for two weeks, take a holiday and just spend some time doing absolutely nothing.' So pause and temporarily lie on a beach in Thailand? That was something I'd have to learn how to do. But time was of the essence, so I had to find some other solution.

You see, the scattered tour schedules of the last few years had really got to me. Instead of organizing my performances in a sensible sequence, I was constantly zigzagging back and forth across time zones. So, after years of chaotic scrambling around, combined with increasing exhaustion, I would have to make sure my performance schedule was better co-ordinated, with concerts grouped into geographic areas. And I did gradually manage this, culminating in the final highlight of that eventful year.

It was the first time I had ever been to Mallorca. I was staying in Sóller, using it as a base from which to make excursions to other parts of the island. I adored the landscape and wondered: why would you fly twelve hours to an exotic beach when you can be in Mallorca in two and a half hours, with this amazing panorama outside your window? As a fan of open houses, I started having a look around and ended up finding a house on that same holiday.

I stepped in and it just vibed with me – super modern, almost sterile, no bells and whistles/nothing too extravagant, but a view of the sunset over the sea from the living room, bedroom and kitchen. 'Mum,' I told my mother on the phone, 'I've found my dream house. No need for any more holiday trips.'

My mother knew me well and tempered my exuberance. 'I'll fly over there myself and have a look at your dream house.' She called again soon after, from Mallorca, and just said, 'I know what you mean.' Since then, I've been flying there whenever I get enough time off between work projects. It's become my favourite home base. The only problem is that, in Mallorca, I run the risk of working myself to death. Sure, I sit on my terrace drinking my coffee, enjoying the privacy, the landscape, the rocky coast, the sea, the gentle breeze, the sun, and everything's wonderful – if only it weren't all so freaking inspiring, so motivating, so unsettlingly beautiful, so infectiously stimulating and restorative enough to make me feel I can tackle anything ...

You can find videos and photos for this chapter here.

Every day is not a Sunday

If you recall, I hadn't had the best of luck with my New York apartments. The first one had been too dark, the second one too bright. With the third one, I wanted to prove to myself that I had learned from those experiences. So I started house-hunting again and found something in 2016.

I hold dual citizenship: American and German. When choosing my Berlin flat, the American in me had come out; one year later in New York, it was the European in me that opted for Soho. This area is the New York of fire-escape stairs, gorgeous façades and streets lined with colourful buildings, of good restaurants, galleries, the art and cultural scene; everything that makes the city what it is. It's a microcosm of life and spirit, and just ten blocks away is the start of Little Germany, where you pass by old metal signs indicating venues and associations such as 'German-American Rifle Club'. So Soho is where I've been living ever since and whenever I'm there, I enjoy experiencing every New Yorker's dream of sitting on the terrace of a rooftop penthouse and taking in the view of the city. In other words, this is where I'll be staying until further notice; everything about the apartment is perfect.

But now back to my busy work life. Most readers will assume I recorded *Viva la Vida* in the studio. But I didn't. *Viva la Vida* was created in a hotel room in Zurich, just like many other pieces that result from ideas that come into your mind at night and gradually take shape between performances. *Pirates of the Caribbean*, for example, was born backstage on one of my concert tours.

This is because Franck van der Heijden always has a microphone and computer with him – and what's even better is that Franck and even John Haywood are always on the same page as me. They actually deserve to be left alone on rest days between performances, but, whenever I need them, it's always, 'When should we come around?' I'm so grateful for this team. They think just like me; they're musicians through and through, professionals through and through, and, whether it be in a hotel room in Mexico or backstage at Lanxess Arena in Cologne, they set up the keyboard and microphone, switch on the computer and tinker around, trying things out with a sense of love and passion, because each of us knows that pieces recorded spontaneously often have that certain magic about them. Recording the same piece later on in the studio, it sounds perfect, and every note comes out crystal clear, but something's missing. So then I go back to the version we recorded backstage or between the bed and the bathroom in a hotel room, and it's back – that inexplicable X factor that you may not be able to hear, but can certainly feel.

Now, for every new piece, you need an initial idea that acts as a spark. If this idea is good, if it's easy to implement, the rest happens instinctively – ninety minutes later you listen to the finished tape and say, 'That works. How did we even manage it?' But if you start tackling something without an idea, it'll never come to anything. That's how it was initially with *Viva la Vida* – I had already given up on it as I hadn't been able to come up with anything. But then came the day in Zurich.

I was sitting in my hotel watching a YouTube video of a singer using a pedalboard to pre-sing her own harmonies before laying the actual melody over the top. She sang eight loops live, then put her foot on the pedal, recorded those eight loops and repeated the process twice to achieve the full triad harmony, thereby creating her own musical framework before finally singing the actual melody. I watched that, paused, and thought, *Viva la Vida* ...

I called Franck in his room. 'I've just worked out how we can do *Viva la Vida* after all!' It was about 1 a.m., but poor Franck went along with it. 'I'll build my own orchestra live on stage!' The next morning, we sat together in my hotel room, me on the violin, Franck next to me on his laptop, and we ended up having not just three, but eight, loops before the melody came in. I will never forget the reactions to that piece the night I played *Viva la Vida* live on stage with the pedalboard for the first time. The crowd went wild. Not at the end of the piece, but rather at the moment the melody finally kicked in. And I know that was also the moment I looked over at John, who hadn't had anything to do up to that point, with the broadest grin on my face, and got an equally big grin back from John.

The backstory of *Purple Rain*, a piece on the 2017 *Rock Revolution* album, is similarly enthralling.

Prince had died a little while before, and, one night, I was in Mallorca rewatching some of his performances on my computer, as I'm sure many of his fans did. Even when listening to his version of Gershwin's *Summertime*, I thought, what a genius! But then came *Purple Rain*. I knew the piece, of course. His guitar solo in the middle is lush enough on the CD, but during his performance at the MTV Awards, he amps it up even more, with even wilder improvisations. And that's when I knew I wanted to play that piece. Never before had a solo given me so many goose bumps.

But it wouldn't work on a classical violin. On that instrument, I would only be able to play the melody – the elemental force, the cosmic sound, of the electric guitar is not something you can achieve on a violin. Because then it ceases to be about phrasing and nuances; then things get beyond my control, so once again I was calling Franck in the middle of the night, 'I'm sending you a link. Have a listen.'

I actually had prejudices against electric guitars, but when I woke up the next morning, something happened in my head, and I called Franck again. 'Please find me an electric guitar. I'm coming to Hilversum!' I had to try to get my instrument to bring to life that brute sound that goes right through you. We met up in Hilversum as per usual. Franck had procured the electric guitar, which he tinkered around on himself as we tried to find the answer to the big question of whether the blood-curdling sound of an electric guitar could be reproduced on an electric violin.

Yes, it could. On an electric violin, you can actually get the desired effect through a long, rich, incredibly stirring vibrato, and, once I had adjusted to the unfamiliar instrument, it ended up being the most awesome track on the album. On stage, the electric violin is lowered from the ceiling in the beam of the spotlight in the middle of the piece, the rest is improvisation. *Rock Revolution*, born of a moment of personal Prince nostalgia under a starry Mallorcan sky, is, quite simply, an elemental force.

The year 2018 started off promisingly. In February, however, I began feeling a numbness in the little and ring fingers on my left hand, followed soon after by back pain. Normally, it would just be a case of 'mind over matter', but having a left hand that wasn't behaving the way I wanted it to was setting off alarm bells. I need fine motor skills in my fingers to get the correct note, and if I'm unable to perform at my usual level, I get quite depressed. Unfortunately, it wasn't just a temporary little ailment. As it turned out, my condition was very serious indeed, because the back pain and numbness proved to be the symptoms of a severe slipped disc. So I had no choice. I had to pull the plug and cancel concerts for the first time in my life.

Was this my body getting its revenge? It had probably had enough of all that excessive, extreme practising over the last ten years – the night-time practice sessions sitting cross-legged at the back of the van driving down the highway, and the hours spent in the plane toilet on the way to Mexico, where I had smuggled in my violin, put the muffler on and sat on the john practising while everyone else was sleeping in their seats. I hadn't given my body a break, and now it was going on strike. Clearly, you can practise yourself to breaking point.

I started my recovery by flying to Bali with my mother for four weeks of Ayurvedic treatment, clearing my mind for the first time in years, slowing the pace and refocusing my mindset. I then moved back to Mallorca for a few months to concentrate on my physiotherapy exercises. I wasn't allowed to touch my violin for the first two months, which was a struggle, but I was rewarded by the realization that I could actually get through a day in Mallorca without music, and, suddenly, work didn't have that all-engulfing presence; nature, the sun, the wind and the sunsets allowed me to think of other things. And my mother made sure I didn't slacken off with my exercises: 'You do want to get back to making music at some point, don't you?' – which brought me back to my senses.

At the end of 2018, I advised my management we could resume working – albeit with a few changes. From now on, I didn't want to only be seeing Tbilisi from the air. I needed breathers; I wanted to experience a bit of the cities I was travelling to. The concert in Abu Dhabi in February 2020, essentially a birthday party, was unforgettable for two reasons. First, because of the extravagant lengths the organizer had gone to: Robbie Williams was there doing a fifty-minute show, followed by American rapper Flo Rida, then I popped up in between with my violin – the entire exquisite programme for a small, select circle of invited guests. Secondly, because it was my last concert before COVID-19 brought the cultural scene in Europe, among many other things, to a standstill.

A year earlier, I had returned to the stage, refreshed and reinvigorated, playing the *Unlimited* album to sold-out venues. Now came another enforced break. Sure, it was annoying, but it also meant I had time, lots of time, and I got used to seeing it as a gift. Maybe it wasn't such a bad thing to work without any time constraints for once. And so it was that, in the summer of 2020, I began an unusual collaboration with Till Lindemann, lead singer of German band Rammstein.

I had met Till years before in New York. My old promoter friend Matt Assante had shown up late one night, and one of the guests he brought with him was Till Lindemann. Till and I ended up having quite a long conversation that night, and we soon discovered we shared a love of music and a love for our work. Since then, we had bumped into each other on various occasions, and, during those times of pandemic-induced downtime, he invited me and my friends to his country home.

Rammstein is of course known all around the world; the band ranks #1 internationally when it comes to German rock music. Whenever I see posters backstage within and even outside of Europe, there will always be one advertising a Rammstein concert. But Till also has his own projects going on the side, and, on that summer's evening, he happened to mention Richard Tauber. I couldn't believe my ears. Tauber? I had grown up with him as a kid! We had constantly put on his recordings during our long drives to and from Lübeck, because my father had also been a big fan. Tauber was a magnificent tenor – someone who, as an opera singer, had embraced both operettas and pop hits, and whose musical curiosity extended well beyond classical. When Till noticed my enthusiasm, he asked me, 'Have you heard of *Alle Tage ist kein Sonntag*?' No, I hadn't. As it turned out, this was the title of a popular German hit from the 1920s and 1930s, and translates as 'every day is not Sunday'. Marlene Dietrich had sung it, and so had Tauber. In the end, Till said to me, 'If we ever do something together, I'd like to do this track.'

And so it was that I unexpectedly embarked on a great project, because no sooner had I arrived back at Franck's place in Hilversum than I recorded a demo for *Alle Tage ist kein Sonntag* and sent it to Till. He suggested a few changes, recorded the vocal part, and then invited me over to Berlin. Just like me, he had a team of people he had trusted for years, and it was in this circle that ideas for a video were now being discussed. Till wanted to do something in the slightly creepy style of an expressionist film – black and white, bizarre and macabre yet simultaneously also darkly dreamy. You should have seen him spending the whole night honing the story, calmly going through everything in his head, then suddenly coming out with brilliant ideas and brainwaves.

I found the basic idea for his video – Till making me, as the violinist, his puppet – particularly awesome. After all, being a puppet, and being defined and controlled by others, was not an alien feeling for me; I was familiar with it from my childhood, and wanted to portray this part of my life, in this format, on screen. Back home, I stood in front of the mirror, picked up my violin and thought about how a puppet would move. Definitely jerkily. But it wasn't just the up and down bowing that had to look fitful; so too did the head movements, and I had to hold the right arm higher because the string would be attached to the elbow ... yep, you could say I know a thing or two about perfectionism.

Till certainly did. With him, everything really did need to be just right, and while I was practising puppet movements in front of the mirror, he was flying to Budapest to learn about the mechanics of puppetry from a puppet-maker. Budapest was also where we shot the clip – in an old café with a bar and ballroom, whose nostalgic atmosphere was very much like what we had in mind for a 1920s vibe.

Till's infinite meticulousness is evident in the finished video. What most struck me during filming, however, was his kindness, his unswerving friendliness. As a veteran pro, Till was always perfectly prepared, laser-focused when he had to be, yet never impatient, equally amiable with everyone, with no airs or graces. Allowing each of the forty extras to take photos with you at 1 a.m. after a tiring day of filming when all you want to do is just get back to your hotel, still taking the time out to do that without showing any irritation – I have to say, that was next-level professionalism compared to anything else I had ever witnessed.

You can find videos and photos for this chapter here.

Not too much serious classical stuff, please

So is my house of cards still standing? Sometimes I do actually wake up thinking about this and am amazed it still hasn't collapsed, that it's still withstanding the elements. As fragile as it looks, it does appear to be pretty sturdy. And it's certainly had to cope with a thing or two. Critics came out of the woodwork after my very first crossover album and, since then, I've borne the brunt of fierce criticism on many an occasion. But I knew from the outset that not everyone would exactly be jumping for joy, and that some people would get very upset about me going on stage with a philharmonic orchestra in jeans and boots.

I take comfort in the fact that everyone has to live with criticism, including the biggest names. Just for a laugh, I've read some of the reviews slating Mozart's compositions that were

In the spotlight, 2017

written at the time ... In short, I feel like I'm in good company. Besides, my benchmark is: who is working with me? Who is inviting me to perform?

The answer continues to be all the greatest names, so there's no reason to worry. As long as Riccardo Chailly from Milan's Scala keeps asking me to play with the Scala's symphony orchestra in front of the Duomo, or Zubin Mehta wants to record albums with me in Israel, or world-famous orchestras like the Vienna Symphony Orchestra, London Philharmonic Orchestra and Israel Philharmonic Orchestra keep inviting me to perform with them, or world-famous conductors such as Christoph Eschenbach, Vladimir Spivakov and Manfred Honeck still aren't turning their noses up at the mention of my name, I don't think I need to worry about my reputation as a violinist. No one can accuse me of becoming undisciplined as a result of my crossover work. When I go on a classical tour, I don't just leave the orchestra to deal with the symphony in the second half on their own; I play through the whole evening from start to finish, performing three successive violin concertos. Whether or not everyone realizes this, who knows, but my fingers are definitely sore after tours like that.

And besides, it's not as if classical musicians only listen to classical music; Itzhak Perlman, for instance, loves klezmer music, while others have a penchant for rock or classic hits. But it is a bold move to indulge your non-classical preferences to the extent that you actually play that sort of music yourself – being a keen, passionate listener is one thing, but having the confidence to play that genre on your instrument is something very different, because you immediately ask yourself the anxiety-inducing question of: how will people in the world of classical music view me now? I took this step nonetheless, and believe I have opened some new doors in the process.

One innocent little example: I was in Mallorca and had a bit of time that particular day to look for music videos online. I came across a young female violinist, fifteen or sixteen years old, participating in a Menuhin competition that was taking place at the time. I was so impressed – which is not something that happens that often – that I sent her a message on Instagram, telling her how awesome I thought she was – 'In my opinion, you deserve to win this competition!' But would she even know who I was? And, if so, would she mind receiving praise from a long-haired crossover violinist? Whatever, she replied within twenty-four hours, saying, 'Thank you! Great to hear from you! I have all your records ...' A response like that can keep me happy for days and weeks.

I know, of course, that my crossover concerts have a big reach. Some of the audience may also attend one of my classical concerts at some point, while others might listen to my music because they think 'he looks cute' or 'I like the funny things he talks about between pieces.' It's all okay by me. But what makes my day more than anything else are experiences like the one I just mentioned: telling someone I think they're really good, and then finding out they're a fan. What can I say? The young female violinist did actually win the competition, and I wrote to her again to congratulate her. In other words, treating an audience to two hours of enjoyment is one thing; encouraging a talented young person, cheering on someone who has the potential to make it big, is another. I consider these among the greatest successes I have been able to achieve as a musician.

Incidentally, none of the great musicians has ever asked me why I got into all this crossover nonsense. Whenever I performed in New York, at the Beacon Theatre, for instance, Perlman would come along with his wife and congratulate me backstage afterwards. 'Of all the violinists out there today, you're right at the top, in my opinion,' he said after one of my crossover concerts. You can't show much more admiration than that. And in Miami, it was ninety-year-old Ida Haendel who sat in the audience and, when asked by a reporter afterwards whether she was disappointed in me, replied with, 'As long as he keeps playing classical music, he can do what he wants. Besides, this music is good to dance to.'

But if you think these are progressive views, you'd be wrong. Long before our time, it was a matter of course for great musicians, composers and artists to pick up on popular music or make it themselves. The reservations we see today were totally unheard-of in the 19th century, and when it comes to the baroque era, I'm reminded of an incident from my early childhood.

At that time, I was working with Isaac Stern on Bach's second *Partita*, a sarabande, and was playing the piece in a measured, solemn manner. In the middle of it, Isaac waved for me to stop. 'Why are you playing so slowly? Do you know what a sarabande is?' I had no idea. 'It's a dance in 3/4 time. So let the music dance in 3/4 time. But no waltzes please, just emphasize the second crotchet.' So the exalted Johann Sebastian Bach hadn't had the slightest issue with picking up on the rhythms of popular folk dances at the time. And you're telling me I wasn't supposed to be including rock tracks in my repertoire 300 years later?

Time to jump to the 19th century now. Unlike today, all great violinists back then composed their own work; that is to say, virtuosos such as Paganini, Sarasate and Wieniawski also saw themselves as composers. This tradition disappeared with Heifetz, which I think is a great shame. When I listen to brilliant young violinists today, I always feel myself wanting them to write their own music, because that's how you bare your stripped-back musical self.

What's amazing now is that this musical self of Paganini and others was definitely still compatible with popular pieces. In the

19th century, for instance, it was not uncommon for popular operatic arias – the equivalent of modern-day pop music – to be adapted for the violin, and audiences devoured them. Fritz Kreisler was one of the last of those to include both classical pieces and *Gassenhauers* – popular songs – in their repertoire, and his violin-playing even went hand in hand with composing.

So what I do is more traditional than what a lot of critics today consider to be traditional, because the idea of someone being purely a performer of only classical music emerged in the 20th century. Previously, people would deliberately put together a programme of folk tunes that would be sung in the streets just like *Gassenhauers* – *Carnival of Venice* is a good example of this – today, there is a song in Germany called *Mein Hut, der hat drei Ecken (My hat, it has three corners)* that uses the same melody but, at the time, was a well-known folksong. And what did Paganini do? He picked up on this theme, wrote variations of it and performed the whole thing at his concerts! He sometimes also took a soprano with him on his tours, just to give the audience a bit of variety.

And while we're at it ... These days, you look like a fool if you clap between the movements of a sonata or symphony – in 'knowledgeable' audiences, no one's hand moves until the very last note has rung out. In my concerts, however, you are allowed to clap in between, and people do, which is something countless critics used at the start of my second career as a reason to spout off about how clueless my audiences were. I just shook my head. Anyone familiar with music history – which is something you'd think critics would occasionally be – will know that, until about 1920, people generally applauded between movements.

One good example is the premiere of Brahms' *Violin Concerto in D Major* at Leipzig's Gewandhaus in 1879. Brahms himself was at the conductor's stand when Joseph Joachim played his famous cadence, namely the ultra-challenging violin solo at the end of the first movement, before the orchestra quietly came back in and ended the movement together with him. And what do you think happened at the point when the violin slipped back into the orchestra after the solo? The audience clapped in the start of the coda! There was spontaneous applause, an eruption of euphoria, before the movement had even finished. What barbarism!

Let's put it this way: I know how depressing it is for a violinist when they've worked up a sweat performing the first movement of a Beethoven violin concerto, playing their hearts out – only for there to be dead silence in the hall. Or, if we take Tchaikovsky's violin concerto, which gets faster and faster towards the end of the first movement, and which was practically written for audiences to go ballistic at that point – are listeners instead supposed to sit rigidly, unmoved, in their seats as if in straitjackets? No, it is not a moral offence for people to express their enthusiasm at the end of a movement, because, first, the applause makes for a good atmosphere and, secondly, the audience feels more comfortable if they're allowed to show their emotions. At my concerts, in any case, I often tell them, 'I don't want to force you to clap, but if anyone feels the need to express their joy, then please, be my guest!'

You can find videos and photos for this chapter here.

Spring in Hilversum

Every family is an alchemist's laboratory where substances are mixed together under intense heat, pots bubble away, things snap, crackle and pop, and odd-smelling vapours are constantly given off. Some experiments fail, while others yield unexpected results; they always produce something new, something that's rarely planned. Then, things eventually settle down. The laboratory has fulfilled its purpose, the fire put out and the pots cooled, but experiments are continued somewhere else, and the bubbling and fizzing resumes.

In the Bongartz/Garrett family, it was no different. It's been thirty-seven years since I sat between my parents in the audience as a four-year-old while a man in black played the violin in the spotlight up on stage. Things have now gotten quieter

A recent family photo

in the Bongartz household in Aachen. Its residents, apart from my father, have all dispersed. My own life experiment took me far, far away from Aachen; I got around, as they say, but the others went far and wide too. We still keep in touch, and I want to make sure this book also acknowledges them; for better or worse, they're the ones who shaped me, and no independence or self-will in the world will change that. So what are the Bongartzes and Garretts doing these days?

Let's start with my brother Alexander. He married his girlfriend in Las Vegas in 2014, in a large hall with a harpist in the background playing *Ave Maria*; I nearly melted with happiness that day. I usually try to control myself in public, but the two of them looked so in love, it was all so romantic, that the floodgates opened when it was time for me to give me speech as the brother and best man. Their happiness was tangible; today they live in New York with their two children and dog. Alexander works there as a lawyer, and I meet up with them whenever I'm in the city.

My sister Elena has also grown into a wonderful, independent woman. She has that same creative gene that seems to feel right at home throughout our entire family. While the hardcore music vibe in our home no doubt helped, she did excellently at school and went on to study jazz in Maastricht; she is also an outstanding pianist to boot. In the end, however, she chose family over a commercial career; today she lives with her husband as a singer-songwriter in Hamburg, writes amazing songs with fabulous lyrics and recently also had her first child. As her big brother, I have good reason to admire her. In other words: I couldn't have asked for better siblings.

As for my mother, she was in charge of all areas of life not directly relating to my violin practice during my childhood and youth. Apart from running the household and managing the logistics of an auction house – which was already more than enough to keep anyone on their toes – there were loads of things she had to organize for me, not to mention the fact that she was always there to encourage or console me when I needed it. Stuck behind the sliding door in my study, I unfortunately didn't get to see or hear much of what she did at the time, which is why I am all the happier that we now live in the same city and can do a lot of things together. When she went through a period of depression – something exceptionally rare for her – in the summer of 2020, I wanted to help improve her mood, so I looked around online for a Karmann Ghia for her. I don't need my own car; I never have, apart from a brief phase in New York, but my mother would go into raptures every time she saw one of these 1960s iconic vehicles. When I stumbled upon a decent enough model in the champagne colour, I couldn't resist. So there's been a Karmann Ghia parked in my mother's garage – unfortunately without power steering – ever since, and, occasionally, when the sun plays along, I ride in it with her when we go for coffee in Charlottenburg or the Grunewald.

And my father?

The timing of my departure to New York wasn't part of the plan he'd had for me. We became less close during my studies. Our relationship wasn't necessarily strained at that time, but it was far from harmonious or relaxed. 'You're doing perfectly' are words anyone would like to hear their father utter at least once, but he never did. Later, it made me so happy when, after one of my crossover concerts, my father came into my dressing room, gave me a hug and complimented me! His reservations probably melted away when he realized I was very successfully performing at both Berlin's Philharmonie and the Mercedes-Benz Arena. And today? I would say we've grown closer again.

And finally back to me. The first month of the pandemic marked the end of gallivanting around, including for me. All concerts were cancelled, and my new album *Alive* was created under very unusual circumstances in March and April 2020. Travel restrictions meant we had to do without John Haywood, and, as I drove from Berlin to see Franck van der Heijden in Hilversum, I didn't even have a clear idea of what my next CD would be. Since all hotels were closed, I rented a small house in Hilversum, and then I gave myself lots of time – more than for any other record I'd ever produced.

Franck's house was actually the perfect place to clear your head. Because, with their little red houses and park-like gardens, the Dutch know how to create urban landscapes that are clean, well-tended, yet also heart-warming – and that was precisely the scene on the outskirts of Hilversum, where Franck lives in one of those red houses. At the back is a little interior courtyard with a patch of lawn and shrubs, where you can constantly hear birds twittering. And right next to this is his recording studio – it's only a few steps back to the house when you want to make yourself a coffee.

And that was the first thing I drank in the morning, at my ease, on the sofa outside his studio. Franck had probably never seen that side of me. Normally I'm giving his wife a quick wave, sprinting into the studio, ripping my violin out of its case, adjusting the microphone and giving the start signal. But this time I myself felt like a different person. Those first few days, Franck would silently gaze at me in amazement as I sat outside on his sofa, coffee mug in hand, legs crossed, bathed in sunlight. 'You let me know when you want to start, okay?' 'Sure. Just don't rush me.' I have no idea what he thought; he was probably totally bewildered. 'The next few weeks are shaping up to be pretty great ... I'll just get myself a coffee.'

Go right ahead. Whatever. It was spring in Hilversum, I was enjoying the coffee, we would have good chats ... And so it was that, as we talked, dreamed and squinted into the sun, we came up with the odd thing or two. Sometimes it would turn into a piece, sometimes it wouldn't, but even that didn't bother me; after all, we had more than enough time on our hands.

I can still remember hearing Louis Armstrong's *What a Wonderful World* on the radio one day as I was driving over to Franck's place in my rental. The road ran through a patch of forest, the foliage greener than ever that spring, and the narrow street lined with its red houses came into view. Soon after, we were sitting on the sofa outside the recording studio, Franck on his guitar, me on my violin ... The sword of Damocles that was COVID-19 may have been hanging over the world, but the two of us played the melody of *What a Wonderful World*. And that's how *Alive*, my seventh album, came about – as a two-man show. Just like my mother used to say: 'When life gives you lemons, make lemonade.'

Having a fulfilling time doesn't necessarily mean having a packed full schedule, though this was a new concept for me. A lot was actually new at the time, and most of it seemed unpleasant at first. Public life had come to a standstill, concerts were out of the question, and if a single day of a holiday in the Maldives without my violin had seemed unbearably long, how was I going to manage entire months, possibly years, without performing? Despite my spring experiences in Hilversum, I would have eventually been climbing up the walls with impatience if I hadn't met a loveable, warm-hearted person not long before, just prior to the outbreak of the pandemic. I've now been happy, content and in love for two years. People might not take you totally seriously when you talk of being 'inseparable', but whatever, that's what we are.

This love is partly thanks to the unusual circumstances that existed then, because, for the first time in fourteen years, I now had the downtime needed for love. This time, nothing had to be rushed, which is a huge advantage. In this relationship, I've felt the support and backing I had so often lacked. In previous relationships, it had been so rare for one of us to be truly interested in the other, for one of us to show the other person things they loved and appreciated – and the amazing side effect of this is that you yourself suddenly see these beloved things in a new light, and they seem more endearing than ever before. I'm basically just happy to have found someone who doesn't put any emphasis on the 'show'. Many of my ex-girlfriends wanted to use me for their own fame – my current girlfriend doesn't.

So, with the days now being so wonderful, they could be as long as they wanted, and, in the spring of 2021, they were long enough for me to get the perfect balance between love and work. I'm not one to lie idle, so I started doing three projects that wouldn't have been possible in my normal concert-performance schedule. The first was something close to my heart. Inspired by my favourite composers, by romanticists like Tchaikovsky, Rachmaninoff and Chopin, I ventured into new territory and composed a piano concerto with John Haywood. Now it's pretty much finished, it's due to premiere soon, and I admit I'm just a little bit proud of this oeuvre.

As for the second one, I recorded a new classical album in May 2021, called *Iconic*. It's become a special album, one that ties into my past on two levels, because, for the first time since my wunderkind period, this CD will once again be released by Deutsche Grammophon, and the tracks on it are intended as a nod to all the amazing violinists I idolized as a child – great masters such as Menuhin, Kreisler, Heifetz and Milstein.

The 1920s and '30s are considered the golden age of virtuoso violin-playing. I painstakingly rummaged through the archives to find out what the famous violinists of those years liked, and which classical pieces they preferred to record. As vinyl records at the time only lasted a maximum of fifteen minutes a side, violin concertos were out of the question, which is why the focus was instead on pieces suitable as encores – between three and five minutes long. So you could say that, from September 2022, this CD will be transporting listeners back to the concert halls of that golden age.

The third pandemic project was this book, and, as we come to the end of this forty-one-year life journey, it might indeed seem as if I've achieved it all. But that's not entirely true, for you keep hoping and dreaming until your last breath.

The sort of life I've led so far is bound to leave traces of wear and tear, and well-meaning people might well advise me to wind down and take things slower. But my response to even the most earnest of them would be: this is who I am, this is where I play; I can't change that. So my own wish for the future would instead be to maintain my curiosity and my love of experimentation, because that moment of discovery, that instant of inspiration and the brief sensation of bliss you feel when something's finished and successful – that's when my life dream comes true. I hope to have many more such moments.

But I find it just as enjoyable to climb the mountain, tackle the ascent and gradually get closer to the summit. In other words: to take on the glorious trials and tribulations of that long, difficult route to the ultimate goal. However, I also hope to have the sense not to overdo things, because, as much as I love it, I don't want to work myself to death. Finally, my dream is to own, in addition to my magnificent Stradivarius, a Guarneri del Gesù – there's certainly still room for one in my collection. It's been one of my childhood dreams, because, since the age of seven, the fragile, deeply human, almost tragic sound of a Guarneri has meant even more to me than the divine sound of a Stradivarius.

THE END

You can find videos and photos for this chapter here.

Appendix

Link to additional material

All the additional material accessible via the QR codes can also be found here:

www.heyne.de/garrett-overview

Picture credits

Text section

P. 11: Philipp Müller (DECCA)
P. 16: Bongartz family
P. 23: Bongartz family
P. 28: Bongartz family
P. 34: Bongartz family
P. 43: Bongartz family
P. 50: Bongartz family
P. 59: Bongartz family
P. 64: Bongartz family
P. 71: Bongartz family
P. 80: Bongartz family
P. 87: Bongartz family
P. 94: Keshet Eilon Center/ Amnon Weinstein
P. 102: Bongartz family
P. 108: Bongartz family
P. 117: Bongartz family
P. 123: Getty Images/Afton Almaraz
P. 128: Bongartz family
P. 136: Bongartz family
P. 144: Getty Images/Rahav Segev
P. 152: Bongartz family
P. 161: Bongartz family
P. 168: Bongartz family
P. 176: Bongartz family
P. 184: Bongartz family
P. 191: Tom Holmes
P. 196: Jörg Kollenbroich
P. 204: Ian Harrison (DECCA)
P. 209: Marcus Wolf
P. 216: Getty Images/Eva Ritchie
P. 223: Karsten Woelk
P. 228: Bongartz family
P. 237: Bongartz family
P. 243: John Haywood
P. 251: Christoph Koestlin
P. 256: Jörg Kollenbroich
P. 263: Denis Ignatov
P. 269: Jörg Kollenbroich
P. 278: Uli Weber@kristinakorb (DECCA)
P. 285: Summerstorm Entertainment/ W.Wehner
P. 293: Joern Gierschke
P. 299: Edel Verlagsgruppe GmbH/ Shai Skiff
P. 306: Magdalena Stanković
P. 315: Jörg Kollenbroich
P. 321: Bongartz family

Picture section

P. 1: Christoph Koestlin
P. 2: Netzhaut/Dirk Hoppe
P. 3: Top and bottom: Bongartz family
P. 4: Top: Summerstorm Entertainment; Bottom: IMAGO/MIS
P. 5: Top: ddp images/J. Luebke; Bottom: Getty Images/Ronny Hartmann
P. 6: Top: Bongartz family; Bottom: Giovanni Hänninen
P. 7: Ananda Siegling
P. 8: Top: Getty Images/Sean Gallup; Bottom: Getty Images/Franziska Krug
P. 9: Top: IMAGO/Coldrey; Bottom: IMAGO/Eventpress
P. 10/11: Getty Images/Marco Mantovani
P. 12/13: David Marschalsky
P. 14/15: Jörg Kollenbroich
P. 16: Jörg Kollenbroich

List of works

Albums and CDs

Mozart: Violinkonzerte KV 218 & 271a
David Garrett with Claudio Abbado (conductor), The Chamber Orchestra of Europe and Itamer Golan (piano)
Deutsche Grammophon Gesellschaft 1995

Beethoven: Frühlingssonate – Bach: *Partita* BWV 1004 – Mozart: Adagio KV 261
David Garrett with Alexander Markovich (piano)
Deutsche Grammophon Gesellschaft 1995

Paganini Capricen
David Garrett with Bruno Canino (piano), No. 1 to 23, arranged for violin and piano by Robert Schumann
Deutsche Grammophon Gesellschaft 1997

Tchaikovsky & Conus: Violinkonzerte
David Garrett with Mikhail Pletnev (conductor), The Russian National Orchestra
Deutsche Grammophon Gesellschaft 2001
Also released as *Pure Ecstasy*

Pure Classics
Deutsche Grammophon Gesellschaft 2002 – A compilation of the first four CDs released by Deutsche Grammophon Gesellschaft
Re-released in 2008 by Deutsche Grammophon Gesellschaft as *The Fascination of David Garrett*

Virtuoso
Released as *Free* by Decca in 2006, as *Virtuoso* by DEAG Music in 2007 and again by Decca in 2008

Encore
David Garrett and band, with Ivan Kozhuharov (conductor) and The Bulgarian Symphony Orchestra
DEAG Music/Decca 2008

Classic Romance
David Garrett with Andrew Litton (conductor) and Deutsches Symphonie-Orchester Berlin
Decca 2009

Rock Symphonies
David Garrett and band, with The City of Prague Philharmonic Orchestra
Decca 2010

Legacy
David Garrett with Ion Marin (conductor) and The Royal Philharmonic Orchestra
Decca Classics 2011

Music
Decca Classics 2012

David Garrett: 14
Deutsche Grammophon Gesellschaft 2013

Garrett vs Paganini
David Garrett and band, with the Munich Radio Orchestra
Decca 2013
Released as *Garrett vs. Paganini* by Decca, and as *Caprice* by Decca UK minus *Erlkönig*.

The Early Years
Compilation of five albums: Mozart: *Violinkonzerte*; Beethoven: *Frühlingssonate*;
Bach: *Partita BWV 1004*; Mozart: *Adagio KV 261*; Paganini *Capricen*; Tchaikovsky & Conus: *Violinkonzerte* and *14*.
Deutsche Grammophon Gesellschaft 2014

Timeless – Brahms & Bruch Violin Concertos
David Garrett with Zubin Mehta (conductor), The Israel Philharmonic Orchestra
Decca 2014

Explosive
David Garrett with Franck van der Heijden (conductor) and The Royal Philharmonic Orchestra
Decca 2015

Rock Revolution
David Garrett and Band, Franck van der Heijden (conductor)
Decca 2017

Unlimited (Greatest Hits)
David Garrett and Band, with other partners
Universal 2018

Alive – My Soundtrack
David Garrett and Band, with other partners
Universal 2020

Alle Tage ist kein Sonntag
Rammstein singer Till Lindemann and violinist David Garrett release their version of the hit *Alle Tage ist kein Sonntag*
Universal 2020

DVDs

David Garrett live in Concert & in Private
Universal 2009 (Germany, Switzerland, Austria)

Rock Symphonies – Open Air Live
DEAG Music 2010 (Germany, Switzerland, Austria)

Legacy – Live in Baden-Baden
David Garrett with Vladimir Spivakov (conductor), Lorenzo Coladonate (conductor) and the National Philharmonic of Russia
Decca 2012

Music – Live in Concert 2012
Universal 2012

Der Teufelsgeiger – The Devil's Violinist (motion picture)
Universum Film GmbH 2014

David Garrett – Unlimited – Live aus der Arena di Verona
Kineskop – Cmajor 2021

Music books

The Best of Violin. 16 Titel arrangiert für Violine und Klavier
Schott Music GmbH & Co KG, Mainz, April 2019

Alive – My Soundtrack. 16 Titel arrangiert für Violine und Klavier
Schott Music GmbH & Co KG, Mainz, September 2021

What I'm currently working on:

www.david-garrett.com
www.fb.com/davidgarrettofficial
www.instagram.com/davidgarrettinsta/
twitter.com/david_garrett
www.youtube.com/user/DavidGarrettMusic